A Short History of Christian Doctrine

"Who do you say that I am?"
Matthew 16:15

"Keeping silent about dogma means denying dogma."
Maximus the Confessor

A Short History of Christian Doctrine

BERNHARD LOHSE

translated by F. ERNEST STOEFFLER

FORTRESS PRESS PHILADELPHIA

Translated by F. Ernest Stoeffler by the German *Epochen der Dogmengeschichte* by Bernhard Lohse, published by Kreuz Verlag, Stuttgart, 1963.

First paperback edition 1978
Second printing 1980

Library of Congress Catalog Card Number 66–21732
ISBN 0–8006–1341–4

8819180 Printed in the United States of America 1–1341

Contents

Preface to the German Edition

To WRITE A HISTORY OF DOGMA in our day is a risk. The great works in this area, which in the German-speaking areas were written around the turn of the century, have not yet been replaced by any new, convincing, and comprehensive alternatives. This despite the fact that the understanding of dogma and of the history of dogma has changed considerably within Protestantism since that time. The idea of writing a history of dogma originated not with me but with the original publisher, Kreuz-Verlag. In undertaking the assignment, however, I have received encouragement from various quarters. Of course, it is hardly enough for evangelical theology to concern itself only with a basically new understanding of dogma and of the history of dogma. We are, in fact, confronted with the additional task of trying to embody this new understanding in a new outline of the history of dogma, and thus to demonstrate its validity.

In the present attempt I have gratefully used many works, among them the great histories of dogma by Harnack, Loofs, and Seeberg. In writing a history of doctrine addressed to an audience wider than the circle of specialists, it is of course impossible to mention all the sources which have been used. I would refer only to J. N. D. Kelly's excellent work, *Early Christian Doctrines,* from which I have learned a great deal about the ancient church. Some important literature is listed under "For Further Reading." In the footnotes I have mentioned quotations and references which are of special importance. Here too, of course, only selections could be offered.

I am convinced that in the current state of research in the history of dogma the present effort can be no more than a mere attempt to expand the new evangelical understanding of dogma and its history into an outline of the various epochs in the history of dogma. It is to be hoped that this attempt will help to reawaken within the Protestant church an understanding of dogma and of its true meaning and significance. In the dogmas of the church we have been given a heritage which must not be neglected and which should not merely be conserved. If it is true that the church of our day is one in faith and confession with the church of our fathers, this heritage should be responsibly accepted and treated as intrinsically valid.

Hamburg, Germany
February, 1963

Bernhard Lohse

Preface to the American Edition

IT IS WITH PLEASURE that I express my sincere and cordial thanks to those responsible for the American edition of this book. I am especially indebted to the translator, Dr. F. Ernest Stoeffler, Professor of the History of Christianity at Temple University, Philadelphia.

It is my hope that the book will be as well received in the United States as it was in Germany. I am all too aware that the book is nothing more than an attempt to break new ground. May it not discourage others from writing their own outlines of the history of doctrine!

Some of the ideas incorporated in this book were discussed with American students during a term as guest professor at the School of Theology at Claremont in 1961. To them and to my many other friends in the United States this American edition is dedicated.

Hamburg, Germany
February, 1966

Bernhard Lohse

Translator's Note

WHILE THE VOLUME before us has considerable value for the experts in the historical field it was not written primarily for them. In the main, Professor Lohse addresses himself to the needs of a broader segment of the contemporary church—churchmen, pastors, seminarians, and theologically alert laymen. In making this translation, and in editing it, the author's intention has been kept in mind.

A few German words have been reproduced in brackets, but only where this seemed to be absolutely essential. The effort has been made to achieve a reasonably fluent English style. In many cases the German idiom had to give way to more customary English usage. Our general aim has been that of giving an accurate translation, though not a literal one.

Though more recent translations of quoted matter were available in many instances, in most cases quotations are taken from well-known and widely circulated English translations, and references have been altered so as to be oriented toward these works. The bibliography has been augmented by listing a number of major English sources. Wherever possible, English translations of works in foreign languages have been cited in the footnotes.

Philadelphia
January, 1966

F. Ernest Stoeffler

List of Abbreviations

ACW – *Ancient Christian Writers.* Johannes Quasten and Joseph C. Plumpe, editors (Westminster, Maryland: Newman Press, 1946-).

ANF – *The Ante-Nicene Fathers.* Alexander Roberts and James Donaldson, editors (Buffalo and New York, 1885-1896; American reprint of the Edinburgh edition).

BC – *The Book of Concord.* Theodore G. Tappert, editor (Philadelphia: Fortress Press, 1959).

CD – *Church Dogmatics,* by Karl Barth. G. W. Bromiley and T. F. Torrance, editors (Edinburgh: T. and T. Clark, 1936-).

CR – *Corpus Reformatorum.* C. G. Bretschneider, H. E. Bindseil, G. Baum, *et alii,* editors (Halle, Braunschweig, Berlin, 1834-).

Denzinger – *Enchiridion Symbolorum definitionum et declarationum de rebus fidei et morum.* H. Denzinger, editor; revised by Karl Rahner. (30th edition; Freiberg im Breisgau: Herder, 1954).

FC – *The Fathers of the Church.* Ludwig Schopp, founder; R. J. Defarrari, editor (New York: Cima Publishing Co., and Fathers of the Church, Inc., 1947-).

LCC – *The Library of Christian Classics.* John Baillie, John T. McNeill, and Henry P. Van Dusen, General Editors (London: SCM, and Philadelphia: Westminster, 1953-).

LW – *Luther's Works,* American Edition. Jaroslav Pelikan and Helmut T. Lehmann, General Editors (St. Louis: Concordia, and Philadelphia: Fortress Press, 1955-).

MPL – *Patrologiae, Cursus Completus, Series Latina.* J. P. Migne, editor (Paris, 1844 ff.).

NPNF[1] – *The Nicene and Post-Nicene Fathers of the Christian Church,* First Series, Philip Schaff, editor
(Buffalo and New York: Christian Literature Co., 1886 ff.).

NPNF[2] – *The Nicene and Post-Nicene Fathers of the Christian Church,* Second Series. Philip Schaff and Henry Wace, editors
(New York: Christian Literature Co., 1890 ff.).

PE – *Works of Martin Luther.* Philadelphia Edition
(Philadelphia: Holman and Muhlenberg, 1915-1943).

TCT – *The Church Teaches.* Translated and edited by John F. Clarkson, *et alii*
(London and St. Louis: B. Herder Book Co., 1955).

WA – *D. Martin Luthers Werke.* Kritische Gesamtausgabe
(Weimar, 1883-).

WA, Br. – *D. Martin Luthers Werke.* Briefwechsel
(Weimar, 1930-).

Introduction: Dogma and the History of Dogma

Christianity without Dogma?

If there is one thing on which a great many people of our day both inside and outside the church are in perfect agreement, it is that Christianity ought to be free of dogma. Ever since the days of the Enlightenment, dogma, at least as it was generally understood, has been for multitudes of men the stumbling block that keeps them from a living faith. Modern ideologies have made the struggle against Christian dogma a part of their declared program. In its initial dealings with the church, National Socialism's ostensible purpose was to "deconfessionalize" it. Thus it opposed particularly what it regarded as the church's outmoded loyalty to antiquated dogmas and confessions. Even within the church, however, the call for a Christianity free of dogma has often been voiced. One thinks, for example, of Adolf von Harnack, author of what in many respects is still the most brilliant history of dogma ever written. In the last analysis, Harnack saw in the development of dogma over the years nothing but a process of decay, which had allegedly led to the Hellenizing of Christianity. Only by reversing this process would it be possible, thought Harnack, to achieve again the kind of undogmatic faith which he believed was characteristic of the beginnings of the church and which alone was consonant with the nature of Christianity.

In our day the cry for a Christianity free of dogma is again being heard. The quest for the so-called historical Jesus, which is currently being pressed with renewed vigor, is supposed to provide a solution to the problem of dogma. Gerhard Ebeling has insisted, "Where Christology is concerned nothing may be said of Jesus which does not have its ground in the historical Jesus himself and does not confine itself to saying who the historical Jesus is."[1] It is an open secret that many Roman Catholics take a similar view with respect to belief in dogmas and that, to say the least, they have no desire for any new dogmas. When the infallibility of the pope was proclaimed as dogma at the First Vatican Council in 1870, there was considerable opposition, particularly from the leading Catholic theologians of Germany and France. Prior to its promulgation in 1950, the new Mariological dogma was likewise sharply criticized by a number of Catholics.

There would appear to be three main reasons for the fact that the call for a Christianity free of dogma is heard again and again, even within the church itself. First, it is frequently said that one can be a good and sincere Christian without believing in particular dogmas. This thought has been voiced repeatedly ever since the days of the more radical kind of Pietism typified by a man like Gottfried Arnold. The most trenchant expression of this point of view is probably found in Leo Tolstoy, who envisioned a reformation of Christianity after the pattern of the Sermon on the Mount. In our century Albert Schweitzer has given us a living example of such a Christianity of practical deeds devoid of belief in specific dogmas. No theologian or leader of the church should underrate the earnestness and the dedication which stand behind this kind of Christianity. The demand for complete freedom from dogmas may of course be voiced also by people who are quite indifferent to the needs of others and wholly unmotivated by love for their neighbor. Still it is our own century in particular which seems peculiarly averse, and not without reason, to mere words, i.e., words unsupported by the involvement of the entire person.

However, it is not merely the tension between a faith committed to dogmas and a Christianity of deeds which leads to the demand for a Christianity free of dogma. No less important is, in the second place, the insight that dogmas have all too often grown out of a particular situation which is unique

[1] G. Ebeling, *Word and Faith,* trans. James W. Leitch (Philadelphia: Fortress, 1963), p. 298.

and unrepeatable in its way, and that such dogmas are therefore historically contingent like everything else in this world. This insight was first attained not by the enemies of Christianity but, quite significantly, within the church itself. It is closely bound up with the rise of historical thinking in modern times. The Reformers, especially Luther, took the first preparatory steps in this direction. In the ancient church and in the Middle Ages dogmas had been accepted largely without question, and such occasional criticism as there was did not yet concern itself with the fact of their historical contingency. Luther, however, while he acknowledged the basic dogmas of the ancient church, nevertheless insisted that one must understand them within the context of the time of their origin.[2] The writing of the history of dogma did not actually begin, of course, until the period of the Enlightenment. Lessing, especially, gave impetus to a number of important developments. Thus, from the very beginning, the history of dogma has been written largely by its critics. One of the first historians of dogma was W. Münscher, who published his *Handbuch der christlichen Dogmengeschichte* during the years 1797-1809. Münscher argued that dogmas have often undergone decided changes and that these changes are sometimes as unmotivated as the variations in women's fashions. Down to the present day the history of dogma has frequently been understood in a similar way. Indeed the very term "history of dogma" appears to point to the historical contingency of the doctrinal pronouncements of the church, for while "dogma" properly denotes something absolute, "history" denotes something relative and subject to change.

Closely connected with the insight that dogmas in the strict sense are historical entities is, finally, the view that all too often dogmas do not stand up well when compared with the Bible. Such a view no longer simply opposes the faith of the theologians to the faith of the laity. Rather, it takes seriously the whole of the biblical witness. It was precisely the scriptural principle of the Reformation that taught men to recognize the difference between the affirmations of the Bible and those of dogmas. Briefly stated, this difference consists in the fact that the Bible uses personal categories, while dogmas employ ontological concepts. In the Bible, man is confronted in his entire

[2] Luther, *On the Councils and the Churches* (1539), *LW* 41, 53.

person by the proclamation of God's saving action in Jesus Christ. Dogmas, on the other hand, represent an attempt to define the nature of God, or of Jesus Christ. The Bible makes man aware of the power of sin, which determines his every action, and calls upon him to be freed from his past by accepting the gospel of salvation. Dogmas, on the other hand, transform this immediacy of proclamation into the remoteness of pure doctrine. The Bible holds before man a mirror in which he sees himself as he really is; in formulating dogmas, however, man pushes this mirror aside and sketches, instead, a picture which can be observed from a neutral point of view or even ignored. The Bible is oriented toward subjectivity; dogma, on the other hand, toward objectivity. Thus it is actually the recognition of the Bible's peculiar way of speaking and thinking that leads to the demand for a Christianity free of dogma.

It is difficult to object to these reasons for desiring a Christianity free of dogma. Under no circumstances may one act as if they did not exist and so attempt to establish the authority of dogmas on the basis of mere traditionalism or confessionalism. To attempt to do so would, in fact, render the Christian faith obsolete, unable to stand up under modern criticism. Still the question does arise whether dogmas really are, or purport to be, what they have so often in the modern period been represented as being. It is significant that this question, too, was not first raised by outsiders, but by historians of dogma. Obviously our assessment of the history of dogma depends upon what we mean by dogma.

What Is Dogma?

To define the nature of dogma might seem an easy task. There is wide agreement to the effect that dogmas are to be understood as doctrinal propositions, analogous to the propositions of a given school of philosophy. It is quite clear that for the Roman Catholic church, dogma has this and no other meaning. In a study of the concept of dogma, the Jesuit scholar A. Deneffe has given the following precise definition, which accords with that of many other Catholic theologians: *Dogma est veritas a Deo formaliter revelata et ab Ecclesia sive sollemniter sive ordinarie definita.*[3] Freely translated this means that a dogma is a truth which, as far as its objective content is concerned, is revealed by God and defined by the church, either through a conciliar decree, or an *ex cathedra* decision of the pope, or by the mere fact that it is generally taught in the church.

The great Protestant historians of dogma have defined dogma in a similar way. Harnack, for instance, writes: "The dogmas of the church are the doctrines of the Christian faith logically formulated and expressed for scientific and apologetic purposes; these doctrines include the knowledge of God, of the world, and of the redemption which took place through Christ, and represent the objective content of religion. They are regarded in the Christian churches as the truths contained in the Holy Scriptures (or in the tradition) and comprising the *depositum fidei,* the acknowledgment of these truths being the precondition of the blessedness held in prospect by religion."[4] Friedrich Loofs and Reinhold Seeberg, two other important historians of dogma of the late nineteenth and early twentieth centuries, are in general agreement with this definition. It only needs to be observed that Seeberg, in contrast to Harnack, does not regard infallibility as a necessary element in the definition of the nature of dogma. Loofs, on the other hand, emphasizes especially that dogmas are propositions of faith "which an ecclesiastical community expressly requires its members, or at least its teachers, to acknowledge."[5]

In contradistinction to this widely held conception, which continues to find many advocates among the experts, a number of Protestant writers have attempted during the last few decades to define the nature of dogma in a much broader sense. Historians of dogma, as well as systematic theologians, have thus abandoned the conception of dogma held by Harnack and his generation. The authors of the two most recently published histories of dogma in the German language, Walter Köhler and Martin Werner,[6] are agreed that one should understand dogma

[3] A. Deneffe, "Dogma, Wort und Begriff," *Scholastik,* 6 (1931), 531.

[4] A. Harnack, *Lehrbuch der Dogmengeschichte* (5th ed.; Tübingen: Mohr, 1931), 1, 3.

[5] F. Loofs, *Leitfaden zum Studium der Dogmengeschichte,* ed. Kurt Aland (6th ed.; Tübingen: Niemeyer, 1959), 1, 9.

[6] Bibliographical details on these and many other works cited in the text are given in the bibliography at the end of the volume.

simply as the prevailing expression of the faith of the Christian community with reference to the content of the Christian revelation. They hold that it is not important whether or not a dogma has been defined, or even ecclesiastically legitimized, since in the last analysis such legitimization cannot at all be regarded as a criterion. What is really important, they contend, is the Christian self-consciousness. Köhler, therefore, has entitled his history of dogma, *Dogmengeschichte als Geschichte des christlichen Selbstbewusstseins* ("The History of Dogma as the History of Christian Self-Consciousness").

Karl Barth also, though obviously for other reasons, defends a very general understanding of the nature of dogma. According to Barth, dogma as such signifies "the agreement of Church proclamation . . . with the revelation attested in Holy Scripture."[7] Thus dogma is initially removed from all concretion and must not be identified with specific, defined dogmas. Dogmas, on the other hand, are nothing other than the forms in which dogma appears. This sharp differentiation between dogma as such and specific dogmas makes it possible for Barth to dispense, even in his definition, with the supposedly infallible nature of dogmas. It thus becomes possible to see the problematical nature of individual dogmas while yet appreciating them as attempts to express the truth of revelation. On the debit side, of course, Barth's "dogma as such" is a quite nebulous thing, which the historian of dogma, at any rate, finds of little use.

The real difficulty besetting every attempt to define the nature of dogma, and one that tacitly underlies the various attempts at definition, is that not only the history of dogma as such but also the very concept of dogma is always historically conditioned and hence subject to change. The Roman Catholic understanding of dogma, which is widely shared by Protestants, was by no means the prevailing concept during the early centuries of church history. It actually developed at a relatively late point in time. During the early centuries the concept of dogma current today was unknown, as was the subject matter later signified by the word "dogma." The first so-called dogma, the decision of the Council of Nicaea in 325 concerning the consubstantiality of the Son with the Father, was, strictly speaking, not a dogma and was not intended to be one, if infallibility

[7] *CD* 1^1, 304.

is regarded as a necessary ingredient of dogma. What the fathers of the Council of Nicaea wanted to do was, rather, to set forth a confession of faith. It was under this heading that they actually published their decision. This is not to deny, however, that the decision of Nicaea makes a tremendous claim and that in a certain sense it was meant to be authoritative. Still there is a difference between claiming infallibility for such a decision (in a strange mixture of philosophical and juridical categories) and indicating through the very language employed that here one is dealing with a confession, which as such can be understood only in relation to the subject matter or person confessed. Recent investigations, at any rate, have demonstrated that Nicaea was not led to define this dogma out of a "hunger for metaphysics."[8] It was Basil the Great who, in the middle of the fourth century, first introduced the distinction between the Christian kerygma and dogmas in the sense of propositions of faith. Of course, it still took some time before the councils made this distinction their own. The didactic significance of dogma is emphasized for the first time in the Chalcedonian formula of 451 which says: "We teach that one should confess . . . ." Dogmas have gained their character as infallible doctrinal propositions at least in part as a result of their acknowledgment in imperial law. Because of this acknowledgment everything pertaining to dogma acquired overtones of compulsion, which it still has for many people today. Yet one cannot say that the ancient church claimed infallibility for its dogmas, since the purpose of dogmas was seen not merely as one of further development of earlier doctrinal decisions, but also as one of imparting to earlier decisions a meaning they did not originally possess. Such a view of dogmas is obviously not in agreement with the modern understanding of the infallibility of dogmas. It was not until the Middle Ages that the Catholic church developed the doctrine of the *depositum fidei,* i.e., the conception that the church had been entrusted with a certain treasure of truths, none of which was to be lost; yet the treasure was capable of further development in the sense of a more explicit ramification of these truths. The full consequence of this

[8] W. Elert, "Die Kirche und ihre Dogmengeschichte," *Der Ausgang der altkirchlichen Christologie,* ed. W. Maurer and E. Bergstrasser (Berlin: Lutherisches Verlagshaus, 1957), p. 323.

conception was that modern Catholicism has claimed infallibility for its dogmas, as it did at the Council of Trent and at the First Vatican Council. The understanding of dogma as a revealed proposition of faith was thus by no means characteristic of the ancient church. It was something that came about only as a result of certain historical factors.

For Protestantism the conception of dogmas as infallible propositions of faith has never had validity. Though Luther and the other Reformers readily acknowledged the authority of the conciliar decisions of the ancient church, they did not do so because such decisions derived from a council which had been authorized either theologically or by canon law, or because these decisions followed necessarily from the *depositum fidei*. They did it because they were of the opinion that such decisions were in material agreement with Scripture and represented a necessary line of demarcation against certain heresies. Consequently Luther, Zwingli, and Calvin did not understand conciliar decisions as infallible dogmas but as confessions, thus recovering, in the main, the ancient church's understanding of conciliar decisions. It is not by accident that the doctrinal formulations of the Reformation churches are called confessional writings rather than dogmas. Hence within the Protestant church the traditional concept of dogma would better be understood in the sense of confession or doctrinal confession. Only then will the constant relation of dogmas to that to which they bear witness be properly recognized.

The Continuity of the History of Dogma

If one thinks of dogmas as confessions, or doctrinal confessions, it should be possible to find a satisfactory answer to the difficult question of the inception of the history of dogma as well as of its further development. As far as the inception of the history of dogma is concerned, there is no doubt that Jesus made a unique claim, that he was not satisfied with the mere attempt to instruct men concerning this teaching or that, but, instead, challenged them to commit themselves to him, i.e., to confess him. In this sense confessions existed during the earthly ministry of Jesus. According to the Gospel of Matthew (16:15) Jesus asked his disciples, "Who do you say that I am?" It is immaterial whether or not Jesus actually put this question to his disciples at a specific point in his career. What this account from Matthew makes strikingly clear is the goal toward which Jesus directed his entire proclamation, namely, commitment to him, or confession of him. The answer Peter gives to this question from Jesus—"You are the Christ, the Son of the living God"—is the first dogma, then, in the sense of a confession.

Since this confession by Peter there has never been a time when Christians did not face the task of expressing their faith in the form of a confession. For various reasons, however, such confession was not merely repeated in the short and simple form in which Peter made it but was further expanded and more fully articulated. The first and most important reason for the fuller elaboration of confession, as well as for the development of doctrine, at least at the beginning, is the fact that very soon after the crucifixion and resurrection of Jesus the primitive community began to pray to its exalted Lord. This is a fact the significance of which can hardly be overestimated. That the primitive Christian community was given to this custom from its earliest days is attested by the Aramaic prayer *Maranatha* preserved in 1 Cor. 16:22 and by the prayer of Paul in 2 Cor. 12:8 as well as by other instances (cf. Acts 9:14; Rom. 10:12-14; 1 Cor. 1:2). Prayers can be addressed only to God. If they are addressed to Jesus Christ, therefore, the question concerning the relationship of the exalted Lord to God necessarily arises. Hence the development of the dogma of the Trinity and of Christology has its beginnings in the early days of the church, even though it took a long time before a doctrine was actually formulated.

Additional reasons can be given for the development of dogmas and confessions. There was, of course, no lack of opportunities to confess one's faith in connection with such events as baptism, the celebration of the Lord's Supper, the proclamation of the gospel, and especially the carrying out of the church's mission. In addition, the fact that the Christian faith often encountered opposition frequently led to new confessions, or at least to an expansion of the existing affirmations of faith. Among the various other reasons which might also be cited is the significant role that philosophy later played in the development of dogma and especially in its interpretation. Certain problems were progressively clarified with the help of philosophical conceptualization. Finally, it should be noted that at times dogma also manifested a tendency toward self-expansion, with new questions being answered by analogy to similar problems that had already found a solution.

It would be hard to deny that under these circumstances dogmas, or doctrinal confessions, at times moved far, sometimes very far, from their beginnings in the New Testament. And yet it is true that the Christian faith could at no time refrain from creating confessions. Confession is by its very nature an essential element of faith. No matter how critically specific dogmas or doctrinal confessions of Christianity may be viewed, this fundamental principle cannot be denied on the basis of the New Testament. Melanchthon, in his *Apology of the Augsburg Confession*, said correctly: "No faith is firm that does not show itself in confession."[9] It must be admitted that confession may lead to an externalizing and formalizing of the faith, and that occasionally this has been the case. Still the fact remains that faith without dogma, without confession, is continually in danger of no longer knowing what it really believes, and therefore of falling to the level of mere religiosity.

The continuity in the development of the history of dogma does not show itself only when one compares the beginnings of dogma in Jesus' ministry with the later development of ecclesiastical confessions. It becomes apparent, also, if the actual development of the history of dogma is viewed from its beginnings to the present. In our century there is considerable skepticism concerning such continuity. The reason for this point of view is to be found in the past century, in the work of Ferdinand Christian Baur, the founder of the Tübingen school of theology, who with the help of Hegel's philosophy of history evolved a universal system of the history of dogma. Even though this system contained a very fascinating element, it was bound to stand or fall with Hegelian philosophy. According to Baur the history of dogma is a continual interaction [*Prozessieren*] of the Spirit with itself. Through thesis, antithesis, and synthesis the Spirit becomes aware of itself and, concurrently, reveals its true being, so that the germinal elements present in Christianity from the very beginning are gradually elevated to consciousness. This concept of history, which takes its position as it were from a point outside the world, has been strongly attacked, and rightly

[9] Melanchthon, *Apology of the Augsburg Confession*, IV, 385, *BC*, p. 166.

so. It is, in fact, much too one-sided to make possible an understanding of the many reasons and motives which have been of significance in the history of dogma. In our day, however, the opposite extreme would seem to be represented in the widespread tendency to see in particular dogmas only signs pointing toward something called "dogma," which is then vaguely characterized as the agreement of the church's proclamation with the revelation recorded in Scripture. For Barth and some of his followers the history of dogma is, ultimately, nothing but a succession of discrete signs pointing to the truth of revelation but bearing little or no relation to one another. It is not clear in Barth to what extent continuity in the history of dogma is possible, since for him dogmas are merely the forms in which "dogma" appears.

Still it seems possible that an unbiased observer can become convinced of the continuity of dogmatic development without having to think Hegelian thoughts. It is hardly an accident that the first dogma to be defined by the Christian church was the doctrine of the Trinity, with special emphasis being placed upon the relationship between Son and Father, and that the development of Christology followed thereafter with the definition, at Chalcedon, of the dogma of the two natures of Christ. Nor was it an accident that at approximately the same time the doctrine of sin and grace was clarified in the West, or that during the Middle Ages the doctrine of the sacraments was further developed, and that at the time of the Reformation the question concerning the appropriation of salvation became the central problem, one which led to the splintering of western Christianity and was then solved differently by Roman Catholics and Protestants. Nor is it an accident that in our day the question of the unity of the church is seemingly moving increasingly to the fore, so that perhaps the next steps in the development of the history of doctrine are to be expected in this area. At no time were the questions that called for dogmatic clarification questions of minor importance. All dogmas, on the contrary, have to do with central problems which are of fundamental importance, both for the self-understanding of faith and for the content of faith. Dogmas and confessions, therefore, are a kind of catechism of the most important Christian truths.

If all this is kept in mind, it becomes difficult to deny that the history of dogma follows an autonomous trend in spite of the manifold motives and influences at work in it. If that is so, then one should not dissolve the history of dogma into a series of confessions which are understood as isolated acts. The continuity in their development must always be kept in mind. In saying this, we are not attempting to support a traditionalism which simply clings to what is past and, as a result, forgets the tasks of the present. Attention must be paid both to the continuity of past development and to the actuality of contemporary questions and tasks.

The Authority of Dogmas

Reflections on the continuity of the history of dogma lead inevitably to the question of the authority of dogma. If the problem of authority is regarded from a purely historical point of view, without raising the question of the theological legitimacy of dogma, it cannot be denied that dogmas, in the historical sense, have possessed authority and still do. The dogmas or confessions formulated in Christendom from time to time have played a special role in the history of the church, a role not to be confused with that played by the opinions of individual theologians. If this special role were disregarded, justice would not be done to the movement of history itself. The Arian controversy, for instance, was little more than a controversy over the Nicene confession of faith. The subsequent christological controversy also was waged, in the main, over the formula of Chalcedon. No less do the decisions growing out of the Pelagian controversy constitute a turning point in the history of the doctrine of sin and grace. The confessions of the Reformation have a similar significance for the doctrinal controversies within later Protestantism. Lastly, the *Barmen Declaration* had overriding significance both for the German church struggle and especially for the stance taken by the Confessing Church. It is the task of the historian of dogma, not only to set forth the historical contingency of dogmas or confessions, but to demonstrate, at the same time, the special significance of particular decisions for a given epoch as well as for the development of the history of dogma.

In the opinion of the various communions, however, the authority of dogmas is by no means exhausted by the fact that in the past they had a significance which cannot be put on the same level with that of individual churchmen and theologians. Actually, both the Roman Catholic church and the Protestant church claim much greater authority for their doctrinal decisions. As is well known, the Roman Catholic church insists that its dogmas are infallible. It should be noted, of course, that according to some Catholic theologians this infallibility does not imply an absolute finality and perfection of defined dogmas. It is often said, in fact, that infallibility does not even imply that a particular dogma is the only correct proposition with reference to a controversial article of faith. Other propositions that are not identical with a given dogma need not be regarded as automatically false. It is also conceivable, according to this view, that the truth expressed in a defined dogma may later be developed or completed; or it may be more fully illuminated by being put into a more comprehensive context.[10] In addition, Otto Karrer has recently emphasized that dogmas of the Roman Catholic church must be understood and appreciated with reference to the period of the development. Infallibility, he says, "means that a given explanation is appropriate and free from error in its answering of certain historically conditioned questions."[11] It would seem, then, that in the Roman church, at least in the opinion of some of its theologians, definite limits are set to the infallibility of dogmas. Only one thing cannot possibly be surrendered by the Roman Catholic church and its theology, namely, the insistence that a defined dogma is without error with regard to its objective content. This implies that the further development or supplementation of a dogma may never contradict the objective content of that dogma and, indeed, by virtue of the infallibility of the teaching church cannot do so. Here the Roman Catholic church has set forth an article of faith which not infrequently can be made to square with historical reality only with great difficulty, if at all.

[10] See P. Lengsfeld, *Überlieferung: Tradition und Schrift in der evangelischen und katholischen Theologie der Gegenwart* (Paderborn: Bonifacius, 1960), pp. 202-204.

[11] O. Karrer, "The Ecumenical Council in the Roman Catholic Church of the Present," in H. J. Margull (ed.), *The Councils of the Church*, trans. W. F. Bense (Philadelphia: Fortress, 1966), p. 301.

In Protestantism such infallibility of evangelical doctrinal affirmations has been maintained by only a few persons standing on the periphery. According to the confessional writings of the Reformation, dogmas and doctrinal decisions of the church belong to human tradition, the dogmatic validity of which cannot be determined on the basis of purely formal criteria. Dogmas are to be judged only on the basis of the content to which they witness and which they confess. Dogmas and confessions are thus, in the strictest sense, subject to Holy Scripture. They must be tested in the light of Scripture and interpreted with reference to it. On the other hand, it is also true that confessions and dogmas are meant to offer guidance toward a right understanding of Scripture by warning against certain conceptions and by setting forth the center of the biblical message. Luther, to be sure, subjected the councils to the authority of Christ when he said, "I do not exalt myself above the doctors and councils; I exalt Christ over all teachers and councils";[12] councils must assemble and make decisions "only when faith is in jeopardy."[13] Nevertheless, he believed that such decisions definitely carry authority: "At a number of councils articles of faith were elucidated by Scripture, as happened at Nicaea, and some things were laid down, drawn out of Scripture and based on Scripture. To hold to these is the same as holding to the Word of God."[14]

In this whole discussion the confessional character of dogmas must always be kept in mind. Such an understanding of dogmas implies that the one who confesses identifies himself with his confession and thus stands or falls with his confession of Jesus Christ. There can never be external, juridical criteria which determine the objective validity of a dogma. This does not mean, however, that dogmas do not have theological authority. But, it is more germane to our subject to speak of the compelling character of dogmas rather than of their infallibility, since it then becomes apparent that dogma, or confession, cannot be either understood or accepted apart from the personal in-

[12] Luther, *Von den neuen Eckischen Bullen und Lügen* (1520), *WA* 6, 581, ll. 14-16.

[13] Luther, *On the Councils and the Churches* (1539), *LW* 41, 136.

[14] Luther, *Von der Beicht, ob die der Papst Macht habe zu gebieten* (1521), *WA* 8, 149, ll. 34-150, l. 4.

volvement of the one who confesses. For that reason, too, it cannot be the task of the historian either to regard dogmas as merely the rudiments or the building blocks of a comprehensive system of doctrine, or to issue general criticisms of them from a supposedly modern point of view. It is his task, rather, to demonstrate that the function of dogma is the continuing actualization of the confession of Jesus Christ in the face of the problems of a given day. Full allowance must therefore be made for the historical situation in which the particular dogmas under discussion originated. Such discussion must proceed with the following questions in view: Did these dogmas serve as a valid confession in their day? Was the differentiation between orthodoxy and heresy that they brought about a legitimate one? Or was the result a false posing of the problem, offering no true alternative?

The church has always been convinced that it does not make dogmatic decisions merely in its own strength, but under the guidance of the Holy Spirit. Of course, there are no formal conditions which would guarantee to the church the help of the Holy Spirit. Even venerable councils may err, and have erred, and it is by no means true that the error can always be blamed simply on human weakness. Still no Christian would doubt that at least some dogmatic decisions were made under the guidance of the Holy Spirit. If this is true, it points to an important implication of the question of the theological authority of dogmas. Every attempt to make such authority wholly relative, so as to favor an undogmatic Christianity, denies the work of the Holy Spirit in the past. Then the continuity of the history of dogma also loses its meaning. An insight which the Christian church has gained, in human weakness and in historically contingent form to be sure, but yet with the help of the Holy Spirit, may and must not simply be discarded as rubbish; nor is it right to make the measure of temporary relevance the measure of dogma. Certain confessions of the past may suddenly regain an entirely unexpected relevance. In the recent struggle of the German church with National Socialism not only the *Barmen Declaration* but also the dogmas and confessions of the ancient church and of the Reformation began to speak to the church in a new way. This continuity of the history of dogma has its basis in the continuity of the church, to which God has promised the

Holy Spirit for every age. The *Augsburg Confession* rightly emphasizes this continuity when it says that evangelical Christians believe there will always be a holy Christian church.[15]

Dogmas Must Be Interpreted

Does not this discussion of the authority of dogmas imply that hardly any difference remains between the Catholic doctrine of the *depositum fidei* and the evangelical conception of dogmas? Not really, for the evangelical understanding of dogmas makes the assertion of infallibility impossible in any case. The continuity of the church and of its history of dogma does not alter the fact that dogmas or confessions, which originated in the past, may become outmoded. The process by which certain decisions and doctrinal declarations become antiquated is unavoidable. This can be observed over and over again. Even in our generation certain confessions that were formulated only yesterday under wholly existential conditions no longer speak to men today because the situation in which men now find themselves has in the meantime changed entirely. But who would on that account deny the truth as well as the continuing validity of confessions? Or who would want to use this fact as an argument against the assertion that many decisions of the church are made with the help of the Holy Spirit? This could be argued only if the incarnation of the divine Word were denied, for there is a similarity between the incarnation of the Word and the aid which the Holy Spirit renders in the formulation of the confessions of the church. In both cases God chooses not to put himself at man's disposal but, instead, to work in secret.

The differences between the Roman Catholic and the Protestant understanding of dogmas do not end with their differing conceptions of infallibility. The Roman view that defined dogmas represent, as it were, a treasure which may and should be increased, is for historical and theological reasons not acceptable to Protestants. This view disregards the significance which must be attributed to the continued reappropriation of the confessions of the past. Furthermore, the idea that something new is merely added to earlier confessions simply does not accord with the facts of history. It is true that in the course of the history of dogma the understanding of the faith has increased

[15] *Augsburg Confession*, VII, 1, *BC*, p. 32.

at many points. But the fact that confessions do become antiquated points up the truth that the center of gravity is constantly shifting in the way dogmatic questions are asked and in the demands laid upon Christians. What is involved is not merely a supplementing of old truths but a repeated reconsideration of the whole of Christian truth. The same truth appears and reappears in the history of dogma, or of confessions, but always in a new light. For instance, in the fourth century the problem of the whole nature of the Christian faith was concentrated in the question of the consubstantiality of the Son with the Father. Similarly, during the Reformation era it was not only the question of the appropriation of salvation, i.e., justification, that was at issue, but also—in and with this question—the whole of Christian faith and doctrine. In the days of National Socialism the church was concerned not merely with certain adiaphora which in the past had not yet been clarified and which could now be explained in the sense that old truths would be supplemented through a mere increase in the Christian treasury of understanding. The fact was that once again, and in an entirely new way, the whole of the Christian faith was jeopardized. It is no different in our day. If occasionally we encounter the opinion that, in the West at least, the alternative between what is Christian and what is not Christian is difficult to perceive, we may reply that this was often true during earlier epochs as well. Only in retrospect do things seem to be clear enough to occasion surprise at the possibility that in the past many people, who really wanted to hold on to the heritage of the Christian faith and confession, could make the wrong decision. It is conceivable that in our day the real decisions as to what is Christian and non-Christian may be made at points quite unsuspected by many people, and that at a later time it will be very difficult to comprehend how the most basic questions remained unrecognized by the majority of men.

It is not enough, therefore, to insist upon the continuity of the history of dogma: it must also be emphasized that in every epoch the totality of the Christian confession again hangs in the balance. Progress in the history of dogma does not mean simply that the treasury of Christian insight grows; it means, rather, that in every new day and every new situation everything that was inherited must be won anew.

This implies that the dogmas, or confessions, which the church has set forth in the past need interpretation if the church is truly to make them its own. It is possible, for instance, to enter fully into the questions and problems of the fourth century, and to side honestly with Athanasian orthodoxy and against Arian heresy, without gaining much thereby for the present. The fact is that the decisions of the past must be interpreted, i.e., they must be, as it were, translated, if they are to be intelligible in our day. This task of translation cannot be, as such, the job of the historian doing research in the history of dogma. To be sure, such research must not treat dogmas as mere entities of the remote past. But the real task of the historian of dogma is to ascertain above all else how certain dogmas, in the sense of confessions or doctrinal confessions, originated, and then to discuss the questions how and in what sense these dogmas have in their day fulfilled their function of pointing to Christ. Among the theological sciences it is systematic theology which is entrusted with the task of the translation of dogmas. The church, too, through its preaching and its confession, must carry the task forward in each new generation.

In all this we do not mean to say that the historian of dogma should not view his task as one in which all the tools of scientific criticism must be employed. No one can prescribe either his methods or his results, nor should anyone be permitted to do so. Every attempt to restrict his freedom would quickly bring its own retribution. Nor does the church really require such restrictive attempts. It would appear, however, that the notion of carrying on research in the history of dogma with the initial and specific purpose of destroying dogma can no longer be scientifically justified. It is apparent that such an attempt rests upon certain philosophical presuppositions which have not been gained through the study of the history of dogma. The history of dogma and the criticism of dogma should at least be methodologically separated; they must not be fused into one. Not infrequently the works of Harnack and his followers, which are otherwise very brilliant, suffer from a fundamental error of this kind, which, despite their great erudition, negates the possibility of arriving at an unbiased understanding of the subject. This is nowhere more evident than in Harnack's thesis that basically only the Father, and not the Son, is part of the Gospel.

The entire New Testament tradition attests just the contrary. Yet it is this thesis which, in the last analysis, constitutes the criterion by which Harnack measures the whole history of dogma. The historian of dogma must not suppose that he should play the same role in the Protestant church as is exercised in the Roman Church by the Holy Office,[16] with only the criteria reversed. Not criticism, but interpretation of dogmas, is the task of the historian of dogma. It is self-evident that this task can be carried forward only with all the tools of critical scholarship.

It should be added that at bottom Harnack himself saw this task clearly, in spite of his own methodology. A good part of what he wrote in a letter to his friend Friedrich Loofs can only be commended: "I believe that we cannot make progress without employing an iconoclastic element. Since we are not permitted to exercise this directly, neither the pulpit nor ecclesiastical instruction being the place for it, it is my opinion that it must not be missing from our books, if we are to free Protestantism from its tinsel. . . . I would not wish to spare any student of theology a profound crisis. The three results which such a crisis might have, namely, the rejection of theology, the undergirding of authority, and [new] understanding, are all to be preferred to that sponginess of mind and thought which their indifference preserves at the university, in order that they may nurture it later with what is called 'experience in the ministry,' and what in most cases is simply routine."[17] Sharp criticism of dogmas is to be preferred in every case to total indifference, since the latter does not even pay them the honor of taking them seriously.

Can There Be New Dogmas?

As we know, for the Roman Catholic church this question can be answered affirmatively. Since the sixteenth century three new dogmas have been defined: in the nineteenth century the dogmas of the immaculate conception of Mary and the infallibility of the pope, and in the twentieth century the dogma of the assumption of Mary. Nor can there be any doubt that the

[16] The Roman Congregation entrusted with the responsibility for the presentation of the purity of the faith and the prosecution of heretical errors.

[17] Cited from Agnes von Zahn-Harnack, *Adolf von Harnack* (2nd ed.; Berlin: de Gruyter, 1951), p. 103.

Roman church can in the future declare new propositions of faith to be dogmas and that it will probably do so. Of course, there is in the Roman church a whole array of voices which have warned for a long time against further dogmatic affirmations. They would not, by any means, deny their church—and in our day this means the pope—the right and the authority to define new dogmas. But they do point to the fact that every new dogma deepens the gulf between Catholicism on the one side, and Orthodoxy as well as Protestantism, on the other. It should especially be noted that every new Marian dogma would heighten the danger that the Roman church might find itself accused, to a greater degree than hitherto, of giving up its Christocentricity in favor of the cult of Mary. We must wait and see, of course, whether or not such voices will make themselves heard in the Roman church. In the period since the great western schism they have not been able to accomplish much. Quite to the contrary, they have not seldom been suspected of representing only a half-Catholicism. This was especially the case during the discussions at the First Vatican Council in the nineteenth century.

How do the non-Roman churches answer the question about new dogmas? The Eastern Orthodox church regards the decision of the Council of Nicaea in 787 as the last dogma. Since then it has refrained from defining any new dogmas, and it would appear that it does not expect to do so in the future. One reason for this, by no means an unimportant one, lies in Orthodoxy's understanding of the authority of councils, which it insists must be ecumenical, something they cannot be in any comprehensive sense, however, after the separation from Rome.

In terms of the Roman Catholic understanding of dogma it is self-evident that Protestantism, too, has not accorded any new propositions of faith the status of dogma. In fact, strictly speaking, Protestantism, as has already been noted, does not recognize a single dogma, if dogmas are understood to be infallible doctrinal propositions. If, on the other hand, dogma is understood to mean an ecclesiastical or doctrinal confession which is not infallible, but which is binding, a new image emerges. Protestantism is not lacking in attempts to arrive at new and binding doctrinal declarations or confessions. Whether or not these have been precisely formulated is not decisive. During the last

130 years, for instance, the Anglican church has gone through a development which has had momentous consequences. This is most apparent in the concept of the apostolic succession, which is given no significance in the basic confession of Anglicans, the Thirty-nine Articles and the *Book of Common Prayer.* Yet, in our day, it has become practically a basic doctrine of Anglicanism.

Within German Protestantism there have also been attempts to formulate new confessions. Even if we disregard the sporadic attempts during the sixteenth century to introduce another confession as a doctrinal norm, as well as the occasional abortive attempts to set forth such norms during the last century, it is still necessary to mention the *Barmen Declaration.* The question as to whether or not this declaration should rank as a confession has led to a lively controversy. On the practical level the member churches of the Evangelical Church in Germany reached different conclusions in the matter. The important thing in this context, of course, is that here German Protestantism, for the first time since the Reformation, clearly recognized and discharged its task of newly confessing its faith in a way that is binding for the present. No matter how individuals may regard the *Barmen Declaration,* on one thing there should be agreement among all evangelical Christians, namely, that here the Protestant church again recognized an obligation which it has. Confessionalists have attempted to belittle the significance of this fact by saying that the confessions of the ancient church were quite sufficient for warding off the heresy of the "German Christians." As a matter of fact these confessions did not accomplish this task. The reason is that, while the continuity of the history of dogma is undeniable, there must also be, ever and again, actual confessing; implicit in such confessing is not only that previously known and confessed truths need to be supplemented, but also that, once again, in a decision now to be made, the entire Christian faith hangs in the balance. The fact that the *Barmen Declaration* came into being signifies, then, a decisive step forward in the history of Protestantism, a step which the Protestant church cannot undo or ignore without inviting retribution. For the absolute dearth of significant new confessional declarations within Protestantism in the period since the Reformation represents a distressing condition which simply must be rectified.

Saying this does not mean we are advocating a greater production of new dogmas or confessions. A surplus of confessions is a distinct possibility. As far as opinions, declarations, and "statements" are concerned, the Protestant church has lately experienced a veritable tidal wave. As urgent as the continual taking of positions may be, if they are published too frequently the statements in question lose their value. Here we are not concerned, however, with taking a position, but with confessions—or whatever one chooses to call them—which formulate the Christian faith in a new and binding way with reference to a given situation, and yet in a way which has more than temporary validity. The church is not given such a confession every year, often not even in every generation or every century. Nor is this really necessary. There is no need to become impatient. Still, the Protestant church should recognize that the confession, even a newly formulated confession, is an essential part of faith. A faith which no longer knows how to confess, and which can no longer express this confession doctrinally, will lose its vigor and become weak. For every epoch must answer anew the question which the Lord of the church and of the world puts to it: "Who do you say that I am?"

I

Canon and Creed

THE FIRST decision of the church which may be called "dogma," in the sense of doctrinal confession, is the creation of the canon and of the creed. To speak first of the canon, it should be noted that its significance is overriding. The fact that Christianity has a canon of sacred writings as the basis for its doctrine and proclamation can be explained, at least from a purely external point of view, on the basis of the example of Judaism. To all intents and purposes the latter had completed the canon of the Old Testament in the days of Jesus, though it was not finally fixed until the Jewish Synod of Jamnia around the year A.D. 100. It is to be noted, however, that the Christian and Jewish understanding of the Old Testament differed from the beginning. Jesus himself, though giving full recognition to the Old Testament, had given a new meaning to some of its sayings. Especially in his "I say to you" of the Sermon on the Mount, Jesus meant to proclaim the original will of God, which was now becoming manifest in him. Thus it is not possible to explain the church's appropriation of the Old Testament canon, as well as the designation of the books of the New Testament as canon, solely on the basis of the example of Judaism. Rather, the establishing of a canon constitutes the first basic doctrinal decision of the church.

The Old Testament

During the first hundred years of the Christian church, its canon, in the strict sense of the word, was constituted exclusively by the Old Testament. Most of the writings which were later gathered together in the New Testament were, of course, already in existence. It must be remembered that with the exception of a few writings the books of the New Testament were written before the year 100. Furthermore, the writings which were later called New Testament Scriptures were in regular use by the churches. They were read in the services of worship, they were regarded as criteria of congregational order, and they were used in catechetical instruction. They were also employed for theological purposes, of course. Still, neither the Gospels nor the letters of Paul were elevated to the status of canon, in the strict sense of the word, until well into the second century. The church regarded itself as the new Israel, and for that reason it clung to the same canon the Jews had. Yet, it was not felt that Christians had the Old Testament in common with the Jews. Quite to the contrary, the ancient church was convinced that if the Old Testament is rightly understood it is a Christian book which testifies in its entirety to Jesus Christ. This point of view was set forth especially by Justin Martyr (d. *ca.* 165)in his *Dialogue with Trypho the Jew.* As a result Christians denied the Jews the right to claim the canon of the Old Testament for themselves.

The notion that the Old Testament belongs not to Judaism, but to the church, has as its presupposition a very special interpretation of Old Testament texts. This was an interpretation which was also repeatedly used as proof of the rightness of the Christian claim to the Old Testament. Of course, even the theologians of the ancient church were aware that the Old Testament does not simply witness directly to Christ. Yet they were convinced that the sense of the Old Testament is not exhausted in a literal understanding of it, but that there is, in addition, a deeper meaning of the Old Testament texts, which can be discerned only when the Old Testament is read from the point of view of its fulfillment in Jesus Christ. Two methods were employed in the ancient church to unfold this deeper sense of Scripture. The one is the allegorical interpretation. It was not an original creation of the church, but was used before the advent of Christianity by the Jewish-Hellenistic theologians of Alexandria. Its purpose was to give to offensive passages of the Old Testament a meaning which would be acceptable to educated Jews, and even to pagans with a philosophical interest.

The church took over this allegorical method of interpretation from Hellenistic Judaism and then developed it, at least partially, on its own. This kind of exegesis often produces results decidedly different from the literal sense of the texts. In fact, sometimes the results no longer bear any relation to the texts.

The second method of scriptural interpretation, which the church used from the beginning in its exegesis of the Old Testament, was that of typology. This was not taken over from Judaism, but—overlooking the typology which is already found in the Old Testament but which did not have very much significance for the scriptural interpretation of late Judaism—was created by the church. This method of interpretation sticks much closer to the literal sense of the text. Not infrequently, of course, typological exegesis became allegorical exegesis. Yet the typological interpretation made possible, in principle, a true historical valuation of the contents of the text. At the same time it was able to show that the sense of the text is not limited to the period of its origin, but that it points toward something yet to come, and can be understood in its dimension of depth only when viewed from that vantage point. This interpretation is seen as according with the divine plan of history, which, stretching from the creation to the last judgment, reaches its climax in Jesus Christ.

Once it had appropriated the Old Testament as canon, the Christian church was henceforth faced with the task of interpreting it in a way which, by comparison with Judaism, was completely new. The church read the Old Testament in the light of its fulfillment in Jesus Christ, even as it also understood Jesus Christ from the point of view of the Old Testament. This reciprocal relation in the understanding of the Old Testament and of the figure of Jesus Christ is already apparent in the Gospels. Texts such as Psalm 22 have influenced the accounts of the passion of Jesus. Matthew, especially, always emphasizes the importance of the so-called proof from prophecy. It is especially significant that according to the early Christian creedal formula about the death and resurrection of Jesus, which St. Paul transmits in 1 Corinthians 15:3-4, everything took place "in accordance with the scriptures." Paul says "that Christ died for our sins in accordance with the scriptures, that he was buried, that he was raised on the third day in accordance with the scriptures." It must not be supposed, however, that the church could reach the insight that Jesus is the Christ only on the basis of the Old Testament. This was known, rather, as a result of his postresurrection appearances. Still the fact of the suffering and resurrection of Christ is disclosed in its total significance only when seen from the point of view of the Old Testament. On the other hand, it is only from the point of view of the eschatological event of the resurrection that the Old Testament can be fully recognized as referring prophetically to Jesus Christ.

It was thus that the first generations of Christians read the Old Testament as the Christian Bible. What is said in the so-called *Epistle of Barnabas,* a treatise which originated, probably in Alexandria, around 135, was the conviction of all early Christendom: "the prophets, having obtained grace from Him, prophesied concerning Him."[1] An especially beautiful example of the early Christian interpretation of the Old Testament is found in the *Homily on the Passover* by Melito of Sardis (*ca.* 170). In this sermon on the exodus of the Jews from Egypt (Exod., chap. 12) the pascal lamb is typologically interpreted as pointing to Christ, the true Pascal Lamb. Melito also touches upon the problem of the law and, echoing John 1:14, penned the profound sentence: "The Law became Word and the old became new, going forth together from Sion and Jerusalem, and the command became grace, and the type became truth."[2] This sentence perceives the difference between the Old Testament and the Christian faith, as well as the unity of the two, a unity which is grounded in the belief that Jesus Christ is the "true" fulfillment of the Old Testament.

The Formation of the New Testament Canon

While the significance of the Old Testament was very great for the ancient church, it must be kept in mind that there were other sayings which the church also considered as "Bible" from

[1] *Epistle of Barnabas,* chap. 5. *ANF* 1, 139.

[2] Melito of Sardis, *Homily on the Passion,* par. 2; ed. C. Bonner (Philadelphia: University of Pennsylvania Press, 1940), p. 168. The sermon is, as I have tried to show elsewhere, a homily on the Passover, not on the Passion; see my edition, *Die Passa-Homilie des Bischofs Meliton von Sardes* (Leiden: Brill, 1958).

the beginning, though they had not yet been set down in writing. The words of the Lord, for instance, possessed incomparable authority, even though the primitive community both preserved and formed the tradition about the earthly life of Jesus in the light of the resurrection. Jesus himself had said, "Heaven and earth will pass away, but my words will not pass away" (Matt. 24:35). St. Paul differentiated carefully between his own opinion and certain words of the Lord (1 Thess. 4:15; 1 Cor. 7:10, 12, 25; 9:14) and, of course, he acknowledged without question the authority of the latter.

The words of the apostles also carried great weight. Their special rank was assured by the word of Jesus, "He who receives you receives me, and he who receives me receives him who sent me" (Matt. 10:40). Furthermore, the apostles were eyewitnesses of him who had been resurrected.

Thus there came into being, alongside the Old Testament, a kind of initial form of a second canon. It is significant that the formula "It is written," with which quotations from the Old Testament were introduced, is used to refer to the words of Jesus as early as *ca.* 135 in the *Epistle of Barnabas*[3] and, at about the same time, in the *Second Epistle of Clement.*[4] This means that the authority of the words of Jesus was equal to that of the Old Testament. Even earlier than this, at the beginning of the second century, the Gospels were regarded as the final court of appeal in the settling of doctrinal differences.[5] Lastly, the letters of Paul also had great significance for the order and life of the Christian communities, and this at an early time. They were read in the services of worship, which naturally indicates that they were also the basis for doctrine.

Thus, in the course of time the New Testament canon developed. It is difficult to say at what point this development began. Certain beginnings are already noticeable in the first half of the second century. In the middle of the second century the process was intensified. The author of 2 Peter, which probably originated between 120 and 150, already equates the letters of Paul with "other scriptures" (3:15 f.). The first writer actually

[3] *Epistle of Barnabas,* chap. 4. *ANF* 1, 138.

[4] *Second Epistle of Clement,* chaps. 2 ff. *ANF* 7, 517 f.

[5] *Epistle of Ignatius to the Philadelphians,* chap. 8. *ANF* 1, 84.

to speak of a "new" testament was Irenaeus of Lyon (d. *ca.* 202). It must be noted, however, that Irenaeus still differentiates carefully between the authority of the Gospels and that of Paul's letters. Not one of Irenaeus' 206 quotations from St. Paul is introduced by the formula, "It is written." Nevertheless, the boundaries of the New Testament canon had been fixed in a preliminary way around the year 200. Of course, the canonicity of some of the Catholic Epistles, as well as of the Book of Revelation, remained controversial for some time to come. The New Testament canon was finally and exactly fixed at a series of synods during the second half of the fourth century. Yet the most important books, i.e., the four Gospels, and the letters of Paul, were regarded from the end of the second century onward, both in the East and in the West, as the New Testament canon.

It has sometimes been maintained (especially by Harnack) that the formation of the New Testament canon was decisively influenced by Marcion. Marcion, who had affinities with certain gnostic ideas, created his own canon shortly before the middle of the second century. He discarded the Old Testament, as well as many writings which the church was later to include in the New Testament. His canon, which included the Gospel of Luke and the first ten letters of Paul, is the first canon of New Testament writings which is extant. Yet the church's canon of the New Testament was, as we have noted, already in process of development. Before Marcion the church already possessed a certain collection (or collections) of New Testament writings that were regarded as holy scriptures. Marcion undoubtedly speeded up the process of the fixing of the New Testament inasmuch as his rejection of the Old Testament and his deletion of everything seemingly Jewish from the New Testament writings forced the church to clarify its attitude toward the God of the Old Testament, toward creation, and toward the New Testament tradition. Since the church, in reaction against Marcion, held fast to the Old Testament and in its development of the New Testament canon did not join him in his arbitrary omission of many writings and portions of writings, it remained true to its tradition and accorded it normative significance by giving the New Testament writings canonical status.

To overestimate the significance of this decision would be

difficult. It is not diminished by the fact that at a time when councils were not meeting and official opinions were not being published, the church gained clarity about its faith and doctrine through its general rejection of Marcion. From the point of view of church history the fixing of the New Testament canon, together with the development of the doctrine of apostolic succession, constitutes the terminus of the movement of primitive Christianity toward the early catholic church. Henceforth there are basic norms for doctrine and order. From the point of view of the history of dogma, too, the formation of the New Testament canon constitutes an event no less significant. Through its recognition of the New Testament Scriptures the church also strengthened its position regarding the Old Testament and creation. The gnostic and Marcionite differentiation between God as Creator and God as Redeemer, as well as the resulting depreciation of creation and of the corporeality of man (which Marcion regarded as a principle other than divine), was flatly rejected by the church. Put positively, this means that the Christian church accepted the unity of the God of the Old Testament with the God of the New Testament as a fundamental doctrinal norm; that, in spite of the church's radical understanding of sin, creation as such was regarded as good; that the unity of the church with the chosen people of the Old Covenant, as well as the general outlines (though certainly not the details) of a particular understanding of the Old Testament, could not be given up. It is thus no exaggeration to say that the fixing of the New Testament canon represents a basic dogma of the church, i.e., it represents a witness to the revelation of God in Jesus Christ, one on which all later doctrinal decisions are based and which, in fact, makes these decisions possible. The fixing of a given New Testament canon indicates that only from these Scriptures can the church gain valid and binding knowledge concerning the revelation in Jesus Christ. No matter how important and profound other writings may be, they cannot claim the same authority in the church as the canonical Scriptures. This basic dogma has remained in force for most Christian communions. To be sure, it has not in fact prevented Christians, at certain times and especially in certain churches, from attempting to find guide lines for affirmations of the Christian faith in other writings and sources.

Scripture and Tradition

The according of canonical status to a certain number of New Testament Scriptures also signified an important decision for certain other questions. Insofar as at the beginning written and oral tradition both possessed authortiy, with no attempt being made to reflect on their relationship to each other, the creation of a New Testament canon was bound to bring about a change. The decisive criterion for establishing the canonicity of the New Testament Scriptures was their age. The attempt was to make normative those Scriptures which had been written by the apostles or by their immediate followers. In the church's opposition to Gnosticism, which claimed to possess a secret tradition coming from the period between the resurrection and the ascension of Christ, the claim of the apostolic authorship of the most important Scriptures was, in fact, both a legitimate and a useful criterion. We know, of course, that the critical scholarship of our day regards the apostolic authorship of some New Testament Scriptures differently from the way the church did in the second century. It is surprising to find, however, with what accuracy, generally speaking, the church of that day included the important and most reliable scriptures in the canon. It is difficult to think of any noncanonical writing that it would seem desirable to add to the canon. There might be some dispute about a few books on the periphery of the canon, but there can scarcely be any doubt about the significance and worth of most of the New Testament Scriptures.

The fixing of the New Testament canon raised the question of the relevance of tradition. In considering this question today, one must disregard modern considerations as to which had the greater significance, the written or the oral tradition. In this form the problem of Scripture and tradition was not raised in the entire ancient church. Things were different during the first centuries of the church from what they were during the Reformation or from what they are in our day. In the ancient church the really important thing was, first of all, that such a special concept as "tradition" should even arise. In the thinking of the apostolic fathers, and even in that of the apologists (which brings us down to about the middle of the second century), Scripture and tradition were not separated from each other. These early Christian writers were convinced that the Christian religion includes certain propositions of faith and certain patterns of life, that Christianity inherited both of these from the apostles, and that in the last analysis both of them go back to Jesus Christ. It was possible to insist, therefore, that it was crucial to "follow God and the doctrines [delivered] by him."[6] Sometimes it was simply emphasized that Christ is our teacher,[7] without raising the question as to the manner in which this doctrine was transmitted. It is true that the Old Testament, as well as the Gospels (which Justin Martyr calls the "memoirs of the apostles"),[8] possessed supreme authority. Scripture and tradition, however, were not set in opposition to each other.

The fixing of the New Testament canon led to a change in this respect. As a matter of fact, at the time when the formation of the New Testament canon was in effect complete, a precise concept of tradition is also discernible in the church. This new concept of tradition is influenced, of course, by the controversy with Gnosticism over what is the right tradition. The word "tradition" in this new sense we meet for the first time at the end of the second century in Irenaeus. For him it is still possible to include in the concept of tradition the entire Christian faith. Thus he emphasizes, for instance, that in spite of all the differences of language and understanding which exist among particular churches, the power of tradition is one and the same in all, so that the entire church proclaims and transmits its doctrine as if it "possessed only one mouth."[9] Yet Irenaeus understands by tradition also the oral tradition which the church took over from the apostles. He holds that this tradition is basically not dependent upon any written fixation of it—many tribes of barbarians believe in Christ and preserve the old tradition without having written documents.[10] In this connection there are several important considerations. First, for Irenaeus this tradition is never something secret; it is always publicly transmitted, and in such a way that anyone is free to examine it. Second, this tradition is at the same time pneumatically wrought, even as the entire church is permeated and led by the Spirit. Third,

[6] Justin Martyr, *Dialogue with Trypho*, chap. 80. *ANF* 1, 239.
[7] Justin Martyr, *The First Apology*, chap. 12. *ANF* 1, 166.
[8] *Ibid.*, chap. 67. *ANF* 1, 186.
[9] Irenaeus, *Against Heresies*, Bk. I, chap. 10, sec. 2. *ANF* 1, 331.
[10] *Ibid.*, Bk. III, chap 4, sec. 1 f. *ANF* 1, 417.

there is no contradiction between the oral and the written tradition, since both go back to the apostles. Of course, as a result of the parallel position of Scripture and tradition the church was faced with the task of bringing them into the proper relationship to each other. Tradition came to be regarded as explaining Scripture, or at least certain difficult passages in it, as, on the other hand, Scripture became the norm for tradition. Thus the theological decision which had been made when the New Testament Scriptures were canonized was bound to lead to further reflection and new decisions.

Another factor was of no less importance. Even though the establishment of a canon, at least in its outlines, represented a decision against gnostic and Marcionite heresies, the church was soon to learn that this decision had not eliminated the threat these posed. The heretics, too, could appeal to Scripture, and often did so with great skill. It is not an accident that the first commentaries upon New Testament Scriptures did not arise within the church at large, but in gnostic Christian groups. In the middle of the second century Heracleon, a disciple of the Gnostic, Valentinus, wrote a commentary on the Gospel of John in which he claimed it for Gnosticism. It was apparent that in its attempt to repudiate Gnosticism the church needed to do something more than include some books in its canon of Scripture. If the gnostic threat was to be met, these books required constant interpretation; furthermore, this exegesis had to be undertaken according to definite principles. As a matter of fact, in the antignostic teachers of the church, especially Irenaeus and Tertullian (d. after 220), one notes that tradition, as over against Scripture, is given special weight because only thus could Gnosticism be warded off. They did not exalt tradition above Scripture, however, as they have sometimes been accused of doing. Rather, they understood tradition as that which summarizes the content of Scripture.

The Creed

Besides Scripture and tradition one finds at the end of the second century another entity of fundamental significance for the doctrine of the church, namely, the creed. There had been creedal formulas in the church from the beginning. To be sure, in the first century there is no one formula, the wording of which is unambiguously recognized as a creed. In the second century, too, there are various formulas of faith. Despite many attempts, scholars have not succeeded in establishing a fixed wording of the creed in Irenaeus and Tertullian, even though both of these men refer frequently to the creed and both cite certain formulas, the wording of which, however, is never uniform. Such divergences notwithstanding, the process of the formation of the creed had come to initial completion already in the second century. One of the oldest creeds to be canonized in a particular church was the old Roman baptismal creed, which is generally designated as *Romanum* (*R*). According to the reconstruction of Hans Lietzmann an early form of this confession read as follows:

> I believe in God, the Father, the Almighty;
> And in Jesus Christ, his only begotten Son, our Lord,
> And in the Holy Ghost, the holy church, the resurrection of the flesh.[11]

In this form the old Roman confession probably originated not later than the middle of the second century. This very simple formula thus originally consisted of three tripartite affirmations. Possibly toward the end of the second century more precise definitions were added to the second and third articles, so that *R* then read:

> I believe in God the Father, [the] Almighty;
> And in Jesus Christ his only begotten Son, our Lord,
> Who was born of the Holy Ghost, and the Virgin Mary,
> Who was crucified under Pontius Pilate and buried;
> on the third day he rose from the dead,
> ascended into heaven,
> sat down at the right hand of the Father;
> from whence he will come to judge the living and the dead;
> And in the Holy Ghost, the holy church, the forgiveness of sins, the resurrection of the flesh.[12]

The lengthy christological insertion was probably directed against certain christological heresies, mainly docetism, but also the adoptionist Monarchianism about which we shall speak in the second chapter.

[11] H. Lietzmann, *The Founding of the Church Universal,* trans. B. L. Woolf (London: Lutterworth, and New York: Scribners, 1938), p. 143. Translations of this creed and the next two creeds used with permission of Lutterworth Press, London, and World Publishing Co., Cleveland.

[12] *Ibid.,* p. 144.

More or less similar creeds were extant in most of the Christian congregations of the West. In Rome, however, the creed was given a fixed formulation earlier than it was in other congregations. Later the wording of *R* became generally accepted in the West. The East, on the other hand, long maintained a much greater variety in the formulation of creeds. Furthermore, it is a characteristic of the eastern creeds that they did not interpret the divine sonship of Christ simply from the point of view of his virgin birth, as did *R*; rather, they understood it from the point of view of his pre-existent generation by God the Father. Their purpose was to set forth the difference between the Son of God and everything that had been created in time. According to Lietzmann the original eastern trinitarian formula read as follows:

> I believe in one God, the Father, the Almighty, of whom everything is,
> and in one Lord, Jesus Christ, the only begotten Son of God, through whom everything is,
> and in the Holy Ghost.[13]

What is the significance of the creed for the history of dogma? The answer is most easily given if one keeps in mind its setting in the life of the church. The assertion has often been made that baptism was clearly the setting. This is true, of course, insofar as creeds were recited at baptism, where it was customary to use the question and answer method. Thus the person to be baptized was asked, "Do you believe in God?" or, "Do you believe in Jesus Christ?" and so forth, with certain elaborations of question and answer being added. If the relationship between baptism and creeds is more carefully investigated, however, the thesis that such creeds have their setting in baptism needs to be stated with greater precision and modified to the effect that they were connected with the instruction of catechumens. At a baptism it is obvious that the recitation of a creed can take place only if the person to be baptized has previously been instructed in the faith he is to confess. Hence the formula of faith was intended primarily for the instruction of candidates for baptism. This leads to a further point, namely, that the creed functioned as a formal summary of the Christian

[13] *Ibid.*, p. 146.

faith. It was the criterion of faith upon which catechetical instruction was based.

Whether or not the creed often quoted in Irenaeus and Tertullian may be equated with the so-called rule of faith remains a problem. Formerly this equation was usually made. In our day certain objections have been raised against it. It may be that the rule of faith did not constitute a fixed formula so much as it did a series of fundamental doctrines of the Christian faith, which actually were largely parallel with the declarations of the creed. Perhaps the rule of faith should be regarded as the theologically deepened, normative understanding of the creed. Certain it is that the creed and the rule of faith cannot be separated from each other. Whatever their relationship to each other may be, it is clear that in them the church had in hand an instrument which was more effective in its controversy with heresy than was mere tradition. The reason is that these formulas were precise, short, and unambiguous. Furthermore, their content was fixed, in essentials, even though varying traditions existed concerning particular affirmations. Because of these characteristics, these formulas were in certain respects even superior to Scripture. It is no wonder, therefore, that a man like Tertullian preferred to appeal to the rule of faith in his controversy with Gnosticism rather than to Scripture. The latter could always be distorted to accord with the private opinions of the heretics. This does not mean that the rule of faith was exalted above Scripture. Yet the rule of faith did in fact attain the rank of dogma. It served as criterion for determining heresy and orthodoxy.

It is not unimportant to note the opinion, which existed even in this early period, that the apostles themselves had transmitted the creed to succeeding generations. Tertullian even asserts that the rule of faith derives from Christ himself, having been transmitted by his disciples.[14] Out of such conceptions grew the later legend about the origin of the Apostles' Creed of which Rufinus of Aquileia speaks in his *Exposition of the Creed* (*ca.* 404). According to this legend, which appears frequently in medieval writings, the apostles, having received the gift of tongues at Pentecost, were instructed by the Lord to proclaim God's Word to all nations. Before they departed, however, they

[14] Tertullian, *Apology*, chap. 47, *ANF* 3, 52.

decided upon a common basis for their preaching, so they would not proclaim different doctrines because of the great distances that would separate them from one another. Hence they set down the Apostles' Creed as a norm for their teachings, each apostle contributing a portion. Thereafter they decided that this creed should be transmitted to later generations as a criterion for faith. This legend, which obviously reconstructs in idealized form the historical process of the origin of the creed, nevertheless hits the mark in one respect, namely, the relative antiquity as well as the importance of the creed. Next to the biblical canon it was, so to speak, the second dogma of the church.

2

The Doctrine of the Trinity

Beginnings

IN THE PRECEDING chapter the rule of faith and the creed were presented as a criterion for the church's preaching and teaching. Both of these, the rule of faith and the creed, constitute an important step in the direction of the development of the church's doctrine of the Trinity, because they summarize briefly the faith of Christianity. It was still a long time, of course, well into the fourth century, before the doctrine of the Trinity was dogmatically clarified. How did this come about? What were the reasons which moved the church to express its faith in God and in Jesus Christ, as well as its experience of the presence of the Holy Spirit, in the form of the doctrine of the Trinity? Is it essential for one who wants to be a Christian to accept this doctrine also?

First, it is important to note that the doctrine of the Trinity does not go back to non-Christian sources, as has sometimes been supposed in the past. There has been no lack of attempts to find the initial form of the doctrine of the Trinity in Plato, or in Hinduism, or in Parsiism. All such attempts may be regarded today as having floundered. It is another question, of course, whether or not the church, in developing the doctrine of the Trinity, had recourse to certain thought forms already present in the philosophical and religious environment, in order that, with the help of these, it might give its own faith clear intellectual expression. This question must definitely be answered in the affirmative. In particular cases the appropriation of this concept or that can often be proved. Unfortunately, however, it is true that particularly in reference to the beginnings of the doctrine of the Trinity there is still much uncertainty. In this area final clarity has not yet been achieved.

As far as the New Testament is concerned, one does not find in it an actual doctrine of the Trinity. This does not mean very much, however, for generally speaking the New Testament is less intent upon setting forth certain doctrines than it is upon proclaiming the kingdom of God, a kingdom that dawns in and with the person of Jesus Christ. At the same time, however, there are in the New Testament the rudiments of a concept of God that was susceptible of further development and clarification, along doctrinal lines.

Judaism, which constituted the environment in which the early Christians lived and from which they themselves had come, has always been an austerely monotheistic religion. From it Christianity inherited monotheism. Over against pagan polytheism Christians and Jews have always had monotheism in common, though their understanding of it differs.

From the very beginning, of course, Christians not only believed in God in the sense in which the Jews did, but they also believed in Jesus Christ. The Holy Spirit, too, was mentioned more frequently by them, and in a different way. Speaking first of the person of Jesus Christ, it should be observed that Christians expressed their faith in him in a great variety of ways. For the primitive church Jesus Christ was the Messiah. As the Gospel of John emphasizes again and again, his early followers regarded him as standing in an incomparably close and indissoluble union with the Father. In other places he is called the likeness of God (2 Cor. 4:4; Col. 1:15). In the prologue of the Gospel of John we are told that the divine Logos, who was in the beginning with God, became flesh in Jesus Christ (John 1:1-18). Here the pre-existence of Christ before his earthly life is asserted. In doing so it was possible for the church to begin with certain conceptions which pre-Christian Judaism had formed about the pre-existence of the figure of Wisdom. But what had been only an ideal within

Judaism was regarded within Christianity from the standpoint of the decisive fact of the incarnation.

Other passages, too, speak of the pre-existence of Christ, or at least presuppose it (e.g., Phil. 2:5-11; Rom. 8:32; 2 Cor. 8:9). A number of passages go so far as to call Christ God. It is disputed, of course, whether in Romans 9:5, for example, the word "God" actually has reference to Christ, or whether the last words in this verse represent a benediction which speaks of God the Father. Most of the objections which are raised against the conception that Paul here calls Christ God are based only on the general consideration that the strict monotheism which Paul inherited from Judaism would keep him from making such an assertion. In reply to these objections it may be said that Paul was able to pray to the exalted Lord. It would follow, therefore, that he could also use the word "God" for Christ. In other passages of the New Testament the predicate "God" is without a doubt applied to Christ.[1] With these affirmations, which for Jewish monotheism were utterly offensive, Christians expressed their faith that it was not merely some heavenly being which encountered them in Jesus Christ, but God himself, and that because of this, his coming, especially his cross and his resurrection, had meaning for the entire world.

The New Testament affirmations about the Holy Spirit are not so clear and univocal as those about Jesus Christ. It was known that the Spirit had spoken through the prophets and that he had descended at the baptism of Jesus in order to equip him for his work. The Johannine affirmations about the Spirit are especially far-reaching. For the period after his departure Jesus promises his people the Paraclete (NEB, "Advocate"; RSV, "Counselor"), who is purposely called "the Spirit of truth" (John 14:17), or "the Holy Spirit" (John 14:26). Since it is asserted of the Spirit that he is "another Paraclete" (John 14:16), it could be supposed that the Spirit is here conceived to be another person distinct from Jesus Christ. But this is hardly the case. The meaning, rather, is that in the Spirit Jesus himself comes to his disciples as the Paraclete. It is noteworthy, of course, and very important for the development of dogma, that Christ and the Paraclete are not simply equated, but that the

[1] At John 1:18 the best manuscripts read, "the only (or, only begotten) God" *(monogenēs theos).* Cf. 1 John 5:20, "This is the true God and eternal life."

Spirit is called "*another* Paraclete." How vividly the early church experienced the reality of the Spirit, and how definitely it was influenced by that reality, can be seen on every hand in the Pauline letters. The Spirit is called the Spirit of God, as well as the Spirit of Christ (Rom. 8:9). Here, too, however, the Spirit is not yet conceived in personal terms, at least not in the sense of the later doctrine of the Trinity.

The New Testament is not satisfied, however, with these sometimes rather far-reaching assertions about God the Father, Jesus Christ, and the Holy Spirit. Some passages present triadic formulas. They are called "triadic," and not "trinitarian," because they name Father, Son, and Spirit alongside one another without reflecting upon the oneness of God and, hence, do not yet contain a doctrine of the Trinity. We have such a formula in 2 Corinthians 13:13, "The grace of the Lord Jesus Christ and the love of God and the fellowship of the Holy Spirit be with you all." It is significant that while in Ephesians 4:4-6 the Spirit, the Son, and the Father are all mentioned and without further elucidation, in each case the "one" is emphasized. There is "one God," not three gods, in whom Christians believe. The baptismal command in Matthew 28:19 is especially striking in this respect: baptism is to take place "in the name of the Father and of the Son and of the Holy Spirit." The significant thing about this formula is not so much that here Father, Son, and Spirit are named alongside one another, which happened frequently at the time, but that mention is made of the "name" of the Holy Spirit. There are not three names in reference to which baptism is to take place, but one name, a name, moreover, which includes the name of the Holy Spirit. The understanding of the Spirit upon which this baptismal formula is based goes much further than that which is otherwise found in the Gospel of Matthew. As a matter of fact the church possessed in this baptismal command an affirmation which went far beyond its comprehension at the time, and the full content and deep significance of which it could appreciate only after a long development had come to fruition. The reason was that the church had hardly begun to realize what the confession of Jesus Christ as God, as well as the presence of the divine Spirit in the church, would mean for its total understanding of God. At the same time it can hardly be doubted that the affirmations of faith which the first Christians made with reference to God the Father, Son, and Holy Spirit, and which were based upon God's act in Jesus Christ and upon the pouring out of the Holy Spirit, simply cried out for fuller elaboration. It was not merely a necessity to point out, in opposition to Judaism, in what sense a Christian is a monotheist. The faith itself demanded greater clarity.

It is not surprising in the least to find that the church fumbled for some time in its attempt to formulate intellectually and conceptually its faith in God the Father, Jesus Christ, and the Holy Spirit. Nor is it surprising that occasionally it took the wrong road, and then found it necessary to retrace its steps and begin looking for the right road again. At times it even seemed as if the task it had set for itself could not be mastered. From the beginning, of course, certain fundamentals were firmly held by the church, namely, that God is one, i.e., that it did not believe in two, let alone three gods; that this one God has revealed himself in a threefold way as Father, Son, and Holy Spirit; that Father and Son may not be equated in a way which dissolves the differences between them, as if the Son were merely a "mask" behind which the Father hides himself. But how were these fundamental articles of faith to be comprehended in a formula? In what concepts could they be appropriately expressed?

When in the second century the church's center of gravity, as well as that of its theology, shifted definitely from the Palestinian realm to the world of Greek thought, the church faced the necessity of expressing its faith in a form that would be intelligible to the Greek mind. The result was that metaphysical concepts which were focused upon being took the place of concrete, biblical forms of speech. As we know, Greek thought differs from biblical thought above all in this, that for the latter the truth of God is revealed in history, while for the former it is grounded in metaphysical being. When related to the concept of God, this meant that the difference between God the Father, the Son, and the Holy Spirit could be understood as one of metaphysical self-subsistence (*hypostasis*). The apologists of the ancient church pioneered in this respect when they united the Greek concept of Logos with the Logos idea of John, chap. 1. Of course, the attempt of a man such as the apologist

Justin Martyr to designate Christ "another God" created its own set of problems.[2]

Against such pluralism stood what was called Monarchianism. Its main concern was to preserve monotheism within Christianity. The basic point at issue was the relation of the Father and the Son to each other. Christology and the doctrine of the Trinity have always been intimately connected, but this was especially true at the beginning. The Monarchians were of the opinion that the problem could be solved by thinking of the divinity of the Son as being merely derived, or by seeing in the Son only a mode of appearance of the Father. According to one brand of Monarchianism, so-called dynamistic Monarchianism, an impersonal divine power was active in the man Jesus. Thereafter Christ was adopted as the Son of God. This dynamistic Monarchianism in its pure form was found especially toward the end of the second century and occasionally still in the third. There is a naïve, adoptionistic concept which is much older, however, and is embodied in many writings of the ancient church which are otherwise thoroughly orthodox.

A second brand of Monarchianism, so-called modalistic Monarchianism, already represents a more developed concept. It, too, was represented among various segments of the church around the year 200. The modalistic Monarchians argued that God is only a single person. The Son and the Spirit merely represent modes of appearance of the one God. Sabellius, who was active in Rome at the beginning of the third century, even used the expression "Son-Father."

It doubtlessly was the concern of Monarchianism, and justifiably so, to insist upon the unity of God. In all ages the danger that in the development of its faith the church might fall prey to polytheism has probably been greater than the danger that the differences between the persons of the Trinity might be leveled. It is deceptive, however, to think that Monarchianism was in a better position to hold to the unity of God than was the church. For either it was forced to see in Christ, after his baptism or after his resurrection, a kind of half-God, as was the case with dynamistic Monarchianism; or else, in the attempt to do away with the differences between Father and Son, it became necessary to disregard entirely the Gospel accounts

[2] Justin Martyr, *Dialogue with Trypho*, chap. 56. *ANF* 1, 223 ff.

which show the earthly Jesus praying to God the Father. This is what happened in modalistic Monarchianism. Both forms of this movement, therefore, abandoned something which, for the church, was absolutely fundamental.

Beyond this, the many gnostic systems which were developed in the second century also exerted an influence upon the formation of the church's doctrine of the Trinity. It is true that the Gnostics did not develop their own doctrine of the Trinity. What they did, rather, was to include God the Father, God the Son, and the Holy Spirit among their many aeons. The Gnostic, Valentinus, professed knowledge of no less than thirty aeons, below all of which he ranked Christ. According to most gnostic systems, Christ had only a phantom body on earth, which he abandoned again before the crucifixion. Therefore it was not Christ, the Son of God, who died, but only the man Jesus. This Christology is called docetism. Over against such systems, the church could not be satisfied with the mere repetition of the baptismal command of Matthew 28:19, or with other New Testament affirmations. It had to develop its faith further.

Early Traces of a Doctrine of the Trinity

A saying of Justin Martyr indicates what lack of clarity there was with regard to the development of the doctrine of the Trinity as late as the middle of the second century. In his *Apology* Justin seeks to weaken the pagan reproach that Christians are atheists. He admits that Christians indeed reject the false pagan gods, but, he goes on to say, they do not deny the true God, who is the Father of justice and chastity and of all the other virtues, and who will have nothing to do with that which is evil. He then says, "Both him and the son who came forth from him and taught us these things, and the host of other good angels who follow and are made like to Him, and the prophetic Spirit, we worship and adore, because we honor [him] in reason and truth."[3] As if it were not enough that in this enumeration angels are mentioned as beings which are honored and worshiped by Christians, Justin does not hesitate to mention angels before naming the Holy Spirit. The sequence in

[3] Justin Martyr, *The First Apology,* chap. 6. [The rendering in *ANF* 1, 164, does not imply angel worship. In translating we have reproduced the author's literal rendering of the passage.—TRANSLATOR.]

which the beings that are worshiped are mentioned (God the Father, Christ, the angels, the Spirit) is noteworthy. Yet we would be doing Justin an injustice if we were to put him on the same plane as the Gnostics such as Valentinus.

Only toward the end of the second century was greater clarity introduced into the doctrine of God. Of importance here was, first of all, Irenaeus, Bishop of Lyons. In his doctrine of God two basic features are evident. First, he spoke of God's inner being, and, second, of his progressive self-disclosure in the history of salvation [*Heilsgeschichte*]. Sometimes Irenaeus emphasizes the unity of God so strongly that he does not shrink from using expressions which sound modalistic, as if Son and Spirit were only appearances of the one God. In his *Proof of the Apostolic Preaching* he says, "Thus God is shown to be one according to the essence of His being and power" even though "as the administrator of the economy of our redemption, He is both Father and Son. . . ."[4] In this way Irenaeus hoped to avoid every pluralistic expression with reference to God. He knew, of course, how to differentiate between God the Father, Son, and Holy Spirit. Irenaeus was of the same opinion as the apologists of the ancient church, especially Theophilus of Antioch, when he taught that God had with him from all eternity his Word and his Wisdom. These were, so to speak, hypostases. God brought them forth from himself before the creation of the world. The Son was begotten of the Father before time. To every further speculation, which tries to enter into the mystery of the begetting of the Son, Irenaeus objects.

In this way Irenaeus developed the basic features of a doctrine of the Trinity. It is, in fact, the most fully developed doctrine of the Trinity during the first and second centuries. Its characteristic feature is that it does not begin with three co-eternal persons, as does the orthodox doctrine of the Trinity in the fourth century, but with the person of the Father who has with and beside himself his Word and his Wisdom. To employ the terminology of a later period, it is not possible to speak of three co-eternal persons in Irenaeus' doctrine of God. Nor should it be expected that the rank of the Son or that of the Spirit would be clearly expressed. The development of the doctrine of the divine persons took place in Irenaeus only from the

[4] Irenaeus, *Proof of the Apostolic Preaching,* chap. 47. *ACW* 16, 78.

point of view of the history of salvation.

Tertullian, who lived in Carthage and was the first theologian of the church to write in Latin, expressed himself similarly on the doctrine of God. He, too, began with the person of God the Father, who has with him Word and Spirit, and who brings these forth out of himself for the purpose of the creation of the world. Yet Tertullian's work proved to be of great significance for the later development of the doctrine of the Trinity, thanks to his coining of precise formulas giving expression to the unity of God as well as to the threeness of the persons. It was his intention to hold to the one substance in three related persons.[5] Three persons exist, he said, in the one substance, and still there is only one God. For the history of salvation, however, there is a threefold differentiation of the unity. God's *oikonomia,* his *Heilsgeschichte,* requires three persons. In a statement formulated with acute precision Tertullian says that they are differentiated *non statu sed gradu, nec substantia sed forma, nec potestate sed specie* ("not in condition, but in degree; not in substance, but in form; not in power, but in aspect").[6] The three are thus one, though not one person. Tertullian thus pithily summed up older thinking concerning the doctrine of God and he rejected, at the same time, the heresies of Monarchianism and Gnosticism. Thus the basic elements of the doctrine of the identity of substance with reference to Father, Son, and Holy Spirit are already present in Tertullian, even though, on the other hand, he strictly subordinates the Son to the Father and at times uses rather unfortunate images, such as his likening of Father, Son, and Spirit to root, branch, and fruit.

Origen (d. 254) went much further than Irenaeus and Tertullian. This acute thinker, who had already engaged in textual criticism of the biblical writings and from whose pen we have the first Christian dogmatics, also made an important contribution to the doctrine of God. This is true even though it must be admitted that his doctrine of the Trinity contains many problems which helped to bring about the beginning of the Arian controversy.

Origen's doctrine of the Trinity is marked by two basic fea-

[5] Tertullian, *Against Praxeas,* chap. 12. *ANF* 3, 607.

[6] *Ibid.,* chap. 2. *ANF* 3, 598.

tures. First, like Irenaeus and Tertullian, he puts great emphasis on the unity of God. Yet he does not set it forth very clearly. The reason is that in addition to his emphasis on the unity of God he lays stress upon the differences between the persons. In doing so he goes beyond his predecessors. Strictly speaking, only the Father is God, though the name "God" may also be applied to the Son and to the Holy Spirit. The divinity of the Son and of the Spirit is derived from the Father. God brings forth the Son in an eternal act. As the Son is subordinated to the Father, even so the Spirit is subordinated to the Son. For the three persons of the Godhead, Origen uses the concept of *hypostasis,* by which he means an individual essence, or individual subsistence. Thus Son and Spirit are other than the Father with regard to their *hypostasis.* At the same time, however, he holds that all three persons are one in the sense that they possess a unity and harmony of will. For this kind of unity Origen already used the concept of *homoousios* ("oneness of being," or in the common liturgical rendering, "of one substance"), which later was given dogmatic status at Nicaea (325), even though he held to the numerical difference between Father and Son. There can be no doubt, however, that although Origen always held to the unity of the three persons, and was thus the first to develop an actual doctrine of the Trinity, he was not so successful in making clear the unity of the three divine persons as he was in defining their differences. Here the tensions in his doctrine of God become evident. It was possible, for instance, for Origen to say that the Son was a creature of the Father, thus strictly subordinating the Son to the Father, while at the same time he insisted upon a unity of substance with regard to Father and Son. The problematical nature of his doctrine of the Trinity is especially evident in the fact that, contrary to both the New Testament and tradition, Origen rejected prayer to the exalted Lord. Only prayer to God the Father is permitted, he insisted, although such prayer has to be made through the Son and the Spirit.[7]

Of no less importance is the second feature of Origen's doctrine of God. He was of the opinion that, since God the Father is perfect in goodness and power, he must always have had objects toward which he exercised this goodness and power. On

[7] Origen, *On Prayer,* chaps. XV, 1-XVI, 1. *LCC* 2, 269-271.

the basis of this presupposition Origen taught the doctrine, reminiscent of certain gnostic systems, that before the creation of the cosmos God called into being a world of spiritual beings which are co-eternal with him. The world of history, he asserted, God created only when these spiritual beings fell away from him. Furthermore, said Origen, these eternal beings were subordinated to God the Father from the beginning. Hence a mediator between God's absolute oneness and this multiplicity of beings was necessary. This mediator is the Son. Origen's teaching concerning the eternal generation of the Son, i.e., a generation which is not yet a completed act, must be seen against the background of this concept of an eternal creation. It has thus an entirely different foundation from that of a similar idea found in the later theology of the Trinity, for which the eternal generation of the Son was founded upon the notion that in eternity there is no past and no future but only an eternal now (Augustine). It is immediately apparent that this second feature of Origen's doctrine of the Trinity is considerably more problematical than the first. The assumption of an eternal creation directly contradicted the church's doctrine, as well as the statements of Scripture. Through its controversy with the various gnostic systems, the church had become fully aware of the fact that the doctrine concerning an eternal creation could not be brought into harmony with the Bible and the Christian faith. As a result, Origen's notion of the eternal generation of the Son as well as his conception of the unity of the Son with the Father had to stand or fall with his insistence upon an eternal creation.

During the decades between the death of Origen and the beginning of the Arian controversy, it became clear that the Origenistic doctrine of the Trinity had to be refined in one way or another. Most theologians rejected the eternity of creation. This made it necessary, however, either to emphasize the strict subordination of the Son to the Father, or to go beyond Origen in strongly asserting the oneness in substance of the different hypostases. All subsequent theology, however, whether it stands to the "left" or to the "right" of Origen, owes to him that which is really decisive. For only through him, and since his time, has the task of actually developing a doctrine of the Trinity which progresses beyond the older theologians' "economic"

Trinity and toward an "immanent" Trinity been recognized, that is to say, a doctrine of the Trinity which sees in the successive revelation of the persons of the divine Trinity at the same time a reference to God's eternal being. Furthermore, as will be pointed out below, only through Origen did the Logos Christology gain universal acceptance. Thus all later generations have learned from Origen, even when they did not share his one-sided emphasis.

Arius

Arius (d. 336), too, had learned some things from Origen. The intellectual world out of which Arius came, the school of Lucian of Antioch, took over much from Origen. But if it is true anywhere, it is true here, that the same things said by two different people are not the same. Arius, more than Lucian, changed and restructured the Origenistic theology. In this endeavor he permitted himself to be guided by certain distinct motives which, in their Arian form, were not present in Origen.

Arius' prime concern was to emphasize the uniqueness and transcendence of God. This must be kept clearly in mind if we are to avoid passing hasty judgments that would keep us from understanding a man like Arius. A confession of faith by Arius says, "We confess one God who alone is unbegotten, alone eternal, alone without beginning, alone true, alone immortal, alone wise, alone good, alone Lord, alone the judge of all." By "God" Arius always means God the Father only. Because His being is absolutely transcendent and absolutely immutable it cannot be communicated to anyone else. Hence, everything that exists besides this transcendent God must have been created, and that means that it must have come out of nothing. Arius resolutely rejects the thought that the Son came forth from the Father. He felt that such thought-forms apply physical categories to God. More than that, such a concept would make of God a "composite," which is impossible.

What, then, does Arius say about Jesus Christ? It is true that Arius, like the apologists Irenaeus and Tertullian before him, held that God has with him from eternity his Word and his Wisdom. But for Arius these two simply coincide with the being of God and have nothing to do with the second and third persons of the Trinity. The Word, on the other hand, which in

Jesus Christ became flesh, is a creature of God, created by him out of nothing before the beginning of time. Not that Arius puts the Son on the same plane with other creatures. According to him the Son is a perfect creature, but he is not a creature in the sense in which other creatures are. In referring to the Son as a creature, says Arius, one should not speak of a generation of the Son, since this would bring him too close to the Father. Only in a derivative sense should the word "generation" ever be used. Under no circumstances may any unity of substance between Father and Son be asserted. This is for Arius the worst heresy. What must be said instead is that God was not always Father, but that there was a time when he was alone and was not yet Father. Only later did he become Father. Immutability may not be asserted of the Son as it can of the Father. The Son may be called God, to be sure, but his divinity is not an attribute of his being. It is something bestowed upon him by God's grace.

Arius, too, recognized the necessity of taking over the Origenistic concept of *hypostasis*. He even talked, and seemingly much like Origen, of three hypostases, i.e., of the three persons—the Father, the Son, and the Holy Spirit. Thus Arius also assumed a supreme Triad, which means that he did not deny or attempt to conceal the distinctiveness of the Son and of the Holy Spirit as did Monarchianism. So Arius, too, was not able to hold himself aloof from the general trend which the doctrine of God had taken since the second century.

Yet even though one may appreciate the concern of Arius and would like to give credence to some of his ideas, it is difficult not to regard his outline of the doctrine of God as highly dangerous. In the last analysis Arius ends up with many unresolved problems, which are really much greater than those which he had set out to solve. He wanted to hold on to the uniqueness of God, and it seemed he had succeeded in doing so. In reality, however, he made out of Christ a kind of demigod, who was neither quite man nor quite God. A similar observation may be made about his understanding of the Holy Spirit, although it should be remembered, of course, that the doctrine of the Holy Spirit was not yet debated in his day. While it was still possible for Origen to unite in his thought the three hypostases which he taught, in Arius they became three divinities differentiated from one another in terms of gradations. In Arius' doctrine of God, therefore, that which had long been present in theology as a latent danger, namely, the strict subordination of the Son to the Father, was now openly expressed. At an earlier period, as a result of the appropriation of certain ideas from Jewish apocalyptic, a so-called angel Christology had actually been developed in which Jesus Christ appeared as an especially exalted angelic being. Prior to Arius this notion had been held in rather naïve form, since no one had yet thought it through to the end. In Arius' doctrine of God, however, which drew upon philosophical concepts and ideas and was more fully developed than earlier notions of a similar cast, the peril of a subordinationist Christology appeared. The dangerous consequence of the Arian doctrine is found in the assertion that Christ, since he is not God, cannot truly know the Father. Hence not even revelation can give a full knowledge of God. This inadequate doctrine of God, therefore, leads necessarily to an entirely inadequate doctrine of revelation.

If one desires to adhere to the uniqueness of God, as well as to the validity of the revelation of God in Jesus Christ, the path Arius took is certainly not the one to follow. It leads to a new form of polytheism. It is praiseworthy that Arius did not seek to preserve the unity of God at the cost of revelation. Yet to follow the path he took means either that one must deny the revelation of God in Jesus Christ or that one must assume there is more than one God. One thing Arius did accomplish, however. With an urgency that could not be ignored, he posed the question for the church whether, according to its faith, Jesus Christ is a creature standing on a level far beneath God or whether he is God himself. This is the basic question in the Arian controversy.

The Council of Nicaea

Arius was pastor of the Church of St. Baucalis in Alexandria. Alexandria had long been the center not only of intellectual life in general, but also of theology. Here Origen, the most famous Greek theologian of the ancient church, had long been active. Thus the opinions of Arius, having been expressed in this city, were bound to attract attention. At first it seemed that perhaps no controversy would arise. Arius' bishop, Alexander of Alexandria, was a peace-loving man who, as far as he himself was concerned, would have preferred to avoid an argument. But things had progressed too far for that. Behind Arius stood many people in all parts of the Greek East who shared his opinions.

When in the year 324 Constantine the Great, after his victory over Licinius, had become ruler also of the eastern part of the Roman Empire, he found the Eastern church embroiled in bitter controversy. The first emperor to become a Christian, Constantine had basically no understanding whatsoever of the questions that were being asked in Greek theology. In the controversy over the doctrine of the Trinity he saw nothing more than unnecessary bickering of theologians, which might best be avoided by eschewing all speculation and by living together in love and harmony. At the same time Constantine was concerned about keeping or restoring ecclesiastical peace. After all, the church had an important service to perform in his empire. It was to rid the people of the immoralities which had made broad inroads among them and to guide men into law and order; it was to be concerned about the extension of the pure worship of God; and above all else, it was to ask and to obtain God's blessing for the emperor and his realm by discharging responsibly its tasks as a church. The emperor therefore stepped into the controversy and extended invitations for a great council to be held at Nicaea (325), the imperial residence not far from the sea of Marmara in Asia Minor.

In order to follow the course of the discussions at the Council of Nicaea, it is necessary to keep in mind the entirely new situation in which the church found itself at this point in its history. After having been persecuted for three hundred years, with only an occasional brief respite, the church was now confronted with an emperor who professed the Christian faith. To add to the novelty, Constantine's conversion had come on the heels of the Diocletian persecution, which had been the most ruthless the ancient church had ever known. For the first time in its history Christianity in the Roman Empire was no longer the persecuted religion; now officially tolerated and recognized, in some respects it was even fostered by the empire. From a purely external point of view the change in the situation was evident to the bishops in the fact that they no longer needed to move about secretly nor did they have to use the normal means of travel to visit one another. They now had the privilege of coming to the council by means of transportation provided by the state, i.e., means which were intended for use by ranking state officials. At Nicaea the emperor provided lodging for the bishops in his palace. It was there, too, that the discussions took place, and in the presence of the emperor at that. The changed situation could not have been brought home more forcefully. It is understandable if the bishops showed their gratitude by generous efforts to oblige the emperor.

In the course of the long discussions which now took place at Nicaea the emperor intervened personally several times. Even though he had a general antipathy to the controversies, and even though he himself had only a rudimentary "theology," he was still not entirely without sympathy for the problems which arose. In any case, he permitted himself to be more fully instructed about many things by his episcopal counselors. The decisive catchword of the Nicene confession, namely, *homoousios* ("of one substance"), comes from no less a person than the emperor himself. To the present day no one has cleared up the problem of where the emperor got the term. It seems likely that it was suggested to him by his episcopal counselor, Bishop Hosius (Ossius) of Cordova, and it was probably nothing more than a Greek translation of a term already found in Tertullian, who used it to express the idea that Father and Son are of one substance.

At the council a solemn confession of faith was formulated, which embodied the results of the discussions. The basis of it was a confession which came from the area of Syria-Palestine, and which probably stems from Jerusalem. This confession of Nicaea must not be confused with the confession which in today's services of worship is often called the Nicene Creed. Actually the latter should be referred to as the Niceno-Constantinopolitan Creed (381). The Nicene confession of 325 reads as follows:

> We believe in one God, the Father almighty, maker of all things visible and invisible;
>
> And in one Lord Jesus Christ, the Son of God, begotten from the Father, only-begotten, that is, from the substance of the Father, God from God, light from light, true God from true God, begotten not made, of one substance with the Father, through Whom all things came into being, things in heaven and things

on earth, Who because of us men and because of our salvation came down and became incarnate, becoming man, suffered and rose again on the third day, ascended to the heavens, and will come to judge the living and the dead;

And in the Holy Spirit.

Immediately upon this confession follow the anathemas upon heretical opinions. They read as follows:

> But as for those who say, There was when He was not, and, Before being born He was not, and that He came into existence out of nothing, or who assert that the Son of God is of a different hypostasis or substance, or is created, or is subject to alteration or change—these the Catholic Church anathematizes.[8]

Most of the bishops who were present at the council signed this creed. Among the signers were those who, judging by their theological presuppositions, could not do so, or could hardly do so, such as Eusebius of Caesarea. What seemed especially objectionable to many bishops and theologians of the East was the concept put into the creed by Constantine himself, the *homoousios,* which in the subsequent strife between orthodoxy and heresy became the object of dissension. Even most of the Arians put their names to the creed. Only Arius and two of his friends refused to sign, for which they were excommunicated.

What was the exact meaning of this creed which had been signed by theologians of such divergent opinions and which, strangely enough, at first served as a formula of concord, only to generate ever new controversy later? It is not easy to ascertain the original meaning of the confession of Nicaea. The reason for this difficulty is not to be found in the paucity of sources, although it is true that the records of the individual discussions at the council are no more available. The real reason it is not so easy to establish the original meaning of the Nicene decision lies in the fact that the church could not stop with this decision, but was virtually forced to move toward further clarifications of its doctrine of God. As a result the decision of Nicaea was given a progressively new and deeper meaning. This later interpretation of the Nicene confession is therefore not necessarily inconsistent with its original meaning. Quite

[8] For the text of the Nicene confession and a detailed commentary on it see J. N. D. Kelly, *Early Christian Creeds* (2nd ed.; London: Longmans, Green, and New York: McKay, 1960), pp. 205-230; also his *Early Christian Doctrines* (London: A. and C. Black, and New York: Harper, 1958), pp. 231-237. Translation used with permission of the publishers.

to the contrary, this interpretation probably sets forth the import of the Nicene decision more profoundly and better than did the council fathers themselves. It becomes apparent here that the history of doctrine is not concerned merely with the historical origins of a series of doctrinal propositions, but with confessions which constantly need to be adapted and interpreted.

This much is certain, of course, that the Nicene confession was meant to reject the teaching of Arius, and did reject it. With great emphasis the council insisted that the Son is not created, but begotten. This concept of "begetting" is meant to exclude the idea that the Son was called into being out of nothing, as well as the idea that there was a time when God the Father was alone, i.e., was not yet the Father. In this way the immutability and eternity of God are attested. The rejection of Arianism meant, however, that this immutability and eternity of God is also asserted of the Logos, i.e., the second person of the Trinity.

What, then, is the positive sense of the Nicene confession? In order to ascertain this the affirmations that the Son is "from the substance of the Father" and that he is "of one substance with the Father" must be kept in mind. The first of these two formulations certainly seems to say that the Logos is in a true sense the Son of the Father, in other words, that we are dealing here with a "metaphysical" sonship. This first formulation emphasizes, then, that the Son has the same divine nature as the Father from whom he came forth. Every other affirmation, which dispenses with the concept of begetting, would necessarily lead to the conclusion that the Son is not only a person other than the Father, but that he is also "something other" than the Father, i.e., that he is not God.

To determine the sense of the expression "of one substance with the Father" is more difficult. It is clear at the outset that this formula cannot assert anything other than what is meant by the expression "from the substance of the Father," and it is undoubtedly not meant to say anything else. The question arises, however, in what sense the unity of substance, which is emphasized, is to be understood. Are Father and Son one in the sense intended by Origen? That is, are they one as the result of the identity of substance, while they are distinct numerically, as Origen asserted during the controversy against the Monarchians?

Or is the formula to be understood in the sense of numerical identity of substance?

For a long time the decision of Nicaea was understood in the second sense. We meet this interpretation already in the ancient church. There is no question but that the concept "of one substance with the Father" allows this interpretation, indeed, even demands it. In that case, "of one substance with the Father" means that the persons of the Godhead are one common divine Being. While this interpretation accords with the later orthodox understanding, it hardly expresses the original meaning of this expression: the concept *homoousios* was not understood in this sense at the time. For the theologians of the third century *homoousios* simply meant "of the same substance." There was as yet no reflection about the question of numerical identity. It would be difficult to imagine that at the synod of Nicaea the concept *homoousios* could suddenly and without preparation have been used in a new sense.

It is probable that with its choice of the expression "of one substance with the Father" the Council of Nicaea meant to strengthen once more its "begotten, not made," and thus the divinity of the Son. The council did not attempt to solve the question of the divine unity and the distinctness of the persons. What it meant to do was to assert, against Arius and his theory, which made a sort of demigod out of Jesus Christ, the full divinity of the Son. Yet, even if the decision of Nicaea is understood in this sense, which is narrower than the customary understanding of an earlier day, it is still of considerable importance. It is true that the proposition that Jesus Christ is God had long been held; we meet its beginnings already in the New Testament. Yet, the subordinationism latent in the church, which in the theology of Arius is raised to its highest point, led to a limitation of this affirmation. This subordinationist development was now warded off, and the full divinity of the Son was set forth. It is clear that as a result new problems were created at once. The two most important of these were, first, the relationship of the various divine persons to each other, and, second, the relationship of the divinity of Jesus, as asserted at Nicaea, to the image of Jesus as it appears in the Gospels. These two problems were to absorb much of the church's energy during the following period.

No less important, however, is the significance of the Nicene confession in another respect. In addition to the theological errors it rejected, the confession also represents a denial of a philosophical concept of God. It was clear that in arriving at the christological propositions he was able to formulate so acutely, Arius had permitted himself to be influenced by certain philosophical presuppositions. Of course, the Christian church cannot escape the necessity of expressing its faith in a language that is clear and conceptually articulate. For that reason it has never been able to dispense with the use of philosophical concepts. It must be remembered, however, that the use of such concepts in theology is not the same as in philosophy. Luther once said that if philosophical concepts are to be used in theology they must, so to speak, be taken "to the bath," i.e., they must be baptized.[9] At Nicaea, at any rate, the church did not attempt to penetrate the mystery of God or to describe it, as did Arius, from the point of view of the philosophical concept of transcendence. It is true that in return the church had to accept the fact that its confession contains a paradox. Yet is this not the paradox which consists in the Word's being made flesh?

More Than Five Decades of Controversy

The Council of Nicaea did not end the Arian controversy. Indeed, it is with Nicaea that the controversy began in earnest. To be sure, most of the bishops who were present at Nicaea signed the creed. But there were widespread differences among the signers in the way the creed was understood. Constantine was content to have the creed signed, leaving its interpretation largely to the individual. Behind the scenes, however, there now began a violent political struggle within the church. The Arians, who for the moment had been forced into retreat, continued to have many followers. They took steps to fill as many vacant episcopal sees as possible with members of their own party. But the orthodox were also not idle, especially Athanasius, who had become bishop of Alexandria in 328 and was to live until 373. The power struggle was fierce, with both sides using means that

[9] Luther, *Promotionsdisputation von Palladius und Tilemann* (1537), *WA* 39[1], 229, ll. 16-19.

were often regrettable and with the actual differences of opinion magnified by rather far-reaching misunderstandings of the opponents' position. Not all who rejected the Nicene confession were true Arians. On the basis of Origenistic theology, however, they were dissatisfied with the creed. It seemed to them that at Nicaea the divine persons had not been sufficiently differentiated. In their opinion Nicaea aided modalistic Monarchianism. The members of the Nicene party, on the other hand, did not always do justice to their opponents either. In the fifth century the church historian Socrates (d. *ca.* 450) was already comparing the Arian controversy with a battle fought in the dark, with the combatants unable to distinguish friend from foe.[10] Yet these often regrettable by-products should not lead one to disregard the actual substance of the discussions.

Among the many persons who over the decades were involved in the controversy, especially in the eastern part of the Roman Empire, a few stand out. There is, first of all, Athanasius, and then the three so-called Cappadocians. Each in his own way, and yet in substantial agreement with one another, and with a view to the real significance of the discussion, these men held fast to the decision of Nicaea even while they were developing it further in a very definite way. They realized, as few others did, that Nicaea, with its condemnation of Arianism, did not merely represent a climax in the development of the church's doctrine, but that it also imposed new tasks.

Athanasius has always been regarded as the real champion of Nicaea. He fought for the *homoousios* as no one else did, yet without a narrowly conceived insistence on it. He endured no less than five banishments, some of them lasting many years, merely because he held fast to the Nicene confession. He does not belong to those theologians who independently and boldly develop a system of their own. Apparently Athanasius never pursued theology for the sake of theology. He gave himself to it only for the sake of polemic. Yet, in spite of these limitations, he was still an acute thinker. Relentlessly he continued to point to the consequences implied in the position one takes toward the problem of the consubstantiality of the Son with the Father.

[10] Socrates, *The Ecclesiastical History of Socrates Scholasticus*, Bk. I, chap. 23. *NPNF*[2] 2, 27.

For the history of the doctrine of the Trinity, Athanasius has above all a twofold significance. First, he became increasingly aware of the need to understand the *homoousios* of Nicaea not only as an assertion of the full deity of the Son but also in its significance for the unity of God. It was in reference to this latter point especially that Athanasius underwent a development. During his early years he had laid no particular stress upon the *homoousios*. In fact a certain reserve with respect to this expression can be noted in his writings. It proved to be of significance, therefore, that during his first banishment (at Treves, 335-337), as well as during his second banishment (in Rome and Aquileia, 339-346), he became acquainted with the old western doctrine of the Trinity. Since the days of Tertullian this doctrine had emphasized the unity of God, and therefore had understood the *homoousios* of Nicaea more in the sense of the western tradition than in that of the council fathers, who were predominantly Greek. From about 350 on, Athanasius was the determined champion not only of the Nicene orthodoxy as such, but especially of the term *homoousios*. While earlier in his career Athanasius had emphasized especially the divinity of the Logos, without expressing himself in detail about the unity of God the Father and God the Son, he now accentuated above all else the unity of God. The *homoousios* formula served this purpose splendidly. On the other hand, Athanasius had to reckon with the fact that emphasis on the *homoousios* meant that the differences between the persons would not appear with full clarity. It is of immediate importance, however, that *homoousios* is henceforth given a new meaning, in that it is made to refer to the unity of God. Consequently Athanasius was now able to point out that the divinity of the Son is identical with the divinity of the Father, that, in fact, the divinity of the Son is at the same time the divinity of the Father, or that the fullness of the divinity of the Father is the being (*to einai*) of the Son.[11] In doing this Athanasius certainly did not wish to fall into the error of the Sabellians, as the Arians were charging that he did. On the contrary, he held firmly to the idea that the Father and the Son are "two." "They are one," he writes, "not as one thing divided into two parts, and these nothing but one,

[11] Athanasius, *Four Discourses Against the Arians*, Discourse III, chap. 6. *NPNF*[2] 4, 396-397.

nor as one thing twice named, so that the Same becomes at one time Father, at another His own Son, for this Sabellius holding was judged an heretic. But They are two, because the Father is Father and is not also Son, and the Son is Son and not also Father; but the nature is one. . . ."[12] What is not yet clearly enunciated in this position is the difference between the divine persons. Here the Cappadocians were to do further work.

Athanasius was of course never concerned with mere speculation. His real interest was not in the doctrine of the Trinity as such, but in soteriology, or the doctrine of redemption. Arius' strict subordination of the Son to the Father, the Son being a creature, meant that through Christ no full knowledge of God was mediated. Athanasius had immediately recognized this consequence of Arian theology and he never tired of pointing it out. Conversely, Athanasius always insisted most emphatically that only in holding fast to the consubstantiality of the Son with the Father is it possible to preserve faith in redemption. If Jesus Christ was only the manifestation of a created being, half-divine in nature, then there is no real redemption through Christ. In his early years Athanasius had already insisted, "It is we who were the cause of His taking human form, and for our salvation that in His great love He was both born and manifested in a human body."[13] Later Athanasius made this connection between the doctrine of God and the doctrine of redemption even more central in his teaching. Unless this connection is seen his struggle for the recognition of the confession of Nicaea cannot be understood.

It is precisely at this point, however, that misgivings have often been expressed. They refer not to the connection of the doctrine of God and the doctrine of redemption as such, but to Athanasius' understanding of redemption. His doctrine of redemption is often referred to as "physical"; that is, it is said to be concerned not merely with freedom from sin and guilt but also, and above all, with the restoration and imperishability of human nature, or, in other words, with the deification of man. Again and again this formula recurs in Athanasius: "He, indeed,

[12] Athanasius, *Four Discourses Against the Arians*, Discourse III, chap. 4. *NPNF*[2] 4, 395.

[13] Athanasius, *The Incarnation of the Word of God*, chap. 1, sec. 4, trans. by a Religious of C. S. M. V., S.Th. (New York: Macmillan, 1946), p. 29.

assumed humanity that we might become God."[14] Later he was to write, "Mankind then is perfected in Him and restored, as it was made at the beginning, nay, with greater grace. For, on rising from the dead, we shall no longer fear death, but shall ever reign in Christ in the heavens. And this has been done, since the own Word of God Himself, who is from the Father, has put on the flesh, and become man."[15] On the basis of such assertions Harnack interpreted Athanasius as saying that mortality in itself was the greatest evil and the cause of all other evils, while the highest good was to live eternally.

Such accusations must be approached with caution. There can be no doubt that even though Athanasius is familiar with the idea that Christ frees us from sin and guilt, his soteriology operates primarily with the categories of mortality and immortality. Death is conquered by life. It should be noted, however, that when the New Testament itself speaks of redemption, it, too, does not limit itself to the conceptions of guilt and forgiveness, or justification, but may on occasion set death and life over against each other. This is true not only of the Johannine writings, but also of certain passages in St. Paul. In this respect the Reformation undoubtedly repeated the thoughts of the New Testament with a certain one-sidedness. In doing so, however, it simply remained true to the entire western tradition, whose thought always inclined more to "ethical" concepts than did that of the Eastern church, which from the beginning gave preference to "physical" concepts. For Athanasius, furthermore, death and life are not primarily "physical" concepts, but concepts which are always filled with content. Death is separation from God caused by guilt. It is the curse which came upon Adam and all mankind. Life, on the other hand, is full communion with God, which consists not simply in the forgiveness of guilt, but which signifies a new being whose nature is no longer transitory but eternal.

In addition to Athanasius the three so-called Cappadocians are also of great significance for the further development and right understanding of the decision of Nicaea. Actually it was

[14] Athanasius, *The Incarnation of the Word of God,* chap. 8, sec. 54. *Ibid.,* p. 93.

[15] Athanasius, *Four Discourses Against the Arians,* Discourse II, chap. 67. *NPNF*^{2} 4, 385.

they who created the intellectual and conceptual means for the full appropriation of the Nicene confession. Their labors are most closely connected with the question of the divinity of the Holy Spirit.

The Divinity of the Holy Spirit

In the Nicene confession relatively little was said of the Holy Spirit. An assertion about faith in the Holy Spirit had been deemed sufficient. The problem concerning the divinity of the Son had been uppermost in the minds of the council fathers as a result of the teaching of Arius. To it Nicaea gave its answer. It did not seem necessary to proceed from the question of the consubstantiality of the Son with the Father to the problem of ascertaining the position of the Holy Spirit in the Godhead.

With the passage of time, however, it became increasingly evident that it was not possible to rest content with the brief affirmation of Nicaea. As the concept of *homoousios* necessarily led to deeper reflection on the unity of the Father and the Son, the church having been forced beyond the assertion of the divinity of the Son to an insistence upon the consubstantiality of the Father with the Son, so the question of the Holy Spirit was now destined to become urgent. Once the alternative between the divine and the created, which had been pointed out by Arius, was seen in its full significance, the related problem of the Spirit could not be avoided. Arius regarded the Spirit as a being which totally lacked any similarity with either the Father or the Son. Among other theologians, too, the uncertainty concerning the doctrine of the Holy Spirit was greater than the uncertainty about the *homoousios* of the Son. A man such as Eusebius of Caesarea subordinated the Spirit to the Father and the Son, teaching that the Spirit was the first of the creatures to be brought forth by the Son. It is true that some theologians, for instance, Cyril of Jerusalem, approximated later orthodoxy in their teaching concerning the Spirit. Even among the adherents of the confession of Nicaea there was still much uncertainty about the question of what position the Spirit occupies in the Trinity. The divinity of the Holy Spirit was especially rejected by the so-called Pneumatomachians, who gathered about Macedonius, Bishop of Constantinople (342-360).

Only at a rather late date did Athanasius have something to

say in his various letters to Serapion (359 or 360) concerning the position of the Holy Spirit. In doing so he emphasizes that according to the unambiguous testimony of Scripture the Holy Spirit is not of a creaturely nature but belongs to God and is one with the Godhead, namely, the Trinity. The Spirit comes from God. He bestows sanctification and, indeed, life itself. The Spirit is immutable, omnipresent, and one, while the creatures are mutable, dependent upon time and space, and many. Through the Spirit we partake of God. On the other hand, it is not true that the Spirit partakes of others. He only communicates himself. Thus Athanasius concludes that, without doubt, the Spirit, too, is God, and that of him, too, consubstantiality must be asserted. Athanasius emphasizes especially the connection between the Spirit and the Son. As it is necessary to gain the knowledge of the Spirit through the Son, so the Spirit is inseparable from the Son. He is the Spirit of the Son, sent by the Son. Everything that belongs to the Spirit belongs also to the Son, as is evident in John 16:13-14. Thus Athanasius developed a complete theology of the Trinity, in which, however, an appropriate concept for that which we call "person" was missing. It was the Cappadocians who led the way to greater clarity on this point.

The term "the three Cappadocians" refers to Basil the Great (d. 379), Bishop of Caesarea and Metropolitan of Cappadocia; Gregory of Nyssa (d. 394), a younger brother of Basil; and Gregory of Nazianzus (d. *ca.* 390). They all came from old, cultured families. They had steeped themselves in ancient classical literature as well as in the church fathers. All three were bishops and had promoted the ecclesiastical life of their dioceses in many ways. Above all else, however, they made an extraordinary contribution as theologians. Without their intellectual labor the Arian controversy would hardly have ended in the manner in which it did.

With reference to their intellectual and theological peculiarities the Cappadocians differ basically from Athanasius. They were not so concerned about ecclesiastical politics as he. Instead they took their cue from Origen. Yet they had moved toward the confession of Nicaea, affirming fully and completely the decision of 325. At the same time they attempted to pursue further the solution of the problems.

Among the Cappadocians the heritage of Origen is evident: in their doctrine of God they proceed less from the unity of the divine Being than they do from the three persons which, they felt, must be differentiated from one another. Even so, they emphasized the *homoousios* of the Son as well as that of the Holy Spirit. Above all else, however, they developed a precise terminology, in order to differentiate between the being of God in general and the individual persons. While the terms *ousia* (essence, substance) and *hypostasis* (essentiality, nature) were used indiscriminately by the older Nicaeans, the younger Nicaeans used the first concept for the common substance and the second for the concrete expression, or personal existence. From now on *ousia* becomes the technical expression for the Godhead as such, while *hypostasis* now no longer means "nature" but "person." Thus *ousia* refers to the common substance of God, and *hypostasis* to the special forms which this divine substance assumes in the person of the Father, the Son, and the Holy Spirit. This precise differentiation between concepts helped greatly to clarify the doctrine of God.

Furthermore, the Cappadocians set forth much more sharply the peculiarity of the persons of the Trinity than had been the case previously. In this endeavor it was natural to begin with the three names which were given to the persons of the Trinity. Basil did this, and accordingly ascribed to the Father "fatherhood," to the Son "sonship," and to the Holy Spirit "sanctifying power" or "sanctification." Or again the differences could be pointed out by saying that the Father is "unbegotten," the Son is "begotten," and the Holy Spirit "proceeds." As a result of such careful differentiation, and as a result of the definition of *ousia* and *hypostasis,* the three Cappadocians actually made possible a true doctrine of the Trinity, a doctrine, namely, which maintains both the unity and the difference of the persons. It should also be remembered that at about the time when these men were developing their doctrine Athanasius declared as orthodox the interpretation of *homoousios* (of the same substance) in the sense of *homoiousios* (similar in substance). Since, as has been mentioned, *homoousios* had meanwhile been interpreted in the sense of a numerical unity of the Father with the Son, it could also be misunderstood in a Sabellian sense. The term *homoiousios* was appropriate for removing this misunderstanding.

The stage had now been set for the conclusion of the long trinitarian controversy. On the eve of the Council of Constantinople (381), which was convoked to put an end to the long arguments, Gregory of Nazianzus declared in a speech that it was the destiny of his time to bring to full clarity the mystery which in the New Testament was only dimly intimated. That was a daring pronouncement, but it outlined the theological task which had been given to that day.

At the council of 381 the definitions of the Nicene confession were largely taken over, though at a few places changes were made. These had to do especially with the third article, which was greatly enlarged in order to witness also to the divinity of the Holy Spirit. Because the resulting creed is not historically attested until 451, attempts have been made in the past to assign to this creed a place of historical origin other than the council of 381, the Second Ecumenical Council. These attempts, however, may be regarded as having been proved to be untenable.[16] The Niceno-Constantinopolitan Creed, as this creed is called, is worded as follows:

> We believe in one God the Father almighty, maker of heaven and earth, of all things visible and invisible;
>
> And in one Lord Jesus Christ, the only-begotten Son of God, begotten from the Father before all ages, light from light, true God from true God, begotten not made, of one substance with the Father, through Whom all things came into existence, Who because of us men and because of our salvation came down from heaven, and was incarnate from the Holy Spirit and the Virgin Mary and became man, and was crucified for us under Pontius Pilate, and suffered and was buried, and rose again on the third day according to the Scriptures and ascended to heaven, and sits on the right hand of the Father, and will come again with glory to judge living and dead, of Whose kingdom there will be no end;
>
> And in the Holy Spirit, the Lord and life-giver, Who proceeds from the Father, Who with the Father and the Son is together worshipped and together glorified, Who spoke through the prophets; in one holy Catholic and apostolic Church. We confess one baptism to the remission of sins; we look forward to the resurrection of the dead in the life of the world to come. Amen.[17]

In this creed a specific assertion of the consubstantiality of the Spirit with the Father and the Son is missing. Yet, in es-

[16] See J. N. D. Kelly, *Early Christian Creeds*, pp. 296-331.

[17] English text taken from J. N. D. Kelly, *Early Christian Creeds*, pp. 297-298. Translation used with permission of Longmans, Green and Co., and David McKay Co.

sence it is there. For one thing, the Spirit is also called "Lord." Furthermore, it is emphasized that, together with the Father and the Son, the Spirit, too, is worshiped and glorified as the giver of life. Again, in the year 382 a new synod at Constantinople specifically affirmed the consubstantiality and the full divinity of the Holy Spirit, as well as his existence as a separate *hypostasis.* In this document, which is addressed to the bishops of the West who could not be present, the one Godhead of the three divine persons is set forth. Based upon the theology of the Cappadocians it says: "According to this faith there is one Godhead, Power and Substance of the Father and of the Son and of the Holy Ghost; the dignity being equal, and the majesty being equal in three perfect essences [*hypostaseis*] and three perfect persons."[18]

With the decision of Constantinople a specific problem of the Christian faith was settled for the first time in the history of the church in an authoritative and final way. While it is possible to see in the creation of the New Testament canon, as well as in the rule of faith, an initial dogma of the church, it must be admitted that the decrees of Nicaea and Constantinople differ from these in the sense that the major concern here is a specific article of the faith, namely, the doctrine of God. Does this imply, as has been so often asserted, a falling away of the church from the Christianity of the New Testament? If the development of the doctrine of the Trinity from its beginnings to the end of the fourth century is seen in its totality, it becomes difficult to make such an accusation. In fact, it is more correct to insist upon the opposite, namely, that by means of this dogma the church erected a barrier against the onslaught of the tidal wave of Hellenism, which threatened to inundate the Christian faith. If the word *homoousios* is taken in its original sense, which has been set forth by recent research, it must be said that in 325 the church confessed its faith in the divinity of Christ, and it did so exclusively in an attempt to reject the Arian heresy. Basil said at one time with reference to the term *homoousios* that, because of the errors of the Arians, it became necessary to choose a clear word, since Arius redefined the words of Scripture to suit his own purposes. Neither at Nicaea nor at Constantinople was the attempt made to plumb the depth of the divine mystery or to

[18] Theodoret, *The Ecclesiastical History,* Bk. V, chap. 9. *NPNF*² 3, 138.

define God's essence. The intention was, rather, to indicate that God himself encounters us in Jesus Christ, and that in the Holy Spirit God himself is present within his church.

The Right Interpretation of the Doctrine of the Trinity

If the council fathers had really been trying to fathom the depth of God's essence with their creed, it would mean, in effect, that every interpretation of their decision is superfluous. In that case it should be possible to see in the Nicene confession and in the Niceno-Constantinopolitan Creed the kind of clarification of the doctrine of the Trinity which would eliminate all further investigation of this segment of Christian doctrine. Neither the council fathers themselves, however, nor later theologians understood the dogma of the Trinity in this fashion. Quite to the contrary, as the declaration of consubstantiality in 325 led, of necessity, to a further deepening of the doctrine of God, so, too, the creed of 381 did not put an end to work on the doctrine of the Trinity. In fact, only after 381 was the necessity felt for a more profound interpretation. This may be shown by citing the example of Augustine.

When the council fathers assembled in 381 Augustine was not yet a Christian. His Damascus hour did not come until 386. From 395 on he was bishop of the little, insignificant North African coastal city of Hippo Regius which today is called Bone. The work of this man, who is, no doubt, the most important Latin church father, covered a great variety of very different areas. He advanced the theological study of the doctrine of sin and grace as well as that of the doctrine of the church, the latter a very controversial issue in the Africa of his day. His teaching in reference to the sacraments set forth the presuppositions for the total subsequent development of this doctrine in the Middle Ages as well as at the time of the Reformation. In *The City of God* he developed, on the basis of the Christian faith, one of the most profound interpretations of history ever offered. It is not surprising, therefore, that Augustine also devoted attention to the doctrine of the Trinity, especially in the fifteen books of his great work *On the Trinity,* on which he worked, with interruptions, from 399 to 419. It is the greatest work which was written about the Trinity in the ancient church.

In summarizing the basic thoughts of this work it must be

noted, first, that Augustine emphasized above all else the unity of God. He saw clearly that the formula of the Cappadocians concerning the one substance and the three persons, and even more their interpretation of this formula, could lead to misunderstandings. Their distinction between *ousia* and *hypostasis,* between the common substance and the distinctive expression of the individual persons, has been mentioned above. As we know, the Cappadocians often emphasized the second alternative, namely, the persons. In doing so they sometimes went very far. For instance, they compared the concept *ousia* with the generic concept "man," while they compared the individual hypostases with certain men such as Peter, Andrew, or John. Using this analogy, they taught that insofar as the *ousia,* the substance common to all three, is concerned, they are human beings. Thus they are of "one substance." On the other hand, this common substance comes to definite expression only through concrete personal existence.

This comparison was, of course, not a very happy one. It emphasizes the difference between the persons of the Trinity much more than it does their unity. It was thus possible for the Arians to brand the Cappadocian doctrine of the Trinity as polytheistic, and to do so with a certain appearance of justice. Augustine, who strongly felt the unfortunate element in such a comparison, sought to circumvent this reef on which the theology of the Cappadocians threatened to run aground. As emphatically as he could, he asserted that the Trinity is one God, not three gods. Nor does God cease to be "simple" (*simplex*) because of his threefoldness. It is noteworthy that Augustine does not use the concept of *substantia* for the being of God, but that of *essentia.* He avoids the expression *substantia,* because it would seem to imply that God's righteousness is attributed only to his substance, whereas all the perfections which are ascribed to him must, in fact, be regarded as one with his being. If the concept of *substantia* were used, God would have to be regarded as the bearer of his attributes. But that is impossible. For instance, the greatness, or the goodness, or the eternity of God are not something which must first be added to his substance. God is great in himself, through his own greatness. The same is true for the other so-called attributes of God. All of them inhere in his essence.

This, however, leads immediately to a further consequence. Absolute perfection and absolute being can be asserted only of one. For that reason Augustine insists that it is the one God, not each of the three persons in himself, who possesses a nature, and who possesses one deity, one majesty, and one glory, as well as one will and one operation. There is no activity, therefore, in which only the Father, or only the Son, or only the Holy Spirit is involved. Over against the world, God (i.e., the three persons of the Trinity) represents "one principle" (*unum principium*).[19] Augustine conceives the unity of the Trinity so stringently that he asserts that not only the Father, but also the Son and the Holy Spirit, were actively involved in the incarnation of the Son.[20] To express this view Augustine created a precise formula to the effect that the works of the Trinity are not separable as regards the outside, which means that the three persons of the Trinity always work in concert.[21]

Of no less importance are Augustine's reflections on the concept of the persons. He always had reservations about this concept. It is indeed a highly problematical element in the doctrine of the Trinity. While the Greek term *hypostasis* refers primarily to a distinct personal existence, the Latin term *persona* frequently includes also a distinct self-consciousness. It was extremely difficult to find a fitting Latin equivalent for the Greek word *hypostasis*. It should have been translated by the word *substantia*. But this would have created the impression that three divine substances were being taught, which would have contradicted the *homoousios* of the Son and the Spirit with the Father. In the Greek the term *hypostasis* had gained acceptance very slowly, gradually forcing out other words which were also problematical, such as *prosōpon* (mask, face). Augustine strongly felt the inadequacy of the term *persona*. He always used it with hesitation, and as a rule substituted for it the concept of *relatio* (relation). The three so-called persons, he said, are not something different, each in himself. They are different only in their relation to each other and to the world. While all absolute properties such as perfection, goodness, and omnipotence belong only to the Trinity in its oneness, the term *relatio*

[19] Augustine, *On the Trinity*, Bk. V, chap. 14, sec. 15. *NPNF*[1] 3, 94-95.

[20] *Ibid.*, Bk. II, chap. 5, sec. 9. *NPNF*[1] 3, 40-42.

[21] Augustine, *Enchiridion*, chap. 38. *NPNF*[1] 3, 250.

refers to the inner life of God, as well as his relation to the created world. For this reason, he held, it is not possible to call the Trinity "Father" in the same sense in which it is referred to as great, or good, or eternal. Such an assertion of fatherhood could be made of the Trinity at best in a derivative sense, e.g., in relation to the creatures adopted by God as his children. Yet even in the derivative use of such appellatives Augustine believed there is a difference between the persons of the Trinity. While it is possible to call the entire Trinity "Father" in a secondary sense, it is impossible to call the Trinity "Son" as well: the concept of sonship does not in any way apply to the other persons of the Trinity.[22] What Augustine means here is that the designations "Father," "Son," and "Holy Spirit" do not express either a substantial, or a quantitative, or a qualitative difference, because these do not even exist. What the concept of the persons expresses is, rather, an eternal relation. But this relation is not an *accidens,* i.e., something that is added to "being," for such a relation would be subject to change. The one God, then, is never Father only, or Son only, or Holy Spirit only. He always was, and always will be, the one triune God, namely, Father, Son, and Holy Spirit.

Thus Augustine, too, clings to the differences between the "persons." Under no circumstances did he wish to deny the unique element associated with each of the persons of the Trinity. He rightly noted, however, that the concept of persons is subject to misunderstanding. Augustine felt that this concept was used only in order that the truth involved "might not be left [wholly] unspoken." It did not express to him the actual state of things.[23]

The West has never left out of account this interpretation which Augustine had given to the decisions of the councils of Nicaea and Constantinople. It was he who played the decisive role in warning Latin theology against the danger of tritheism and in keeping it from succumbing to this danger. Appealing to Augustine, Karl Barth rendered the concept of *persona* by the use of the word "mode" [*Seinsweise*].[24] There is yet another sense, however, in which Augustine sets an example for

[22] Augustine, *On the Trinity,* Bk. V, chap. II, sec. 12. *NPNF*[1] 3, 93.

[23] *Ibid.,* Bk. V, chap. 9, sec. 10. *NPNF*[1] 3, 92.

[24] *CD* 1^1, 400.

our day. He closed his great work on the Trinity with a prayer in which he asks God's forgiveness in case he should have said something which does not accord with the truth. "O Lord, the one God," he prayed, "God the Trinity, whatever I have said in these books that is of Thine, may they acknowledge who are Thine; if anything of my own, may it be pardoned both by Thee and by those who are Thine."[25] No one should speak of the mystery of the Trinity unless it be with such reverence. But in our day it is perhaps even more essential to emphasize that mere silence about this mystery is not enough.

[25] Augustine, *On the Trinity*, Bk. XV, chap. 28, sec. 51. *NPNF*[1] 3, 228.

3

Christology

Beginnings

In giving an account of the development of the doctrine of the Trinity it was also necessary to mention briefly certain christological problems. Christology and the doctrine of the Trinity cannot be separated from each other either in the history of doctrine or in systematic theology. Every christological affirmation always contains a certain understanding of the Trinity and, conversely, every trinitarian affirmation contains, at the same time, a christological one. Still it is necessary that the trinitarian and the christological problems be carefully differentiated from each other. While christology and the doctrine of the Trinity have always influenced each other, it is no accident that in the fourth century there was first a controversy about the doctrine of the Trinity, and only thereafter about Christology. The doctrine of the Trinity is concerned with the question of the unity of God in the context of a faith which, in the same breath, asserts not only the divinity of the Father, but also that of the Son and of the Holy Spirit. Christology, on the other hand, is concerned with the question of the relation between that which is divine and that which is human in the person of Jesus Christ.

It is obvious at the outset that the problem here is a specifically Christian one. While it is certain that the doctrine of the Trinity does not stem from non-Christian sources, it is still true that the problem of the unity of God is by no means merely a Christian one; it is also a philosophical one. In Christology, on the other hand, we are concerned with a purely Christian problem. The question how the divine and the human are related to each other in a given person is not a general concern of mankind, or of philosophy as such. It is a question only for the person who has encountered Jesus Christ, and who then wants to express his faith that Jesus Christ is truly man, but that, on the other hand, God himself is present in him, indeed, that he himself is God.

In the New Testament there is no conceptually and intellectually developed Christology, any more than there is an actual doctrine of the Trinity. Yet it is a fact that with reference to Christology forms are already present in the New Testament which are more developed than those that provided the starting points of the subsequent doctrine of the Trinity. The reason is to be sought in the fact that Christology was given decisive impetus by the Christians' immediate confrontation with Jesus Christ, while for the development of the doctrine of the Trinity delicate conceptual explanations were necessary. For the disciples and for the authors of the Gospels there could not be the least doubt concerning the true humanity of Jesus. They had known Christ "according to the flesh." They had walked with him through Galilee and Judea. With him they had experienced his trial and condemnation, his torment and, at last, his death on the cross. Their faith in the resurrection did not stand in opposition to this experience. They felt, rather, that, by resurrecting Jesus Christ, God had testified that he who had been crucified was also the one sent from God.

At the same time the disciples were sure that Jesus Christ was not just another man sent by God. They knew that in him God meets us in a unique and incomparable way, i.e., in a way which is absolute and ultimate; they knew, in fact, that in a certain sense Jesus is himself divine. This faith did not result merely and exclusively from their confrontation with the risen Christ. Even the earthly Jesus had come with an authority which broke through everything men had been accustomed to. They were shocked by his preaching, "for he taught them as one who had authority, and not as the scribes" (Mark 1:22). By God's commission Jesus could forgive sins. He set himself above the Old Testament and insisted that he was declaring the original will of God. Nor was the law a final authority for him. He healed the sick and announced the judgment of God to the scribes and the Pharisees. The category of the prophetic was obviously not sufficient to explain the secret of his person (Mark 8:27-33). What, then, were the concepts which might be employed to express the Christians' faith in Jesus Christ? How could that which is more than prophetic be formulated so that, on the one hand, it is appropriate and, on the other hand, does not endanger the unity of God?

It is noteworthy that the New Testament, while in a few places it calls Jesus "God," usually displays great reserve toward this form of address. The reason for this was the strict monotheism of the Jewish environment, which would not tolerate such a designation. As a matter of fact, however, the primitive church regarded Jesus as God from the very beginning. This is evident from the fact that it prayed to him. It may be said, therefore, in a general way, that the authors of the New Testament believed in "the divine character" of Jesus Christ from the outset. Beyond this, even the pre-existence of Jesus was asserted at an early date. In St. Paul we meet this idea as something taken for granted. In this respect the primitive church was able to draw upon certain conceptions which had already been developed in Jewish apocalyptic and, using them, to express its faith in Jesus Christ.

Obviously the development which led from the christological ideas of primitive Christianity to the two-nature doctrine of later times was not unilinear. In the history of Christology, as in the history of the doctrine of God, many groping attempts were made which did not gain acceptance. At the beginning there was a great variety of christological conceptions. Gradually these congealed into a few patterns, which were sharply differentiated one from the other. Since here we can follow only the line of development which leads to the later two-nature doctrine, two other types should at least be mentioned. The one is the so-called Ebionite Christology. The Ebionites were Jewish Christians who adhered to many ancient traditions of the primitive church but, under the influence of Jewish and gnostic currents, separated themselves from the church at large and did not participate in its development. They stood in strenuous opposition to St. Paul, as well as to John the Baptist. The name they applied to themselves, "Ebionites" (poor ones), had reference to an honorific title given to the primitive church at Jerusalem (cf. Gal. 2:10; Rom. 15:26). They believed Jesus to be the human son of Joseph and Mary. He was destined to become the Messiah, and would one day return to establish his kingdom. The basic characteristic of the Ebionites was their belief that Christ was a mere man who, however, had been equipped by God with special gifts. A similar Christology could, at times, be found among Christians of non-Jewish origins. An example is the adoptionism mentioned in the previous chapter, which found learned proponents far into the third century.

Another christological type which developed in opposition to the doctrine of the larger church is what came to be called "docetism." Its proponents maintained that Christ was a man in appearance only, who united himself for a limited time, namely, to the day of the crucifixion, with the man Jesus but left him before his death. A developed docetism is found especially in the gnostic systems and in Marcion. Even a considerable number of ecclesiastical authors of the second and third centuries occasionally betray docetic leanings. In later times, also, docetic tendencies showed themselves ever and again within the church. Docetism had reached its zenith, however, in the first and second centuries.

Early ideas which point most strongly in the direction of the Christology of the later church are found in St. Paul and St. John. In Galatians 4:4 Paul writes, "But when the time had fully come, God sent forth his son, born of a woman, born under the law." Here the pre-existence of Jesus is clearly asserted. He was the Son of the Father even before he came into the world. His sonship, therefore, does not date only from his earthly birth. Another assertion, which may represent an early Christian confession of faith cited by St. Paul, goes even further: "the gospel concerning his Son, who was descended from David according to the flesh and designated Son of God in power according to the Spirit of holiness by his resurrection from the dead" (Rom. 1:3-4). St. Paul, or the confession which he cites here, speaks of Jesus Christ as having two modes of being. The one is earthly and carnal, the other heavenly and spiritual. According to the one he is like us men, according to the other he is plainly superior to us. According to the flesh Jesus Christ descended from David; according to the Holy Spirit he is designated Son of God in power. This assertion that Jesus is "designated" Son of God should not be understood in an adoptionist sense, as if he had become the Son of God only as a result of his resurrection. The word "designated" should here be understood in opposition to the word "descended." In both cases a basic datum is given concerning the origin of Jesus Christ. The one has reference to the beginning of his earthly existence, the other to the beginning of his heavenly existence "in power." It is certain that we do not yet have a developed two-nature doctrine here. Still the important presuppositions for it are present, and basically the problem has already been raised. This is apparent if one considers that this confession cannot be interpreted to mean that during the days of his flesh Jesus was mere man. The subject of the entire affirmation is the Son of God. He is initially with the Father, he comes into this world, and he does so in order to return again to the Father. The declaration in question actually demands further consideration of the problem as to how the divine and the human in the person of Jesus Christ are related to each other.

The hymn of Christ found in Philippians 2:5-11, and which again was not created by Paul but is merely cited by him, goes a step further than the confession in Romans 1:3-4. This hymn says more about the mode of existence of the Son of God, inasmuch as it speaks of his being "in the form of God," and of having "equality with God" (v. 6).

The Johannine affirmations also point in the direction of future christological development. We are concerned here especially with the prologue of the Gospel of John and the affirmations concerning the divine Logos which are found there. Scholars are not in agreement as to which particular philosophical or religious concept of the Logos forms the background to the Gospel. The Stoics spoke of the Logos as the divine reason in the world, which at the same time is active in man. Philo, the Jewish theologian of Alexandria, accorded the Logos a place of supreme importance in his system. To him the Logos was the divine mediator of creation and revelation, though again it was not conceived of in personal terms. Within Gnosticism there was a mythological Logos figure, though it is questionable whether this concept was already present in pre-Christian times. Up to the present day the attempt to establish with certainty which of these conceptions of the Logos was employed by the writer of the Gospel of John has been unsuccessful. This question, however, is not really very important for the later development of Christology. For whether John's conception of the Logos has reference to Philo or to Gnosticism, at the decisive point it parts company with all prototypes, culminating as it does in the confession, "the Word became flesh" (John 1:14). The introduction of the concept of the Logos into Christology was bound, sooner or later, to open up enormous possibilities for the further development of the doctrine of Jesus Christ. The entire ancient heritage of this concept could now be sifted to find that which might prove useful. It was still some time before an actual Logos Christology established itself in Christian theology. But the presuppositions for it were already present in the New Testament itself. Once again the New Testament affirmations called for further reflection and fuller elaboration.

During the second century the further development of Christology came not with the apostolic fathers, but with the apologists, among whom Justin Martyr is pre-eminent. We have seen that the apologists looked for new points of departure in connection with the doctrine of the Trinity; they did the same with reference to Christology. First and foremost, they appropriated the concept of the Logos which, from the beginning, they brought into relation with Greek philosophy. This concept made it possible for them to explain further the relation between Christ and God the Father. Stoic philosophy distinguished between the Logos insofar as it inhabits the realm of Spirit and the Logos insofar as it communicates itself, i.e., insofar as it is expressed (*logos prophorikos*). This differentiation was well suited for the purpose of explaining more fully the relation between God the Father and his Son.

The apologists found the concept of the Logos no less important for the understanding of Jesus Christ himself. They no longer understood the Logos in the sense of the Gospel of John, namely, as the Word of God which appeared in history. They thought of the Logos as a universal mind and cosmic principle. That is, they equated the pre-existant Christ with the Logos concept of Greek philosophy. For the educated classes the way into Christianity was thus made easier, for now the acceptance of the entire Greek heritage had been made possible. On this basis the apologists could assert that all truth which the Greek philosophers possessed came, in the last analysis, from the Logos, namely, Jesus Christ. They insisted that while in ancient philosophy the Logos appeared in fragmentary and imperfect fashion, it had now revealed itself finally and fully in Jesus Christ.

Thanks to the influence of Origen the Logos Christology established itself everywhere in the third century. It had become the universally acknowledged presupposition of further christological thought. Even Arius accepted the concept of the Logos, though his interpretation of it differed from that of the apologists and from that of Origen. Still, the acceptance of the Logos Christology did not mean, in itself, that the christological problem had been satisfactorily resolved. Even if Arius' doubling of the Logos, which was described above, was rejected, even if the Son of God was understood to be the eternal Logos of the Father, and even if, with Athanasius, the consubstantiality of the Son with the Father was maintained, not all questions were answered. Actually the problem of how the divine and the human in the person of Jesus Christ are related to each other became all the more pressing. As long as the Son was strictly subordinated to the Father it was possible to see in the earthly Jesus a kind of superhuman, nearly divine being. If, on the other hand, the unlimited and full divinity of the Son was asserted, then his true humanity was bound to become a problem. How could both positions be reconciled?

Once again it was Tertullian who at the beginning of the third century had already found a solution that was far in advance of his time, one that still had significance in the fifth century for the decision of the Council of Chalcedon. It had been Tertullian who had created a clear conceptual terminology for the doctrine of the Trinity. Now he pioneered in finding christological formulations. His controversy with the Gnostics, as well as with the Modalists, had forced him to further reflection on the inherited problems in Christology. In his treatise against Praxeas he asks how the incarnation is to be understood. Does the divine Logos undergo a change? Or should we speak of the Logos assuming flesh? Tertullian decided, as did later Christology, in favor of the assertion that in the incarnation the Logos assumes human flesh. If the flesh were said to undergo a transformation, it would follow that the Logos ceases to be what he is. God, however, can never cease to be what he is. By the same token, the assertion that Jesus Christ undergoes a transformation would also call into question the true humanity of the incarnated Logos. In that case it would be impossible, Tertullian held, to adhere either to the divinity or to the humanity of Christ. The result would then be some third entity, which would neither be true God nor true man. Hence it is possible to say only that the divine Logos assumed human nature.[1]

This means, however, that Jesus Christ has two "natures" or, as Tertullian puts it, two substances. According to Tertullian each of these two substances is undiminished and has its own characteristics. Furthermore, each of them has its own distinctive functions. Thus the Logos works the miracles, while the human substance suffers afflictions. Still it would be wrong to separate the two substances from each other. There is only one Jesus Christ, who is the Son of God and at the same time the Son of man. Following this line of reasoning Tertullian arrives at the precisely stated formula, "We see plainly the twofold state [*status*], which is not confounded, but conjoined in One Person—Jesus, God and Man."[2] Thus in the one inseparable person, Jesus Christ, are present God and man, divinity and humanity, divine Spirit and human flesh. That being the case, immortality and mortality, power and weakness are also conjoined in him. Here Tertullian sometimes touches upon the theses which were later set forth by the Nestorians, according to which particular happenings in the life of Jesus are ascribed to the one or the other of the two natures. In spite of his differentiation between the two natures, however, Tertullian was extremely careful not to question the unity of the person of Jesus Christ.

In view of later controversies it is worth noting that according to Tertullian, Christ was a real man, and as such had a human soul. The Logos did not take the place of the human soul, for then the work of redemption would not have been accomplished. Rather, Christ became wholly man. On the other hand, Tertullian asserts that, even as man, Jesus is still the Son of God, i.e., the divine Logos.

Tertullian's ideas, though very profound, were not able to spare the church its lengthy christological controversy. Some problems were still in need of further clarification. Even more important, the Greek East did not take further notice of the

[1] Tertullian, *Against Praxeas,* chap. 27. *ANF* 3, 623-624.

[2] *Ibid.,* chap. 27. *ANF* 3, 624.

Christology of Tertullian. The reason was that from the third century on the East was obviously the center of theological work while, generally speaking, the West did not make any contributions of its own either to the trinitarian or to the christological controversy. Most western theologians were unfamiliar with problems of eastern theology at the time.

In the development of Christology, as in the history of the doctrine of the Trinity, the thought of Origen occupies a place of supreme importance. It was his work that provided the basis, even in details, of the approaches to the problem of Christology in the later christological controversy. Once again the opposing parties were substantially indebted to the great Alexandrian.

Parallel with Origen's speculative doctrine of the Trinity runs a speculative element in his Christology. To the question which later on became so highly controversial, namely, whether or not Jesus had a human soul, Origen gives a strange answer. He maintains, to be sure, that Jesus had such a soul. Yet, in line with his notion concerning spiritual beings and their pre-existence, Origen asserts pre-existence also of the soul of Jesus, which he believed had been in existence before the incarnation. But while the other pre-existent souls fell away from God, the soul of Jesus was united, already in its pre-existent state, with the divine Logos. This union was so close that the pre-existent soul of Jesus took the Logos wholly into itself, so that from the Logos it received its light and its glory. Already in its pre-existent state, therefore, it became of one spirit with the Logos. As a result, the soul of Jesus lost its capacity to sin. At the time of the incarnation the divine Logos, already united with this soul, entered into the body of Jesus. The soul now played a mediating role between the eternal Logos and the finite body of Jesus. As the soul could contain the Logos, so the body could contain the soul, and through it the Logos. Jesus, then, was a true man, quite like all other men. Since Origen asserted the pre-existence of all souls Jesus did not differ from men even with respect to such pre-existence. On this basis Origen could, on the one hand, assert the difference between the divinity and the humanity of Jesus Christ (to some extent he used formulations similar to those of Tertullian). On the other hand, he could also emphasize the unity of the God-man. Thus the two natures are connected with each other not merely through "communion" with each other, but in true "oneness" or "union."

This theory was able to subsume many biblical conceptions. Yet it did not stress sufficiently the idea of the incarnation. In the last analysis human nature has no place in this system. This shows itself, not only in the mediating role Origen assigned to the soul, but also in Origen's assumption that after the resurrection there was a progressive absorption of the resurrection body of Jesus. Actually it was the gnostic opposition to the body which, in a mitigated form, here found entrance into Christology. For that reason Origen's Christology was unacceptable to most theologians. Above all, the theory of the pre-existence of the soul of Jesus was discarded. In the process, however, a difficulty arose. What about the human soul of the incarnated Logos? The choice here was basically between two possibilities. On the one hand, adherence to Platonic anthropology, according to which man is a body animated by a soul or a spirit, would lead to the conclusion that no soul could be ascribed to the earthly Jesus. Adherence to Aristotelian anthropology, on the other hand, would mean that body and soul must be regarded as constituting a unity. In both cases special problems resulted. The question was, How is it possible to express both the unity of the divine Logos and the human body, and the difference between them? In the history of dogma the line of thought which put the emphasis upon unity asserted itself in Alexandria under the catchword "Word-flesh Christology." The second line of thought, which put the emphasis upon the difference between the divine Logos and the human body, was centered in Antioch and utilized the concept of "Word-man Christology."

Apollinaris of Laodicea

During the Arian controversy the significance of the question whether or not Jesus had a human soul was not yet recognized. In fact, it is even possible to note a certain agreement between Arius and the Nicene party in their position on this problem. The Arians denied the presence of a human soul in the incarnate Logos. In their opinion the Logos took the place of the soul, so that the body of Jesus was, in itself, without a soul. It is significant that for Athanasius the offensive element in this line of argumentation was not the denial of the human soul.

What repulsed him was the conclusion of the Arians that if the Logos takes the place of the human soul the former is thereby proved to have the character of a creature. For if the Logos takes the place of the human soul, everything that is said about the passion and death of Jesus Christ must have reference not to his human soul but to the Logos himself. Yet, if the Logos suffered he cannot be immutable. He must, in fact, be a creature.

Basically Athanasius, too, stood for a Word-flesh Christology, though his point of departure was opposite to that of Arius. To be sure, Athanasius never denied the presence of a human soul in Jesus. Still there is no question but that at least during the first decades of the Arian controversy he did not succeed in attributing to that soul any actual significance. Athanasius was in danger of insisting upon the consubstantiality of the Son with the Father at the price of the full human nature of Jesus Christ. His basic concern was the full divinity of the Son. As yet he did not regard the incarnation as a problem.

At quite an early date many of the orthodox theologians also began to see the seriousness of the problem concerning the human soul of Jesus. This is true especially of Eustathius of Antioch (d. 337). In contradistinction to the Arians, Eustathius held to the divinity of Christ, but recognized at the same time the consequences of denying that Christ had a human soul. Unfortunately Eustathius was in danger of falling into the other extreme, namely, of sundering the divinity and humanity of Christ. He taught that Christ had a human soul and that it had been the subject of his sufferings. It is necessary, he thought, to conceive of the connection of the Logos with the full humanity of Jesus in a way which thinks of the Logos as dwelling within the man Jesus. The man Jesus thus carried God within him. In saying this Eustathius anticipated the basic elements of the later Antiochene Christology.

Apollinaris of Laodicea (d. *ca.* 390) very quickly recognized the danger of the rending of the divinity and the humanity of Christ. A stanch defender of the confession of Nicaea and one of Athanasius' comrades in arms, this courageous thinker was in many ways ahead of his time; he perceived the issues that proved to be the actual problems of the christological controversy of the fifth century. He saw in the ideas developed by

Eustathius a dualism which would cleave the unity of the person of Jesus Christ. In opposition to it, therefore, he developed a very precise Christology of the Word-flesh type, which was much more one-sided than that of Athanasius. He charged his opponents with teaching two sons, the Son of God and the son of Mary, the former being the Son of God by nature, the latter only by adoption. In contradistinction to this view, he said that the Holy Scriptures know only of one Son of God. Apollinaris, very much like Athanasius, was prompted here by soteriological considerations: as a mere man Christ would not have possessed the capacity to redeem men. Apollinaris states: "If we call him who was born of Mary, and who was crucified, a man, then we make him a man instead of God. And in a man the life which is given by God cannot be found."[3] Furthermore, how could we be baptized into the death of a mere man? As a man Christ would have been subject to error and consequently would not have brought us redemption.

To avoid these dangers Apollinaris often spoke of a "God made flesh," or a "flesh-bearing God." He did not understand these expressions docetically, as if the flesh were merely a cover for a God who walks upon earth. He presupposed a union of God and flesh beginning with the moment of conception. The flesh is thus not something added, but it forms one single reality with the divinity in Christ. The Christ who became flesh is therefore a composite being in the form of a man. Thus there is only "one nature of the divine Logos, which [nature] became flesh."[4] This means that Jesus Christ was a single, indivisible being or, to say it more pointedly, that the body of Jesus was dependent upon the Logos as its guiding principle. The Logos is active, the flesh passive. Only thus is it possible to speak of the one nature of Jesus Christ.

This was the foundation of Apollinaris' Christology. Up to this point many theologians were able to follow him; certainly Athanasius could. From the point of view of later orthodox Christology there are hardly any objections which can be raised against it. The trouble was that Apollinaris attempted to finish what he had started. In doing this he understood the incarna-

[3] H. Lietzmann, *Appollinaris von Laodicea und seine Schule* ("Texte und Untersuchungen," No. 1; Tübingen: Mohr, 1904), p. 202, ll. 5-10.

[4] *Ibid.*, p. 251, ll. 1 f.

tion of the Logos, not in a broad sense, as referring to his being made man, but literally: the Logos took on only flesh, only a body. For this reason no human intellectual activity can be asserted of the earthly Jesus. For if it were, it would mean, first, that the human nature of Christ would be exalted to the level of a discrete entity. As a result its full unity with the Logos would be diminished to a mere connection between the two. Second, it would imply that the human nature could, because of its own freedom, sever its connection with divinity. In that case the permanence of the unity between divinity and humanity would be called into question.

From this Apollinaris deduces that the Logos did not take on a "spirit," but that the Logos took the place of the spirit. During his early period Apollinaris probably denied that Jesus even had a human soul. Later on, however, he changed his mind and admitted the presence of a soul in the earthly Jesus, but he now put the Logos in the place of the human spirit. What we thus have in Jesus Christ is a "mixture" of God and man. As Apollinaris sees it, there is here the kind of connection which obtains between fire and glowing metal.

This conception has an important consequence as regards the flesh. Apollinaris was of the opinion that the flesh of Jesus was glorified by this union. It became divine flesh. For that reason Apollinaris has sometimes been accused of teaching the preexistence of the flesh of Christ. This is unfair to him, however. For him the glorification of the flesh was solely the result of its union with the Logos. He always maintained that the flesh of Jesus came from the Virgin Mary. It is significant also that Apollinaris arrived at conclusions similar to those of Origen, even though he began with different premises. In the last analysis, neither of these men succeeded in maintaining the full humanity of Jesus.

It took some time before the danger lurking in Apollinaris' teaching was recognized by the church. During the last years of the Arian controversy the Christology of Apollinaris was rejected by various synods, above all by the Second Ecumenical Council, held at Constantinople in 381. Of course, a final clarification of the controverted problems of Christology was not achieved at that time. It is obvious, however, that Apollinaris could defend himself only with great difficulty against the charge of docetism. It is equally clear that his doctrine flatly contradicted the biblical records, which frequently speak of Jesus as not knowing something, and which also mention his suffering (e.g., in Gethsemane) and other human traits. In a word, Apollinaris did not give expression to the reality of the incarnation of the Logos.

Antiochenes and Alexandrians

On the one hand, the great theological schools of Antioch and Alexandria accepted the older christological ideas while, on the other, they established the outlines of the two basic concepts of Christology which were destined to stand opposed to each other during the christological controversy. During the heated discussions which took place the two starting points which are possible in the development of Christology were clearly brought to the fore. In this connection it is important to note that in one essential point the christological controversy of the fifth century differs very decidedly from the trinitarian controversy of the fourth century. It is true without a doubt that in the fourth century Athanasius and the Nicene party were generally in the right, so that the arguments of Arius did not carry nearly the same weight. In the fifth century, however, the decision as to who was right is much more difficult to make. Both the Antiochenes and the Alexandrians represented points of view which are absolutely indispensable to the Christian faith. Hence the decision which emerged from the christological controversy did not clearly favor one or the other of the opposing parties, as had been the case in the Arian controversy.

A second difference between the christological and the trinitarian controversies is equally important. In the latter the discussions often revolved around questions of ecclesiastical politics, so that dogmatic differences at times became merely an excuse for a scarcely concealed power struggle. This was true to a much greater degree, however, of the christological controversy. During the course of it Nestorius, the Bishop of Constantinople (deposed in 431, d. after 451), defended the opinions of the Antiochenes; and Cyril of Alexandria (d. 444), the Christology of the Alexandrians. At the same time both were exponents of the rival patriarchates of Constantinople and Alexandria. As such they did not shrink from using almost any means at their disposal in order to assert themselves against their rival. In this respect Cyril surpassed his opponent by a few degrees. We cannot enter here into this power struggle and the reasons underlying it. These accompanying circumstances, however, regrettable as they might be, do not alter the importance of the basic issues contested by Constantinople and Alexandria.

We have seen how Apollinaris of Laodicea maintained a Word-flesh type of Christology, and how, as a result, he arrived at those extreme conclusions for which his doctrine was finally condemned. Positively as well as negatively all the subsequent theologians who figure prominently in the christological controversy actually began with the problematics created by Apollinaris. Furthermore, most of the theologians who participated in the polemic against Apollinaris were also adherents of the Word-flesh Christology. This fact is responsible for the weakness of their line of argument. Within this christological scheme it was extremely difficult to avoid the heretical one-sidedness of the conclusions to which Apollinaris had come. What was needed was a Christology which, on the one hand, maintained the full, real humanity of Jesus, but which, on the other hand, succeeded in setting forth the connection between the divine and the human in the person of Jesus. The church is indebted to Antiochene theology for having produced that kind of Christology. Nor is this debt diminished by the fact that the Antiochenes, in their justifiable polemic against Apollinaris, happened to move too far in the opposite direction. What they accomplished is the substitution of a Word-man Christology for a one-sided Word-flesh Christology.

The Antiochene Christology goes back in its rudiments to the ideas of Eustathius of Antioch, which we have already discussed. It was developed further by Diodorus of Tarsus (d. before 394) and then by Theodore of Mopsuestia (d. 428). Only in the form in which Nestorius maintained it did it lead to controversy with the Alexandrians. Common to all these theologians is their emphasis on the full, undiminished human nature of Jesus Christ. Their primary concern was to safeguard the assertion that Jesus had a human soul as well as a human mentality. If the Logos and the flesh had formed one substantial unity, as Apollinaris taught, this would have called into question not only the wholeness of the human nature but that of the divine nature as well. Diodorus, for instance, emphasized that the Scriptures differentiate sharply between the activity of the Son of God and that of the son of David. The unity of the two, he felt, is not a mixture of Logos and flesh. Rather, their unity must be understood in such a way that the Logos is regarded as dwelling in the flesh as in a temple. In this respect Diodorus sees a certain similarity between Jesus and the prophets, although there is also a difference. To be sure, the Spirit of God occasionally dwelt in the prophets, but only temporarily. Christ, on the other hand, was steadily and permanently filled by the divine Logos. Under no circumstances can it be maintained, however, that Jesus was only a single *hypostasis,* although, as regards worship, the Son of God and the son of David are united: the son of David participates in the veneration which is given to the Son of God.

Theodore of Mopsuestia went considerably beyond Diodorus in his criticism of Alexandrian Christology. He saw clearly that the Word-flesh Christology, whether or not it is taken to the extremes of the Apollinarian conclusions, is always based upon the presupposition that the Logos is the dominant principle in Jesus. It is this conception that Theodore criticizes. In doing so he points out that, if this position were correct, the humanity of Jesus would have been free from all weakness and sufferings, such as hunger, thirst, and dejection. This not being the case, Theodore concludes that the Logos did not merely adopt a body, but a perfect man. Here the concern of the Word-man Christology is clearly apparent. On this basis it is possible for Theodore to emphasize that two perfect entities are united in Christ, namely, the perfect man and the perfect God.

The Christology of Theodore exhibits a series of weaknesses. First, there is basically no room in his Christology for the thought that the divine Word became man. The basic idea is that of adoption, rather than incarnation. The result is that Theodore's Christology cannot do justice to the basic affirmation of John 1:14, "The Word became flesh." As it was impossible for Apollinaris to maintain the full humanity of Jesus, so it was impossible for Theodore to maintain a true incarnation. Second, it was equally impossible for him to give adequate expression to the unity of God and man in Jesus Christ. He, too, made use of the idea that the Logos dwelt in man. This indwelling, said

Theodore, was so intimate that it made possible the true unity of the two entities. As a rule, however, he spoke only of a "conjunction" of the two or of a "connection" between them, which was brought about because the man Jesus willed what the Logos willed, and vice versa.

Neither Diodorus nor Theodore were attacked for their Christology during their lifetime. Only later did opposition arise to their teaching, and both were condemned as heretics many decades after their death, Diodorus in 499 and Theodore at the Fifth Ecumenical Council, at Constantinople, in 553. Such a posthumous attempt to brand someone a heretic is, of course, unjust, since it does not afford the accused an opportunity to defend himself against misinterpretations of his teaching. Furthermore, in this case it does not give credit to the two Antiochenes' legitimate concern to emphasize our Lord's full humanity. It was no accident that these two men engaged in biblical exegesis to a degree unparalleled in their day, and that in doing so they set forth the true humanity of our Lord.

It was the theology of Nestorius, however, which triggered the reaction to the Antiochene Christology. Had it not been for his assertions, which were often quite reckless, the orthodoxy of Diodorus and Theodore might never have been questioned. This was true even though Nestorius hardly taught anything which was substantially different from the positions of the two older heads of the Antiochene school of theology. The controversy was precipitated by the question whether or not it could be said of Mary that she was "God-bearing" (*theotokos*).

It seems that soon after Nestorius had become Bishop of Constantinople (428) he was asked to take a position on this question. *Theotokos* was actually a shibboleth: To affirm it would mean, above all, that the unity of the divinity and humanity of Jesus would be established. To reject it would lead to the questions: If divinity and humanity were not united in him from birth, from what moment on could Jesus be designated as God? In what manner were divinity and humanity united in him? Nestorius attributed Apollinarianism to the people who used the expression "God-bearing." He felt, furthermore, that such a title made Christianity ridiculous among pagans. Finally, he noted that it cannot be found either in Scripture or in the confession of Nicaea. The result was that he attacked it in several sermons, granting its valid use only if it were supplemented with the expression "man-bearing" (*anthrōpotokos*). He thought that it would be better in any case to designate Mary as "Christ-bearing" (*christotokos*). What Nestorius meant to accomplish here is apparent. He meant to establish that Mary did not give birth to the divine Logos, but to the man Jesus who was united with the deity. Unfortunately, in his discussions of this theme Nestorius made use of provocatory phraseology. He argued, for instance, that a woman could not carry the deity for nine months in her womb, or that the deity could hardly be wrapped in diapers. Nor could it have suffered, died, and found itself buried.

Long after he had been condemned Nestorius wrote a polemical tract defending himself against the accusation that he had dissolved the unity of the person of Christ and had maintained the heretical doctrine of the "two sons." In the decision of Chalcedon, of which he heard during his banishment and shortly before his death, he also saw a confirmation of his own teaching. In this assessment Nestorius was certainly not wrong, insofar as the Chalcedonian creed did not simply sanction the Christology of his opponent, Cyril of Alexandria. It is another question whether it was Nestorius or Cyril who might have discovered his own thinking in the Chalcedonian creed. But this does not change the fact that Nestorius succeeded only very inadequately in his attempt to express the unity of divinity and humanity in the person of Jesus Christ. His protestations to the contrary, the suspicion is not unfounded that he understood the unity only in a moral or ethical, but not in a substantial or personal sense.

In contrast to the Christology of Nestorius, that of Cyril of Alexandria is developed strictly according to the Word-flesh scheme. In Nestorius' Christology Cyril saw a denial of the affirmation that the divine Word truly became man. This would imply the conclusion that there can be no true redemption. Thus, in Cyril very much as in Athanasius, a pronounced soteriological interest is present. In Cyril this is oriented largely toward the Eucharist. It is his concern that, if Nestorius were right, only the body of a man would be resting on the altar in the Eucharist. This would rob the Eucharist of its life-giving, deifying power.

Proceeding from this soteriological base Cyril emphasizes over and over again that the divine Logos himself became man in Jesus Christ. In doing so Cyril was not so much interested in the question of how the two natures of Christ are to be related to each other. Much like the theologians who stand at the beginning of the history of the church he thought mainly in terms of two successive modes of the Logos: first his pre-existence and then his incarnation. In both cases the same Logos is involved. Cyril gave terminological expression to this differentiation of the modes as well as to the unity of the Logos in both modes. He distinguishes between "the Logos outside the flesh" (*Logos asarkos*) and "the Logos enfleshed" (*Logos ensarkos*). Cyril liked to portray the unity of divinity and humanity by means of the formula, "One nature of the divine Logos, which [nature] became flesh," a formula he believed to be orthodox. As luck would have it, however, this was precisely the fomula Apollinaris had used as a catchword for his heretical Christology. In the meantime some of the disciples of Apollinaris had published the writings of their master under the name of Athanasius. Such forgery was frequently practiced in the early church in order to save the writings of a heretic from possible destruction.

According to Cyril it is not possible to distinguish or to separate the two natures of the incarnated Logos. The Logos truly became flesh. By "flesh" Cyril means the full human nature, which definitely includes a human soul. In spite of his unwitting use of the Apollinarian formula mentioned above, Cyril would have nothing to do with the Christology of Apollinaris. For Cyril the divinity and humanity of Christ are not one as a result of a "conjoining" of the two, but "hypostatically." This means that the human nature of Jesus Christ never had a separate existence, but, from the moment of conception, belonged entirely to the Logos, and was nothing more than the human nature of the Logos. The body of Jesus was the body of the Logos, not merely the body of a human being.

Thus the Christology of Cyril exhibits a wholeness which makes it superior to that of the Antiochenes. Cyril emphasized more strongly than they that salvation was not wrought as a result of God's gracious act toward a man, namely, Jesus, but as a result of God's coming into the world himself. From this standpoint it was possible for him to accept without limitation the expression "God-bearing" as a predicate of Mary. It seemed to be, in fact, the only appropriate designation. Still, Cyril's Christology, too, is not without its difficulties. A certain affinity with Apollinarianism cannot be denied, since Cyril occasionally spoke of a "mixture" of divinity and humanity. Nor did he succeed in emphasizing the true humanity of Jesus quite as much as the Antiochenes. In fact, he was not really able to answer more satisfactorily than they the actual questions with which the scholars of the Antiochene school had dealt. If Cyril had proceeded with the development of his Christology beyond the point to which he actually did go, he could hardly have escaped the consequences of Apollinarianism or those of the later Monophysitism, which acknowledged only a single nature in Jesus Christ. Perhaps the greatness of Cyril is found precisely in this, however, that in the presence of more profound and speculative questions he limited himself to a repetition of the biblical witness and of the faith of the church. The question of how divinity and humanity were united in Christ can presumably not be answered in a satisfactory way by any theologian. When Melanchthon was preparing himself for his death he wrote on a piece of paper, for his own comfort, the words, "You will come to the light, you will see God, you will know his Son, you will discern the wonderful secrets which in this life you could not understand, namely, why we were created thus and not otherwise, and wherein consists the unity of the two natures in Christ."[5]

From Ephesus to Chalcedon

After a series of keen literary exchanges between the rival patriarchs, Cyril of Alexandria and Nestorius of Constantinople, the Council of Ephesus met in 431. Contrary to law, Cyril and his followers opened a rump synod and had Nestorius condemned. The predicate "God-bearing" was asserted of Mary. The countersynod of Nestorius, formally convened according to the law, paid back in the same coin. At first the emperor supported both judgments. Cyril, however, by the use of questionable means succeeded in re-establishing himself in his patriarchal see. It was a still greater victory for him when he suc-

[5] Melanchthon, *CR* 9, 1098.

ceeded in getting his synod acknowledged as the Third Ecumenical Council, an action that flew in the face of the legal situation, which definitely favored the legality of the synod convened by Nestorius. For a discussion of the problem in hand the details of this rivalry are not very important, nor are the various attempts which were later undertaken to reconcile the two parties and which met with some success. Nor do we need to go into the reasons which led to a new flareup of the christological controversy toward the middle of the fifth century and thus to the decision of Chalcedon. Of importance, however, is both the content and the meaning of the decision of Chalcedon.

The Council which met in 451 at Chalcedon, a city on the eastern shore of the Bosphorus, opposite Constantinople, is known as the Fourth Ecumenical Council. In its dogmatic decisions it was decisively influenced by a doctrinal letter, or *Tome,* which Leo I of Rome wrote on June 13, 449. Over against the long and difficult discussions which had taken place in the Greek church the *Tome* summarized briefly and succinctly the Christology of the West. It included not only the Christology of Tertullian, which always remained basic for the West, but also its further development at the hands of Hilary (d. 367), Ambrose (d. 397), and especially Augustine (d. 430). Leo emphasized, first, that the person of the God-man, i.e., of him who became flesh, is identical with the person of the divine Logos; and, second, that in this one person of the incarnated Logos the divine and human natures are coordinate, but not intermingled. Leo put it this way: "Without detriment therefore to the properties of either nature and substance which then came together in one person, majesty took on humility."[6] The unity of the two natures, said Leo, is essential because of the bearing it has upon redemption. He felt that the one mediator between God and man, Jesus Christ, had to be able, in one sense, to die and, in another sense, not to die. By the same token, he thought, it is possible to say that the Logos dies, that is to say, that he dies according to his human nature, but not according to his divine nature. Leo emphasized further that the two natures of Christ have separate modes of operation, although at the same time one always acts in unison with the other. Finally, he maintains the so-called doctrine of *communicatio idiomatum.* This doctrine,

[6] Leo I, Letter 28 (= *Tome*), 3. *NPNF*[2] 12, 40.

which in its rudiments had been set forth by earlier theologians but was expressed with telling clarity by Leo, implies that because of the unity of the person there is an exchange of properties or attributes (*idiomatum*). It is therefore proper to say that the Son of God was crucified and buried, or that the Son of man came down from heaven.

The clarity with which Leo's letter treated important and basic issues, as well as its breadth of treatment of individual issues, made it especially suited to prepare the way for the decision of Chalcedon. At first the majority at the council was even willing to restrict itself to the confirmation of the Nicene faith and to the recognition of the dogmatic letters of Cyril, together with the pope's *Tome.* The fact that a new creed was finally drawn up must be attributed to the emissaries of the emperor, who insisted upon the formulation of a new creed to which the bishops could be bound. Thus while the council executed its original plans, it also acceded to the wish of the emperor.

Under these circumstances the following creed was constructed:

> In agreement, therefore, with the holy fathers, we all unanimously teach that we should confess that our Lord Jesus Christ is one and the same Son, the same perfect in Godhead and the same perfect in manhood, truly God and truly man, the same of a rational soul and body, consubstantial with the Father in Godhead, and the same consubstantial with us in manhood, like us in all things except sin; begotten from the Father before the ages as regards His Godhead, and in the last days, the same, because of us and because of our salvation begotten from the Virgin Mary, the *Theotokos,* as regards His manhood; one and the same Christ, Son, Lord, only-begotten, made known in two natures without confusion, without change, without division, without separation, the difference of the natures being by no means removed because of the union, but the property of each nature perserved and coalescing in one *prosopon* and one *hupostasis*—not parted or divided into two *prosopa,* but one and the same Son, only-begotten, divine Word, the Lord Jesus Christ, as the prophets of old and Jesus Christ Himself have taught us about Him and the creed of our fathers has handed down.[7]

In order to ascertain the exact meaning of the Chalcedonian creed it is necessary to look at the discussions which preceded

[7] English version taken from J. N. D. Kelly, *Early Christian Doctrines* (London: A. and C. Black, and New York: Harper, 1958), pp. 339-40. Translation used with permission of the publishers.

its final formulation. Some bishops expressed concern that the *Tome* of Leo differed but slightly from the teaching of Nestorius. For that reason a first draft of the creed spoke of "one Christ from two natures" (*ek duo phuseōn*) rather than of "one Christ in two natures" (*en duo phusesin*). The unity of the person of Christ was thus more strongly set forth, and the concern of the Alexandrian Christology was safeguarded. Later the formula "one Christ from two natures" became the slogan of the Monophysites. The fact that the council finally did speak of one Christ "in two natures" indicates its adoption of the concerns of the Antiochene Christology and its desire to preclude any interpretation of the Chalcedonian creed that savored of Apollinarianism. On the other hand, in confirming the predicate "God-bearing" with reference to Mary, and in emphasizing the unity of the person of Christ, the basic features of Alexandrian Christology were also adopted. For this reason it is not easy to say whether the Chalcedonian creed is closer to Antiochene or Alexandrian Christology. It actually adopted the decisive elements of both christological conceptions, while it carefully avoided their one-sided features. The creed contains neither the Cyrillic insistence upon "hypostatic unity" nor the Antiochene opinion that the Logos dwelt in the man Jesus. Instead emphasis is laid both upon the unity of the person and the individuality of the natures. This is accomplished by insisting that Christ is to be acknowledged in two natures "inconfusedly, unchangeably, indivisibly, inseparably"; i.e., the unity is not to be understood in the sense of an intermingling of the two natures.

In view of the host of controverted questions, the Council of Chalcedon made a most sane decision, which, morever, it expressed in masterful language. In the Chalcedonian creed the West gave its answer to the East. On the same basis of their tradition the Greek theologians would hardly have been in a position to take such a balanced point of view. The traditional western Christology, on the other hand, acquired its sharp contours as a result of this confrontation with the problems of the East. Finally, it must be said that the Chalcedonian creed took up the questions which were being debated by Antiochenes and Alexandrians and attempted to answer them, but in doing so it rightly elected to take a position midway between neutrality, on the one hand, and, on the other, a speculative attempt to plumb the depth of the mystery which meets us in the person of Jesus Christ. No one who examines the Chalcedonian creed against the background of the christological controversies which preceded it can charge it with attempting to define the person of Jesus Christ or to force the inexpressible into conceptual forms. The opposite is the case. In the face of the endless discussions concerning the relationship of divinity and humanity in Jesus Christ the Chalcedonian creed witnesses to the faith of Christianity. It does this in a way that is simple and yet unsurpassably clear and striking by asserting that Jesus is one person and that he is at the same time God and man. In doing so it does not eliminate the speculative questions. What it does is to give them a direction in which alone every attempt to speak correctly about the divinity and humanity of Jesus Christ must proceed. One cannot say, therefore, that with the defining of this dogma Greek speculation emerged victorious over the Christian faith. On the contrary, it is precisely this dogma which erected a dam against speculation or, at least, against an exaggerated form of it.

The Sequel

The Chalcedonian creed did not put an end to christological debate. It was not able to bring about the union of the rival groups; indeed, it revived the conflict. Many disciples of the Alexandrian Christology felt that the Chalcedonian creed did not take sufficient account of their concern. They thought that the unity of the natures in the person of Christ should have been more strongly emphasized. This rejection of Chalcedon by the extreme adherents of the Alexandrian party resulted in a controversy which was to last for centuries. The discussion, in fact, came to an end only when Islam wrenched away from the Byzantine Empire those sections, notably Egypt and Syria, in which the conflict was carried on. In the areas under its domination Islam condemned the church to a wretched and marginal existence, which robbed it of the capacity for great intellectual achievements. Only a few segments of the lengthy conflicts over the Chalcedonian creed can be described here.

First, it should be pointed out briefly that even now the conflict between the various opponents of the Chalcedonian creed and its defenders was not merely based upon the matter in hand, namely, the variations in Christology, but that other motives played a considerable role. It was now no more a matter of rivalry, of course, between the patriarchs of Constantinople and Alexandria. That was a thing of the past. The reason was that the successor of Cyril of Alexandria, namely, Dioscurus (deposed 451, d. 454), had carried the christological position of Alexandria to such extremes, and had engaged in such arbitrary power politics, that he had come to grief in Chalcedon itself. If the christological controversy of the fifth century is viewed from a purely political point of view it is apparent that victory belonged neither to the Patriarch of Constantinople nor to the Patriarch of Alexandria but to the eastern emperors, who knew how to subject the church to their authority. As a result, however, the national passions of Egypt and Syria were enflamed. Both defended themselves against a creed which had been forced upon them by the emperor, and tried to free themselves from Byzantine overlordship.

Because of this twofold opposition, christological as well as national, pitched battles ensued. Frequently opponents of the Chalcedonian creed succeeded in placing bishops in patriarchal sees. In the fifth century Monophysites were elevated to the position of patriarch both in Egypt and in Syria. This party called itself "Monophysite" after the formula of Cyril which spoke of the "one nature of the divine Logos, which became flesh." In the fifth century several emperors tried to curry the favor of the Monophysites. In doing so they more or less publicly flouted the Chalcedonian creed. The radical Monophysites, however, were not willing to be pacified by a formula of compromise. In addition, the Roman pope condemned these attempts. The result was the first open schism between East and West (484-519).

Like the Monophysites the Nestorians, too, separated themselves from the imperial church. The church in Persia, whose development had long been separate from that of the imperial church, accepted Nestorianism, so that the latter now stretched from Syria to India. During the following centuries the Nestorians developed an exceptionally active missionary enterprise, which brought Christianity to India as well as China. To the unity of the empire and the church the Nestorian split was no less of a blow than was the resistance of the Monophysites.

In the sixth century Justinian I (527-565) continued efforts at union. The Fifth Ecumenical Council, which met at Constantinople in 553, gave renewed attention to the christological question. Here, too, the attempt was made to move a considerable distance toward accommodating the Monophysites, although not quite as far as during the abortive endeavors of the late fifth century. At Chalcedon the West had dictated its Christology to the East; the East now answered by giving this Christology its own interpretation. In the records of the Fifth Ecumenical Council much is said about the unity of the two natures. While the Cyrillic expression "hypostatic unity" had not been adopted at Chalcedon, it is precisely this term which was now introduced as the proper interpretation of Chalcedon. The Christology of Theodore of Mopsuestia and of Nestorius is contradicted and condemned in great detail, since it allegedly leads to the maintaining of two persons. The expression "two hypostases," which are present in Christ, is also rejected, and it is emphatically asserted that this expression constitutes a distortion of the Chalcedonian creed. Of course, the decision of the Fifth Council is not opposed to the actual wording of the Chalcedonian creed. Still, the tension between the decisions of the two councils cannot be ignored. For that reason one hears of a "Neo-Chalcedonianism," which led to a reinterpretation of the Chalcedonian creed, and which found expression in the decision of the Fifth Ecumenical Council. It is true that in this interpretation of the Chalcedonian creed Justinian did not reach the political aims which he was pursuing. The Monophysites also rejected the Fifth Ecumenical Council, and the movement toward the establishment of two great national churches, the Monophysite church and the Nestorian church, continued afterward as before.

Later christological conflicts became even more problematical. In the seventh century Emperor Heraclius attempted once more to win the Monophysites for the imperial church. In the year 633 he achieved union with them on the basis of a formula which stated that the Christ who consists in two natures performs all things "by one theandric energy." This formula resulted in new and bitter controversies. The concept of "one energy" aroused considerable opposition, especially in the West. For a time there was agreement that the phrase "one will" should be substituted for "one theandric energy." This formula was even approved by Pope Honorius I. The expression, however, could not satisfy the adherents of the Chalcedonian creed. Keen opposition arose in East and West against this Monotheletism (doctrine of one will). The theological leadership of this opposition was provided by Maximus the Confessor, whose tongue was cut out and whose right hand was severed as a punishment for his resistance to the compromise formula favored by the emperor. In the end, however, the opposition to Monotheletism gained the victory. The Sixth Ecumenical Council, which met at Constantinople in 680-681, sanctioned Dyotheletism (doctrine of two wills). This council decided that in reference to the question whether Jesus Christ had one or two wills the assumption that he had two was made mandatory by the Chalcedonian creed. Analogous to the Chalcedonian creed, however, the assertion is made here that the "two natural wills" and the "two natural energies" in Christ are to be acknowledged "inconfusedly, unchangeably, indivisibly, inseparably." Any opposition in the incarnated Logos between the divine and human wills is unthinkable. The reason given is that the human will of Jesus is subject to his divine will without resistance.

It is difficult to be happy about this decision, though formally no objections can be raised against it. Within the lines of the Chalcedonian development the only possible conclusion was the one which was reached by the Sixth Ecumenical Council. Especially the assertions in Leo's *Tome*, to which Constantinople had appealed, did not permit any other conclusion. If, therefore, one affirms the Chalcedonian creed, one must also affirm inwardly the struggle of Maximus the Confessor, as well as the decision of this council. This is especially the case since in the Aristotelian philosophy of the day activity and will were thinkable only as a function of concrete substance. From the point of view of the two-nature doctrine, therefore, no other decision but the one which asserted two wills in Jesus was possible.

Still, it is difficult to avoid the impression that the discussion between Monotheletism and Dyotheletism was a mistake from the very beginning. Though the confession of the full divinity and the full humanity of Jesus is basic to the Christian faith, it is not possible to set off against each other the activity of his divine and his human nature. By comparison, the concern of the Fifth Ecumenical Council, namely, to put emphasis upon the unity of the person of Jesus Christ, was far better justified. Finally, it must be said that this latest decision simply continued the zigzag course upon which Christology had embarked after Chalcedon.

In making such criticisms, however, it should not be forgotten that this problem was not arbitrarily selected at the time, but that the Monothelite controversy was forcibly brought about within the context of the emperor's efforts at unity. No age can select the questions and problems to which it would address itself. To a large extent these are posed for it by the course of history and of the history of thought. The men who defended Dyotheletism would rather hold to the whole truth as they believed it than make politically motivated compromises.

The lengthy christological discussions had a sequel in the iconoclastic controversy, which rocked the Greek church in the eighth and the ninth centuries. It is true that the causes of this controversy are many. Nor did the two sides only emphasize christological points of view. Yet, in the ebb and flow of the controversy christological problems were constantly involved. It is to be noted, for instance, that a number of the opponents of images argued strongly from the point of view of the unity of the God-man. Because of this unity, they would maintain, an isolated representation of the human nature of Christ is impossible, while a representation of his divine nature comes under the prohibition against images which is found in Scripture. The iconoclastic council of 754 made its decision along these lines and in so doing underscored christological motives. The proponents of images, on the other hand, appealed to the affirmation that the divine Logos did, in fact, become man. Besides these christological elements, however, there were other ideas which played a role no less important. Among these was especially the philosophical idea of archetype and antitype. Mention should also be made of the folk piety which clung to the veneration of images, the latter having arisen during the later phases of early Christianity.

Thus the christological controversy lasted much longer than the trinitarian controversy, and did not find the clear-cut conclusion of the latter. Yet, if in the history of dogma the aim is not merely that of defining certain dogmas, but also that of their acceptance, the difference between the two is not very great. In that case only the form in which the church lived with the dogma it had defined is different. Augustine, for instance, succeeded in refining the trinitarian dogma and in protecting it against misunderstandings without provoking a conflict. In the case of the christological dogma the same process of refinement and demarcation was much less placid and far more uneven. Above all, however, the basic decisions in the trinitarian controversy and the christological definitions of Chalcedon are alike in this, that in neither case was any attempt made to unravel the mystery of God. What was attempted was the reformulation and confession of the inherited faith of Christianity *vis à vis* the questions which had been raised.

4

The Doctrine of Sin and Grace

Faith and Works

In the history of Christian doctrine a new chapter begins with the development of the doctrine of sin and grace. The characteristic feature of this new chapter is not found merely in the fact that to the authoritative confessions of the church already formulated a new one is now added. Its characteristic is to be found rather in this, that, in contradistinction to the older dogmas, a new underlying theme emerges. For the first time in the history of the church it is not an article about God, or the Trinity, or the two-nature doctrine which constitutes the subject of discussion. It is a problem which in a special way has as its content the concept of man as well as the doctrine of redemption. The attempt is now to clarify dogmatically a certain affirmation of faith which is distinct from the doctrine of God. In doing so the Christian faith exhibits its full peculiarity as well as its difference from other religions, notably Judaism. In general, the latter knows no dogmas or, at least, only one, namely, that the Lord alone is God and that beside him there are no other gods. Christianity and Judaism are similar in this, that faith in God, though differently understood, is the basic dogma, the basic confession. The Christian faith departs markedly from Judaism, however, in its dogmatic assertion of certain conceptions of sin and grace. It is true, of course, that the Christian doctrine of original sin is not only based upon the New Testament, but also upon certain affirmations of the Old Testament, notably Genesis, chap. 3. Yet the account of man's fall is quite isolated in the Old Testament. Furthermore, Judaism never accorded a doctrine of original sin dogmatic status, though in many respects it arrived at conceptions similar to those of the Christian church. The fact is that the Christian doctrine of sin, as well as the Christian doctrine of grace, were developed in their decisive aspects from the perspective of Christology. Though the Old Testament says a great deal about sin, as well as about grace, both of these were revealed in their deepest sense only through Jesus Christ.

To the modern observer the road from the New Testament to trinitarian and christological dogma often seems shorter than the road to the dogma of sin and grace. It is easier to see that Jesus knew himself to have been sent of God in a special way, that God, as it were, was actually present in him, than it is to understand the rightness and necessity of the doctrine of original sin. Opponents of the doctrine of the Trinity have of course never been lacking. Yet criticism of the dogma of original sin is obviously even more widespread. Even renowned theologians have insisted that the doctrine of original sin is alien to the gospel of Jesus Christ, having originated later with St. Paul. Basically the same is true, they said, of the doctrine of grace. While they realized that Jesus often promised salvation to people who were laden with guilt, they pointed out that the phrase "by grace alone" is not found in the Gospels. Quite frequently Jesus simply appealed to the good in man.

Of course, if we take into consideration the totally different settings of the proclamation of Jesus, on the one hand, and of the theology of St. Paul, on the other, then most of the differences which a superficial study of the two alleges to find disappear. Anyone who makes an earnest attempt to live according to the Sermon on the Mount will, in the end, find it impossible to say about himself and his sinfulness anything other than what St. Paul wrote in Romans, chap. 7. A similar statement could be made about the concept of sin and grace. While it may be missing from the proclamation of Jesus, the communion which Jesus had with sinners is nothing other than that which St. Paul formulated doctrinally in his affirmations about grace. Furthermore, St. Paul does not occupy an isolated position among the authors of the New Testament. Even though the mode of expression in the Gospel of John, or in the catholic epistles, is at many points quite different from that of St. Paul, there is still far-reaching agreement among them with regard to their basic concept of the redemption wrought by Jesus Christ. In spite of various differences in matters of detail, it has been the thoroughgoing conviction of all the fathers of the church that Jesus Christ offered men deliverance and salvation. In fact, this has been the general conviction of the church in all ages. Even Pelagius was capable of exalted language when it came to describing the redemption offered by Jesus Christ.

If, then, most of the fathers of the church emphasize the necessity of redemption and grace, how did it come to a discussion of these questions in the first place? The answer is that here the issue was (and still is) whether the doctrine of grace is simply one article of faith among others, or whether through this doctrine the totality, the very heart of the Christian faith, is asserted once again. It was not a debate over whether or not Jesus Christ redeems us that divided Augustine and Pelagius. The question was whether Christ is our redeemer exclusively, or whether our redemption is dependent also upon other persons or things. It is precisely the debate over the doctrine of sin and grace which demonstrates that during no period of the history of dogma was it the concern of the Christian community simply to add another declaration of faith to the existing treasure of the faith. It was always the totality of the Christian faith that was at stake.

In spite of their far-reaching agreement in essentials, considerable differences exist in the theology of the fathers with respect to the actual significance of grace. It was possible for them to have faith in the redemption of Jesus Christ and, at the same time, to pay homage to a confirmed moralism which really amounted to nothing more than a pure righteousness of works. The germs of such moralism are found in the New Testament itself. The Letter of James, for instance, has a good many things to say about faith; yet, not much is said about what this faith means. Instead, there is repeated mention of the necessity of works. Over against a self-satisfied faith, it was indeed necessary to emphasize works. Even St. Paul did that. Yet, he did it differently from the author of the Letter of James. This movement toward a stronger emphasis upon works and toward a Christian moralism which differed but imperceptibly from the philosophy of that day gained even greater momentum in the third and fourth centuries. The early fathers of the church placed more emphasis on developing the doctrine of God, of Jesus Christ, and of the Holy Spirit in a way that would accord with the New Testament than they did upon comprehending the New Testament's profound understanding of the redemption wrought by Jesus Christ.

There are any number of good reasons for this development of Christian moralism; they do not excuse this development, but they do make it understandable. During the second century the church was involved in a decisive struggle with Gnosticism; even the first decades of the third century are overshadowed by this conflict. Over against Gnosticism the unity of God the Creator and God the Redeemer had to be emphasized. The theologians of the time did this circumspectly and thoroughly, so that ever since that day the danger that the doctrines of creation and redemption would be separated has hardly ever become as acute as it was then. It is understandable, however, that as a result other problems were given less attention. Furthermore, in opposition to Gnosticism the necessity of works had to be set forth in no uncertain terms. Most Gnostics were of the opinion that the redemption offered by Christ affects only a part of man, his divine spirit-substance, which is encased in nonspiritual matter. Man, they taught, is redeemed if he comes to know his true self and thus initiates the return of his divine spark to God the Redeemer. The emphasis here was upon "knowledge." With regard to everyday life many Gnostics might permit complete freedom, while others might exhort to ascetic practice or might even recommend a weird mixture of license and self-denial. Against such a notion, man's responsibility had to be stressed. The unremitting and pronounced conflict with pagan folkways and customs had similar results. Frequently the treatise of one of the fathers of the church is, at least to a considerable extent, nothing other than an ethical admonition, which certainly was very necessary, but in which it is often difficult to find anything specifically Christian.

For these reasons it is understandable that the fathers succeeded in clarifying the doctrine of God before they could do the same for the concept of sin and grace. Among the apostolic fathers, as well as among the apologists, there is hardly an inkling of the later doctrine of original sin. Nor should the few remarks which point in this direction be given any significance. There are, to be sure, the classical passages of the New Testament regarding redemption and grace. Yet the generally prevailing conviction among the early fathers is that man is equipped with a free will, and that no sin can effectively keep him from deciding for the good and from avoiding the bad. For a man like Justin Martyr sin consists essentially in a misguided faith and in ignorance of the good.[1] It is true that Justin did ask how this ignorance originated. But he solves the problem by blaming the demons who through their machinations forced mankind into subjection.

Very similar is the case of Tertullian, the great North African theologian who exerted such a positive influence upon the development of the doctrine of the Trinity and of Christology. It is true that in Tertullian one finds stronger traces of a doctrine of original sin than in any other theologian of his day. According to him evil finds its seat in the soul and becomes almost a constituent of man's nature. For that reason he felt that even little children must be regarded as unclean. In spite of these views, however, Tertullian, no less than Justin and others, emphasized the freedom of man's will. There is, he felt, something good which is intrinsic to the soul, and which remains unspoiled by the vitiated nature of man. Tertullian is even able to say that the soul is Christian by nature,[2] meaning by this that by nature the soul has at least a darkened understanding of the Christian God. As regards redemption, Tertullian obviously knew the New Testament well and cites it often. Repeatedly, however, formulations flow from his pen to the effect that Christ is basically a new lawgiver. In a detailed discussion of the rule of faith, he points to its content in these words, among others: "thenceforth He preached the new law and the new promise of the kingdom of heaven. . . ."[3]

Where we find detailed treatments of original sin in the theology of the second and third centuries, these have frequently

[1] Justin Martyr, *The Second Apology*, chap. 14. *ANF* 1, 193.

[2] Tertullian, *Apology*, chap. 17. *ANF* 3, 32.

[3] Tertullian, *The Prescription Against Heretics*, chap. 13. *ANF* 3, 249.

been developed under the influence of Gnosticism and its negative view of matter and of the body. This is especially true of Origen. His opinion that the pre-existent souls who have fallen away from God are punished by imprisonment in created matter has already been mentioned. It is precisely the extreme one-sidedness with which Gnosticism developed a certain concept of original sin that made it difficult for the church to distinguish between the true and the false. For the same reason the church found it equally difficult to interpret the declarations of the New Testament in a way which would restrict the error of Gnosticism but which, at the same time, would do justice to the radical nature of the New Testament concept of sin. Little wonder, then, that the church searched gropingly for a season, now giving preference to the concept of free will, and then again to the condemnation of matter. In the Cappadocian theologians of the fourth century, especially in Gregory of Nyssa, it is noticeable how an attempt was indeed made to avoid the Origenistic concept of evil, but how easy it was to fall prey to it, almost unwillingly.[4]

It was not by accident that Pelagius, when he offered his teachings to the public, was accorded wide acclaim both in the West and in the East. In the East it was especially the adherents of Antiochene Christology who welcomed his theses, finally dragging Pelagius with them to their doom. Theodore of Mopsuestia, for instance, roundly denied the assertion of original sin. In fact, he even wrote a tract against this doctrine. He rejected the idea that death became man's lot only after it had been decreed by God as a punishment for Adam's sin. Man, he insisted, is mortal by nature, even as the human will is, by nature, capable of sinning. What Christ has offered is not freedom from original sin, but the possibility of attaining immortality, and with it, of course, sinlessness.

Besides the reasons already mentioned, there was another which impeded and delayed the development of the doctrine of sin and grace. This was the ascetic element, which is apparent in the church from the second century onward, but especially during the third century, and which became progressively stronger. True asceticism was alien both to Jesus and to the

[4] See E. Ivánka, *Hellenisches und Christliches im frühbyzantinischen Geistesleben* (Vienna: Herder, 1948), pp. 62-65.

whole New Testament. It must be granted that Jesus could, upon occasion, demand absolute self-denial "for the sake of the kingdom of God." Yet such self-denial possessed no value in itself, but simply served to free man from his ties to the world. Nevertheless, as the hope of Christ's immediate coming receded, and the influence of the environment made itself felt in the church, a more pronounced ascetic element is already found among the apostolic fathers. It is this element which finally culminated in the development of monasticism. With asceticism an ethic of graded values penetrated the Christian church: the ascetic carries out the instructions of the Lord in a manner more perfect than the Christian who lives in the world. The latter is, in fact, basically still "worldly." For his greater achievements the ascetic also receives from God a greater reward. From the second century on this was the unanimous opinion of almost all the fathers of the church who wrote on asceticism (though there were exceptions). The spread of the ascetic ideal was bound to revitalize faith in the unimpaired ability of man to lead a pure and sinless life before God. As a matter of fact, the fathers of the church, and especially the monastic theologians, repeatedly liken the life of ascetics here on earth to that of angels. Only occasionally did opposition to this kind of an exaggerated valuation of the ascetic ideal dare to make itself felt. Usually, however, such opposition was quickly crushed.

Pelagius

Pelagius was born in Britain, the son of Christian parents, about the middle of the fourth century. Whether his native land was Ireland or England is a matter of controversy. Having received a higher education in the country of his birth, he studied law in Rome beginning *circa* 380. According to the custom of the day he was not baptized as a child. While in Rome, however, he soon permitted himself to be baptized, and accepted with full seriousness the responsibilities of the Christian life. He did not become a monk, as is often erroneously asserted. He remained a layman. He wanted to be nothing else but a Christian, and to live according to the law which is binding upon all Christians. The way he understood this law becomes evident in the fact that, to the sorrow of his parents, he gave up his worldly career and began to live a life of asceticism and of constant self-scrutiny. His opinions appear to have made a considerable impression upon educated pagans, and seem to have found many adherents among the very lax segments of the church as well. His influence reached far beyond the borders of the city of Rome. In Rome itself Pelagius established a friendship with a highly placed lawyer, Coelestius, which later was to have unfortunate results for him. Through the spoken and the written word Pelagius tried to win followers for his conception of the seriousness of following Christ. Outstanding among the many works of Pelagius is a commentary on all the letters of St. Paul, and a letter to a prominent, ascetic young woman named Demetrias, to whom he dedicated an outline of his teachings. As long as Pelagius remained in Rome he could work without impediment. The dogmatic conflicts which ended with his condemnation ensued only when, as a result of Alaric's conquest of that city in the year 410, he was forced to leave Rome.

If the work and teaching of Pelagius are to be rightly understood, it must be kept in mind that he meant to be anything but a heretic. It is true that both Arius and Apollinaris had the same wish. Yet, it would seem that Pelagius had greater justification in rejecting any suspicion of heresy attaching to his teaching than the heretics associated with earlier dogmatic conflicts. Arius, after all, had denied basic aspects of the Christian tradition. And Apollinaris had indeed recognized the Nicene confession fully and completely, but he had expressed very one-sided views of the actual incarnation of Christ. With Pelagius it was different. He accepted without reservation the dogmatic decisions of the great councils. It was his honest desire to be orthodox. He could assert this wish with even greater justification because his interests, as he himself said, were not oriented toward dogmatic problems as such, but toward the daily life of the Christian.

The center of his theology is the idea of the omnipresence and righteousness of God. This is a concept which he gained less from Holy Scripture than from philosophy or, to put it more broadly, from human reason. To be sure, Pelagius regards the righteousness of God as a demanding and judging righteousness. But at the very beginning of his theology stands the almost rationalistic proposition that God cannot possibly demand of man that which the latter cannot give. God is the righteous judge of all men. No unrighteous man can escape from him. In principle, therefore, man is in a position to live according to God's laws. If this were not true there could be no punishment of the unrighteous; hence God's demands upon men would not be just.

Pelagius was concerned about only one thing: to make all Christians of his day aware of God's demand for a holy life, and to make each individual conscious that he is held responsible should he break the divine law. Everyone, he held, can truly turn to God. Even a sinless life is not outside the realm of possibilities, though there has probably hardly ever been a man who really lived without sin. In preaching to the wealthy, Pelagius demanded that they renounce their property. While he did not absolutely reject material wealth, he warned most emphatically against its dangers. To unmarried and married people alike he hammered away at the obligation to keep the body holy and to live a pure life. Not that he rejected matrimony, but he sharply condemned all lack of discipline. Without compromise he demanded of all Christians that they keep the commandment not to take oaths. Generally speaking, then, Pelagius preached to a worldly church an ethic like that of the Sermon on the Mount. The help necessary to live according to this ethic was to be gained through meditation upon scriptural themes and through prayer.

Pelagius took up dogmatic problems only in order to be able to give the needed emphasis to his practical demands for reform. In itself the reform which he desired had nothing to do with these problems. It was impossible for him, however, to avoid taking a position with regard to the doctrine of original sin, a doctrine which in one form or another was already present in the church. Pelagius rejected the idea that there is such a thing as original sin inherited by all men from Adam by way of sexual reproduction. According to Pelagius it is impossible for God to hold a person accountable for the sins of another when He is willing to forgive the sins which a person has himself committed. Pelagius believed that the concept of original sin supports Manichaean dualism, which regards the body, as well as all matter, as the principle which is opposed to God and which holds the soul a prisoner. It is true that Pelagius, too, attributes to Adam an evil influence upon subsequent generations. He feels, however, that this is not a matter of inherited sin but merely the result of the poor example given by Adam and imitated by most people. In spite of Adam's fall man still has the very real possibility of living a sinless life. Anyone who denies this negates the freedom of the will, as well as man's responsibility for his actions.

How, then, can sin be avoided? Only by instructing men very expressly concerning the requirements of the divine law. Since Adam's fall the knowledge of the law has been forgotten. Even Moses' giving of the law did not basically change this situation. Now, however, Christ has instructed man anew concerning the true law of God. The Sermon on the Mount, especially, leaves no doubt as to what God demands of us.

In this connection Pelagius even used exalted language in speaking of divine grace. At times his theology has been represented as displaying a total ignorance of grace. This, however, is not the case. To be sure, he understands grace quite differently from Augustine. For Pelagius grace means, on the one hand, that man is endowed with reason and, on the other, that he has been given the law. It is grace that man is able by nature to fulfill God's law. In Pelagius, therefore, grace is associated with creation, while in Augustine it is associated with redemption. Beyond this, Pelagius understands grace to be something more, namely, the forgiveness of sin. Such forgiveness did not exist during the period between Adam and Christ. Through and in Christ, however, it is now a fact. To believers Christ gives the gift of the forgiveness of sins. He also instructs them that they must avoid the errors of the flesh and must grow in wisdom. At this point Pelagius develops his characteristic fervor. "A Christian," he says, "is he who is not merely such in name but in works, who in all things imitates and follows Christ."[5]

In the teachings of Pelagius there is hardly an opinion for which some confirmation could not be found among the earlier fathers of the church. Tertullian, to be sure, had an embryonic doctrine of original sin. He did not develop it, however, with reference to the daily life of the Christian. Hence it did not really possess any significance in the realm of theological endeavor. Then, too, Tertullian's doctrine of original sin did not

[5] Pelagius, *Liber de vita christiana*, chap. 6. *MPL* 40, col. 1037.

find any subsequent advocates. The position generally held at the time was that baptism blots out previous sin, and that the Christian is obligated not to incur new sins. Pelagius was in a position to learn much from Tertullian, or from Cyprian and Lactantius, as well as from the so-called Ambrosiaster who, during the second half of the fourth century, was an anonymous commentator on the letters of St. Paul.

It must be granted that the form in which Pelagius communicated his insights was somewhat new and without precedent, as was also the content. For one thing, Pelagius accepted rationality as a criterion of doctrinal truth; and, second, he constructed a kind of system from notions which at an earlier day had been only casually held. Even though Pelagius meant to be anything but a systematic theologian, his discussions moved in the direction of a unified system of dogma.

This sets Pelagius apart from the various ascetic movements of his day. It is not difficult to find parallels for his thoughts in Jerome or in later monastic theologians such as Cassian. In spite of their Pelagian tendencies, however, these men were not really Pelagians. They developed their thoughts solely for a small circle of ascetics. Jerome, too, despite the imbalance which is found in his ideas, generally tried to observe the same limits. The basic attempt of Pelagius, on the other hand, was to elevate the difficult ascetic demands which were then permeating monasticism to the position of a fundamental principle for all Christians. Despite the strong ascetic tendencies which were noticeable everywhere at the time, the church recognized this as a danger. Accordingly it tried to prevent the distortion of the gospel in the direction of a program of ethical reform which was based on the principle of free will. It is Augustine who must be given almost sole credit for this achievement.

Augustine

Augustine was more than fifty years old when, after 410, the fierce controversy erupted over the doctrine of sin and grace. Born in the year 354, he strayed in various directions until at last, in 386, he embraced the Christian faith and was baptized the following year. Thereupon this former professor of rhetoric, who was steeped in the intellectual heritage of antiquity as were few others of his day, lived with some of his friends in a monastic community he had founded. Upon the insistence of the congregation at Hippo in North Africa, which is today the town of Bone, he exchanged the cowl of the monk for the robe of the priest in 391. From 395 on he served as bishop in this insignificant little sea port. As is often the case, the assumption of ecclesiastical office, especially that of a bishop, proved to be of considerable importance for Augustine's theological development. After the middle of the last decade of the fourth century a change can be observed in him. Although it had many facets, the basic characteristic of this change was that in his thinking the empirical church with its tasks took the place of the somewhat exuberant humanism to which he had been given in the early days after his conversion. An intensive study of the Scriptures, which Augustine undertook because of his ecclesiastical duties, also helped him to develop his concept of sin and grace.

As is to be expected, when Augustine became a Christian he began to know and accept the concepts of sin and grace which were current in the West at the time. Thus, in his early tract *On Free Will* Augustine, very much like Ambrose, his spiritual father, said that man's will is basically free and that sin is a motion of the will. Otherwise, it would not be possible to understand God's punishment of sin. One can speak of a compulsion to sin, he said, only in the sense that God knows a man's sins before they are committed. As Augustine points out in this early tract, however, this does not suspend the freedom of the will. Yet Augustine was not given to Pelagianism at the time. He did not merely recognize a bad example in Adam's deed, as did Pelagius. To the contrary, even at this time he had a well-developed concept of original sin, though he still held to the freedom of the will.

As a result of a renewed study of Paul's Epistle to the Romans, which Augustine undertook after he had become bishop, he was led to a more profound understanding of the doctrine of sin and grace. The fruit of this study is found in the tract *To Simplician–On Various Questions* (396). Augustine here takes up in detail the problem of the election of Jacob (Rom. 9:10 ff.). He now has a great deal to say about the comprehensive character of sin. Not only has sin brought mortality upon all men but, in effect, a desire for new sin. No one can, by his own resources, escape from the devilish round of sin and the desire for sin. Salvation from this sinful state is possible only through grace, a grace which, however, is grounded wholly in the election of God. This gracious election precedes every merit on the part of man. In saying this Augustine did not deny the freedom of the will altogether. To be sure, man's will cannot of itself find salvation. Divine election is decisive. Still, the will must will, for without this volitional act the offer of grace would be futile. Even in this tract, however, Augustine already says, "Clearly it is vain for us to will unless God have mercy. But I do not know how it could be said that it is vain for God to have mercy unless we willingly consent."[6] Here are the first traces of the idea of the irresistibility of the operation of divine grace in the elect which Augustine develops later.

Thus Augustine had developed the basic outline of his doctrine of sin and grace even before the beginning of the Pelagian controversy. He did not arrive, therefore, at his characteristic—and in the light of tradition somewhat new—understanding of this doctrine through his opposition to Pelagius, but as a result of reading Scripture. During his days in the episcopacy Augustine developed this concept in a way which was bound to lead to controversy with Pelagius.

To Augustine the nature of sin is a dual one—pride, on the one hand, and concupiscence, on the other. In his original state man himself could have avoided sin. However, this would necessitate not simply a constantly virtuous will on the part of man but the aid of divine grace as well. Adam, therefore, could have remained sinless only if he had been willing at all times to accept the aid of the divine grace which was promised him. Because of his pride Adam wanted to be more than such a situation allowed. He not only wanted to cling to God, he also wanted to follow the desires of his own heart. The result was the fall, through which Adam forfeited the aid of divine grace. That which led him to the fall, however, was not a casual act of disobedience which, as Pelagius thought, could be nullified by a new act of obedience. Through his pride, so Augustine felt, man destroyed the natural and proper constitution of his will. It was a sin which, in the last analysis, carried with it its own punishment. At this point a profound psychological

[6] Augustine, *To Simplician—On Various Questions,* Bk. I, question 2, chap. 12. *LCC* 6, 394.

insight of Augustine's becomes apparent. He could see that all disorder of the human will is at the same time both conscious deed and divine punishment.

Since Adam was not merely a single individual but also the ancestor of mankind, this implies that his entire posterity must also remain in this same sinful condition. Augustine can even say that human nature has been corrupted by sin. Such assertions must have appeared to the Pelagians as being only a thinly veiled Manichaeism. Yet Augustine usually distinguishes between nature and guilt. Nature as such he does not regard as corrupt. How then could Adam's deed result in corruption? Augustine thinks that it must be regarded as a special punishment of God, who imputes to the entire human race—which was represented in Adam—the punishment which, in the first instance, was meant for Adam alone. Romans 5:12 Augustine regards as the exegetical foundation for this position. It asserts that "sin came into the world through one man and death through sin, and so death spread to all men because all men sinned." In the early Latin version of the Bible the word here rendered "because" was translated "in whom" (namely, Adam). Augustine thus understood this biblical assertion to mean that all men sinned "in Adam," because they were virtually contained in him.

In this it becomes apparent that for Augustine sin did not merely consist in pride, but also in concupiscence. The latter, too, is not merely an expression of Adam's evil volitional acts, but is, at the same time, a punishment for Adam's sin. Augustine does not regard concupiscence, or lust, as being merely sexual. He speaks of lust also when referring to the wrongful striving of the soul. Quite to the point is the following definition which he gives: "I mean by charity that affection of the mind which aims at the enjoyment of God for His own sake, and the enjoyment of one's self and one's neighbor in subordination to God; by lust I mean that affection of the mind which aims at enjoying one's self and one's neighbor, and other corporeal things without reference to God."[7]

There can be no doubt, however, that for Augustine concupiscence was operative predominantly in the area of sex. To the

[7] Augustine, *On Christian Doctrine,* Bk. III, chap. 10, par. 16, *NPNF*[1] 2, 561.

point of disgust he had experienced in his own life its great force, which seemingly overpowers even the faculties of the spirit. It therefore appears to him as the force which really tyrannizes man. He says at one point that concupiscence, which is in itself the "daughter of sin," has become the "mother of sin." According to Augustine it is actually concupiscence which is responsible for transmitting original sin. Through it even the children of a Christian marriage are subjected anew to original sin. This is especially serious because by original sin Augustine always means at the same time original guilt.

It is clear that Augustine imparted to the traditional doctrine of sin a profundity which it had not had before. For him sin is not merely this or that wrongful deed. Hence sin is not something which can be removed by a mere appeal to the good in man, or through instruction. Sin is, rather, the wrong orientation of all human existence since Adam's fall, an orientation from which no one can free himself. It is the form of existence in which we, as humans, find ourselves. In insisting upon this, Augustine overcame the moralism which had hitherto dominated the concept of sin.

Yet Augustine's definition of sin is weighed down by his concept of concupiscence and does not permit the principle of pride which is present in his conception to assert itself. The whole problematic of Augustine's conception becomes apparent in his assertion that the act of procreation is not sinful in itself, but it becomes sinful if it is associated with lust. Furthermore, it was not possible for Augustine to explain why the lust of Christian parents, the guilt of which has been forgiven them in baptism, still transmits original sin to their children. At these points Augustine's understanding of original sin is influenced by the low estimate of the body which was characteristic of his age, as well as by his own experiences. For theology to recognize and overcome this imbalance without falling prey to the opposite imbalance of Pelagius took a long time. In actuality it was not accomplished until Luther and the Reformation.

Similar to his radical definition of sin is Augustine's understanding of grace. He emphasized both the necessity and the work of grace as no one before him, and only very few after him.

First and foremost is Augustine's emphasis upon the fact that

God's grace is given gratuitously, purely as a gift of his love. "But a gift," he says, "unless it be gratuitous, is not grace."[8] There is no possibility that man can merit this grace. It is not possible for him either to break out of, or to leave behind, the vicious circle of evil in which he is caught. God alone can free him from it. God alone can save man from the unrest in which he finds himself as the result of wrong orientation of his will. God alone can give him rest. From this Augustine concludes that in relation to grace there is no freedom of the will.

Taking up the matter in greater detail Augustine speaks first of prevenient grace: "It [grace] predisposes a man before he wills, to prompt his willing. It follows the act of willing, lest one's will be frustrated."[9] Through this grace, which can be equated with election, the will of man is prepared. From this prevenient grace Augustine distinguishes accompanying grace. Here he is concerned about sanctification, about growth in faith, in knowledge, and in love, until man becomes a new creature. In this area the human will is no longer excluded. On the contrary, the will is now freed and can therefore act in concert with grace; it can even earn merit. Finally, there is an operation of grace which has to do with the gift of perseverance. Without this gift the action of divine grace could not arrive at its goal. Without the gift of perseverance a person is damned, even though he may seemingly have been elected by prevenient grace. The important thing is perseverance in grace to the end.

Accordingly Augustine does not regard the work of divine grace primarily from the point of view of the forgiveness of sins, but rather from that of man's restoration, or his healing. Justification is thus a process in the course of which man is actually made just. Strictly speaking, it is possible only to say that man is justified at the end of this process, although at times Augustine includes his entire doctrine of grace in his concept of prevenient grace.

The great emphasis Augustine laid upon the necessity of "the gift of perseverance," as well as upon his concept of the bondage of the will, would seem to indicate that his doctrine of grace was bound to proceed almost ineluctably in the direction of a doctrine of predestination. As a matter of fact, he very

[8] Augustine, *Enchiridion*, chap. 28, sec. 107. *LCC* 7, 404.

[9] *Ibid.*, chap. 9, sec. 32. *LCC* 7, 359.

quickly drew this conclusion himself. At the time of the Pelagian controversy, therefore, he had arrived at the following view. From the total number of angels which constituted the heavenly city, a fraction fell away from God. In order that the city of God might not be permanently impaired God predestined to salvation as many men as there were angels who had fallen away. At the end of this tremendous drama of fall and redemption, the number of inhabitants of the heavenly city would perhaps be even somewhat greater than at the beginning. According to Augustine, then, the gracious working of God is subordinated to this eternal predestination and is entirely oriented toward it.[10]

It is not true that Augustine taught a double predestination. If his concept of predestination is carried to its logical conclusion, this deduction may become necessary. Augustine, however, always emphasized that those who are lost suffer a destiny which they have earned. But why does God elect only a given number of men, while he leaves the rest to a damnation which they deserve? In the last analysis, Augustine, too, had no answer to this question. He felt that God's mercy toward those who had been elected to salvation shows itself in its true nature only if it is accompanied by God's justice toward the great mass of sinners. Without such justice, he held, God's mercy would be misunderstood. Hence the people who came under his grace might fall anew into pride.

Finally, it is important to point out that, in spite of his emphasis upon the necessity of God's gracious acts and upon the bondage of the will, Augustine held to the psychological freedom of the human will. In reference to the process of salvation he never thinks of divine grace as being substituted for human decision. Grace always works in such a way that it moves the human will to action. In this way Augustine differentiated between his insistence upon the bondage of the will and the philosophical concept of determinism. In a similar way he also developed his concept of merit. In the last analysis, merit does not have to do with something man can do himself. Under no circumstances would Augustine permit man to attribute to himself the merits which he begins to possess. In a letter he says,

[10] B. Lohse, "Zu Augustins Engellehre," *Zeitschrift für Kirchengeschichte*, 70 (1959), 278-291.

"What else but His [own] gifts does God crown when He crowns our merits?"[11] Basically, then, Augustine speaks of merits only because he wants to emphasize the responsibility of man.

The importance of Augustine's doctrine of grace can hardly be overemphasized. Not only is this true with respect to the overarching influence of his thought upon the Middle Ages, upon the Reformers, and upon certain recurring tendencies within Catholicism. The accomplishments of Augustine assume their full dimension only when they are seen against the background of the moralism of the ancient church and its latent Pelagianism. It was Augustine who for the first time clarified theologically the important questions of sin, grace, and forgiveness. It was he who saw that the Christian, too, falls into sin again and again, and that therefore a sinless life on earth is impossible. Above all, however, he overcame the previous, widespread uncertainty concerning the authority of the church to forgive sins. According to Augustine the unpardonable sin does not consist in a given deed, but in the lack of faith relating to the possibility of forgiveness. Here, as in his doctrine of grace and predestination, Augustine emphasized the element of certainty of salvation. Of course, he could not teach this in the way in which Luther did. An element of uncertainty remains, since, in the thought of Augustine, justification must be understood with its end always in view, and since in the last analysis everything depends upon the gift of perseverance. However, in comparison with the tremendous step forward which is represented by Augustine's doctrine of sin and grace, such defects are minor.

The Pelagian Controversy

The teaching of Augustine still faced the task of gaining acceptance in the church. Whether or not it could have accomplished this without the Pelagian controversy is a question. Even as it is, Augustine's position was not accepted by the church in all details.

For years, both Pelagius and Coelestius had been able to teach their doctrines in Rome without ever being opposed by the hierarchy. The leaders of the Roman church had apparently seen nothing heretical in the teaching of the two men. Things began

[11] Augustine, *FC* 30, 313, letter 194.

to happen only when the invasion of the Goths forced these two to flee to North Africa. Pelagius, whose utterances were somewhat more guarded than those of his friend Coelestius, proceeded east, while the latter applied for a position as priest at Carthage. Here a charge of heresy was brought against him before the North African primate. As a result his request was denied and, in addition, he was excommunicated (411). The propositions which were ascribed to him, and for which he was condemned, were the following: that Adam was created mortal and would have died even if he had not sinned; that Adam's sin hurt him only, not the rest of mankind; that newborn children are in the same state in which Adam was before the fall; that the whole of mankind does not die because of Adam's death, even as through the resurrection of Christ all mankind does not rise again; that unbaptized children are given eternal life; that man can live without sin; that it is easy for man to fulfill the laws of God, since even before Christ there were men who lived without sin, and since the law is quite as adequate for the attainment of the kingdom of heaven as is the gospel.

It seems that the problem of the baptism of children played an important role in the controversy from the outset. It appears to have been held against Coelestius from the beginning that his teaching called into question the necessity of infant baptism. Here we note again, as we did in connection with the doctrine of the Trinity, the importance of the inherited faith of the church for certain doctrinal decisions. One could argue equally well from the baptismal formula or from baptismal practice. Coelestius, on the other hand, tried to demonstrate that he was not attacking the baptism of children; such baptism, he said, not only vouchsafes eternal life, but also salvation. The distinction between these two, however, he was not able to demonstrate convincingly.

Pelagius, in the meantime, tried to win followers for his teaching in Palestine, though in the East there was little understanding of the questions involved in the Pelagian controversy. The reason for this is not to be found merely in language difficulties, even though these were serious enough. In the East the theology of Augustine was not known in detail. A more important reason, however, is that all Greek theology since Irenaeus, and especially since the days of the three great Cappadocians, did not think in terms of achievement and reward, as did western theology since Tertullian. Rather, it thought in categories of a continuous progress which would never end on earth, i.e., in categories of ever greater approximation to God. Furthermore, in the East these conceptions were fitted into the grand scheme of a theology oriented toward a history of redemption. This theology saw in the total history of mankind the realization of a divine plan which, while interrupted by the fall, had been restored through Christ and would finally be consummated in eternity. Within such a frame of reference ideas of achievement and reward, which were also present in the East, could not lead to the same fateful consequences they had in the West.

This difference between western and eastern theology meant for Pelagius, for one thing, that in the East he met no opposition. In 415 he was able to justify his position before two Palestinian synods. It is true that he had to drop his erstwhile friend Coelestius and to disassociate himself from those propositions of the latter which had been condemned at Carthage in 411. To the accusation that he, too, had declared the attainment of sinlessness to be a possibility, Pelagius answered that this possibility is dependent upon the aid of divine grace. However, the concept of the gracious aid of God always remained strangely indefinite in Pelagius. In fact, Pelagius occasionally appropriated other concepts which could be understood in the sense of his theological adversaries but the meaning of which remained unclear in his own thought.

The decision of the Orient, however, did not quiet the situation in North Africa. As late as 416 two synods met which, while they did not condemn Pelagius and Coelestius, did picture them as originators of serious heresies. Furthermore, in North Africa a most important step was taken, which gave a new turn to the entire controversy. It was decided to ask the Bishop of Rome, Innocent I, to add the authority of the apostolic see to the African decision in the controversy. For the Africans this step was probably not easy. In an earlier day it had been precisely the bishops of Carthage who, though respecting the Roman bishop, had always put emphasis upon their own independence and rejected every submission to a Roman decision. Now, however, there may have been fear in Africa, and rightly so, that the still numerous followers of Pelagius in Rome might win over the Roman bishop to their position. It was the intention of the Africans, therefore, to obtain a favorable decision in Rome by submission to the Roman see.

This action of the Africans did not miss its mark. In his answer Innocent I began by praising the obedience of the North Africans to the apostolic see. He also praised their zeal against the heretics. Finally he declared it to be sacrilege to deny divine grace or to promise eternal life to children without baptism. Coelestius and Pelagius were excommunicated.

Soon after this answer Innocent I died (March, 417), and as a result the course of events took an unexpected turn. Pelagius had in the meantime set forth and sent to Rome a confession of faith which was to be a proof of his orthodoxy. In it the controversial questions were hardly touched upon, while infant baptism as well as the freedom of the will were acknowledged. The chief emphasis was upon the affirmation that "we always need the help of God." In addition to this, Pelagius, too, was now eager to demonstrate his submissiveness to the pope. Innocent was no longer able to make a decision concerning this confession, but his successor, Zosimus, regarded the confession as satisfactory. Even before this Coelestius had already smoothed the way for a change of the Roman climate in his favor by surrendering the harshest of his earlier utterances. The result was that in the year 417 a Roman synod confirmed the orthodoxy of Pelagius as well as of Coelestius. Zosimus communicated this decision to the Africans, not neglecting to chide them for their levity in this entire controversy.

Catholics have often said that this decision was rendered only because Coelestius and Pelagius had deceived the pope. This contention is true insofar as both Coelestius and Pelagius had sought to express themselves in a manner which would arouse as few suspicions as possible. Yet, in penning their apologias they did not discard any basic opinions. They specifically rejected the idea that man is sinful from birth. That the two were declared orthodox by Zosimus can be explained only by the fact that they were still highly regarded in Rome and that, at the time, Rome was really closer to the theology of Pelagius than to that of Augustine. While during the trinitarian and christological conflicts Rome usually was on the side of orthodoxy, this cannot be said of its position in the Pelagian controversy.

With this decision of Rome, Carthage was not satisfied. It informed the new pope that it planned to adhere to the decision of his predecessor. Afraid of the determined opposition of the Africans, Zosimus was willing to resume negotiations. The result was the synod of Carthage, which met in the year 418, and settled the Pelagian controversy, at least for the time being. Among other things it made the following decisions: The position that Adam had been created mortal, which had already been condemned in 411, was condemned again. Furthermore, it rejected the opinion that little children "are not involved in Adam's original sin" and that their baptism is therefore not for the purpose of forgiveness of sin. Against this view the synod asserted that through one man sin came into the world and that from him it was transmitted to others. Beyond this the synod decreed: "Whoever should say that the grace of God, by which a man is justified through Jesus Christ our Lord, avails only for the remission of past sins, and not for assistance against committing sins in the future, let him be anathema."[12] It is expressly emphasized that this grace of God does not consist only in instruction concerning the content of God's commandments, but that, above all, it imparts power for their fulfillment. The notion that grace simply facilitates our accomplishment of that which we could do by our own free will is also rejected. It is further stated that the saints do not merely pray for the forgiveness of their sins out of humility, but that they must truly pray this prayer for themselves.

In order to avoid any future difficulty with Roman bishops the synod published a canon[13] threatening with excommunication anyone who appealed from Africa to Rome. So as to be quite sure of achieving their goal, the Africans, prior to the meeting of the synod, had intervened against the two heretics at the imperial court. The result was that an imperial rescript decreed their banishment from Rome, as well as that of their followers. Against these various pressures Zosimus could not avail. He agreed to the condemnation of both Pelagius and Coelestius.

The significance of the decision of Carthage can best be evalu-

[12] The Council of Carthage, Canon III=Canon 111 of *The African Code*. *NPNF*[2] 14, 497.

[13] The Council of Carthage, Canon 17=Canon 125 of *The African Code*. *NPNF*[2] 14, 502.

ated if it is compared, on the one hand, with the Carthaginian synod of 411 and, on the other, with the teaching of Augustine. In comparison with the earlier synod many propositions were elaborated upon. What is most important, however, is that the concept of the aid of divine grace, which has to do not only with the forgiveness of earlier sins but with the whole course of the Christian life, is reasserted. According to this concept, the Christian is constantly dependent upon the aid of divine grace, and such aid consists of much more than instruction concerning the demands made of man. On the other hand, there can be no doubt that Augustine was unsuccessful at the time in asserting his doctrine of sin and grace as a whole. The Carthaginian decision not only lacks a careful definition of the nature of sin but, what is more important, its declarations about grace leave room for very different interpretations. While it is granted that free will alone is not sufficient for the attainment of salvation, there is nothing said about prevenient grace, about the gift of perseverance, about the relation between the work of grace and man's volitional activity or, finally, about divine predestination. The Augustinian doctrine of sin and grace was, by no means, given dogmatic status at Carthage. The synod merely set forth a few basic propositions concerning the universality of sin and the necessity of grace for salvation. Still, it is a decision which has considerable significance. Its judgment upon Pelagius and Coelestius was accepted by the Third Ecumenical Council at Ephesus in 431. Consequently the most important results of the Pelagian controversy became the common property of both the Greek and the Latin churches.

The Semi-Pelagian Controversy

With the decision of 418 the controversy concerning the doctrine of sin and grace was not finally settled. What made for new difficulties was the fact that at Carthage many of the ideas of Augustine, from whom so much had been learned, had not been declared binding. The decision of Carthage could be interpreted in various ways. Not all who had agreed to the condemnation of Coelestius and Pelagius were ready to follow Augustine's daring ideas in all respects. Consequently there appeared very quickly a group of people who rejected Pelagius, to be sure, but who were also dissatisfied with the sharp contours of Augustinian theology. In the modern era they have been labeled "semi-Pelagians," because they are allegedly "half-Pelagian." This label, which first appears in the Lutheran *Formula of Concord* (1577) and which subsequently found wide acceptance, was not a happy choice. The so-called semi-Pelagians wanted to be anything but half-Pelagians. It would be more correct to call them semi-Augustinians.

In Carthage opposition to Augustine's doctrine of grace arose already in the year 420. It did not become active until 426, however, when the monks of the convent at Adrumetum, located on the east coast of modern Tunisia, rebelled against the teachings of Augustine. When the monks of southern Gaul joined in the controversy it became even more heated. In this latter group the names of John Cassian (d. between 430-435) and Vincent of Lérins (d. before 450) are especially noteworthy. These men defended the semi-Pelagian point of view with much more circumspection and facility than the North African opponents of Augustine. The controversy they enkindled was to last for another century. In fact, in later centuries the controversy erupted, in other forms, over and over again.

What did these men teach? They were not overly concerned with theological problems as such. Nor did they broadcast their opinions on their own initiative, as Pelagius had done. It was Augustine's teachings which first goaded them into an opposing opinion. They took exception to a number of points in the Augustinian doctrine of sin and grace. The assertion of the total bondage of the will, of the irresistible operation of the power of grace, and of predestination was especially obnoxious to them. Such conceptions, they feared, would stifle all human initiative from the very beginning. On the other hand, these men were in full agreement with Augustine as to the seriousness of sin. As monks they were used to examining themselves critically and they had good insight into the secret, sinful inclinations of the heart. With reference to original sin, too, there was no difference of opinion. But they did reject the doctrine of predestination, because it seemed to make all human effort superfluous.

Something else needs to be added. The men who opposed Augustine were, for the most part, conscious of tradition. They had the feeling, and rightly so, that the teaching of Augustine, at least in its distinctive emphases, represented a new departure not in keeping with the traditional position of the church. For this reason, among others, they were suspicious of Augustine's theology.

In opposition to Augustinianism, Cassian taught that free will in man has not been entirely obliterated. He would grant that Adam's sin is inherited by succeeding generations in the sense in which a sickness is inherited. As a result the will is weakened. With Augustine, Cassian could go so far as to say that God gives to man the beginnings of a virtuous will. Even Augustine's concept of prevenient grace was not devoid of meaning for him. Yet he would emphasize that grace does not necessarily need to precede the free will. Since man still has a free will, even though weakened, it may come about that this will takes the initiative toward God. Cassian felt Augustine was wrong in thinking that the sinful will is held prisoner by the basic orientation which it itself wills. The free will, he held, can on its own initiative take the first step toward God. By the same token man has the freedom to reject God's grace. Man's will is always free and can either prize God's grace or neglect it. Cassian thus holds in balance the necessity of grace and the natural freedom of the will. To say it differently, grace and free will must work together. When Cassian speaks of grace he by no means thinks only of instruction, as did Pelagius, but of the infusion of grace, that is, of the actual assistance of grace. In opposition to the stark predestinarianism of Augustine, the monks of southern Gaul specifically held to the doctrine of God's universal will to save. Predestination they regarded as nothing but predetermination on the basis of merits which God knew in advance; that is, predestination is simply foreknowledge.

In his last writings, in which he dealt with the views of the monks of southern Gaul, Augustine's tone is quite different from that which prevails in his anti-Pelagian books. He knew very well how to differentiate between Pelagians and semi-Pelagians. For him the men of southern Gaul were not heretics but erring brethren. He says specifically, ". . . I myself also was convinced when I was in a similar error, thinking that faith whereby we believe on God is not God's gift, but that it is in us from ourselves, and that by it we obtain the gifts of God, whereby we may live temperately and righteously and piously in this world."[14] In spite of the winsome form in which Augustine clothed his answer, he did not give in. In fact, he argued his case more strongly than ever.

This debate with the Gallic monks had not been in progress long when Augustine died (430). After his death the controversy became more heated. The followers of Augustine, who continued the conflict, did not have the intellectual breadth of their dead master, and often caused unnecessary resentment. Among them it is especially Prosper of Aquitane who deserves mention. Upon his request the Roman bishop, Coelestine I, sent a letter to the bishops of southern Gaul in which he exhorted to unity. Unnecessary questions were not to be debated. Regarding Augustine, Coelestine rendered the ambiguous judgment, "Because of his life and work Augustine is held in high esteem among us; we always had fellowship with him and no suspicion of him ever arose." Equally ambiguous is Coelestine's demand that the new attempt to attack the ancient tradition should cease.

At this time, that is, in the year 434, Vincent of Lérins wrote his famous *Commonitory* [*Exhortation*] *for the Antiquity and Universality of the Catholic Faith Against the Profane Novelties of all Heresies.* It contains the clearest formulation of the Catholic principle of tradition found anywhere in the ancient church. The important thing about the treatise is that in writing it Vincent permitted himself to be guided by his opposition to Augustine. His polemic against Augustine's doctrine of grace is considerably more skillful than that of the other theologians of southern Gaul. In his book Augustine's name is not found even once. For Vincent the criterion for judging the Augustinian doctrine of grace is the concept of tradition, which he defines as follows: "In the Catholic Church itself, all possible care must be taken, that we hold that faith which has been believed everywhere, always, by all. For that is truly and in the strictest sense 'Catholic,' which, as the name itself and the reason of the thing declare, comprehends all universality."[15] Referring to the example of prominent teachers of the church, such as Origen, he shows that even the wisest may fall into dangerous errors

[14] Augustine, *On the Predestination of the Saints,* chap. 7. *NPNF*[1] 5, 500.

[15] Vincent of Lérins, *The Commonitory,* chap. 2, sec. 6. *NPNF*[2] 11, 132.

and must then be shunned by the church. The following sentences are quite unambiguous and must be understood to have been written with Augustine in mind: "With accompanying promises, the heretics are wont marvellously to beguile the incautious. For they dare to teach and promise, that in their church, that is, in the conventicle of their communion, there is a certain great and special and altogether personal grace of God, so that whosoever pertain to their number, without any labor, without any effort, without any industry, even though they neither ask, nor seek, nor knock, have such a dispensation from God, that, borne up by angel hands, that is, preserved by the protection of angels, it is impossible they should ever dash their feet against a stone, that is, that they should ever be offended."[16]

It is obvious that for Vincent it was only possible to understand Augustine's doctrine of the gift of perseverance, and his doctrine of predestination, to mean that the elect of God cannot sin. This, however, appeared to him as a satanic temptation. His reference to the Gospel account of the temptation, in which Satan demands of Jesus that he throw himself from the pinnacle of the temple so that he may be borne up by the angels, is unmistakable. That Augustine's doctrine of predestination is here not rendered correctly, and that at least its intention was not understood by Vincent, admits of no doubt. And yet the men of southern Gaul were not entirely wrong. They recognized many dangers which are inherent in the Augustinian teaching and against which Augustine himself was not sufficiently on guard. Certain it is that the great pastoral concern voiced by the theologians of southern Gaul about the consequences of Augustinian theology cannot be disputed.

The debates about semi-Pelagianism lasted for another century. They came to an end in 529 at the Synod of Orange, where Caesarius of Arles (d. 542) succeeded in bringing about the dogmatization of a number of propositions against the semi-Pelagians. In doing so, however, the synod did not accept Augustine's whole doctrine of grace. Its most important decisions were the following: Through Adam's sin he himself as well as his posterity have been corrupted in body and soul. Sin and death go back to Adam's disobedience of the divine command. As a result, the free will is so weakened that, left to oneself, no

[16] *Ibid.*, chap. 26. *NPNF*² 11, 151.

one can either love God or believe in him as one ought. Of himself alone man cannot obtain the grace of God. Even man's appeal to divine grace is the work of grace itself. In the same way grace brings about faith and the desire for purity. In this context "grace" refers to the infusion of the Holy Spirit and to his work. "The will is prepared by the Lord," it is asserted. "Faith" means assent to evangelical preaching. The faith which is inspired by God in this particular manner moves us to submit to baptism, which, in turn, restores the freedom of the will. Yet the baptized, too, are in constant need of the aid of divine grace. Without it they cannot persevere in good works or reach the desired end. All that is said about predestination is that there is no predetermination to damnation.

In general the decision of the Carthaginian council of 418 was here underscored once more. Of course, man's total lack of freedom in relation to God is now more clearly expressed and the necessity of divine grace is more strongly emphasized. But the full Augustinian doctrine of grace was not accepted by the synod, and especially not his concept of divine grace which works irresistibly in the predestinated. Generally speaking, however, semi-Pelagianism, too, had now been rejected. Since Boniface II confirmed the decisions of Orange, they gained general acceptance. It was in this way that semi-Pelagianism, which counted the greater number of adherents, was forced into retreat.

The Result

The significance of the Pelagian and semi-Pelagian controversies can hardly be overestimated. It extends further than one would guess on the basis of the dogmatic decisions which were made at the time.

The decrees of the councils of 418, 431, and 529 are, of course, important. A new area of affirmations of the Christian faith had now been clarified dogmatically and took its place alongside the doctrine of God and Christology. It was an area which had long been rife with ambiguities. From now on a radical concept of sin, consisting in man's lack of freedom insofar as he is related to God, a belief in the necessity of the divine work of grace, and an understanding of the primacy of grace rather than of human merit, are definitely among the basic affirmations of the Christian faith. Henceforth the assertion of man's radically fallen estate, and of the work of grace, are never disassociated from appeals to man's will. Nor are they divorced from a pastoral concern which insists that human responsibility should not be diminished. Furthermore, this assertion must be understood in a truly theological sense and must not be confused with considerations of the psychological process which operates in the call and conversion of man. Of course, neither semi-Pelagianism nor Pelagianism, as they existed in the fifth century, were simply excised from the world by the decisions of these councils. Both appeared ever and again. Yet the decisions of these councils did erect a barrier beyond which the church as such can no longer go.

The significance of the Pelagian controversy, however, extends to still other, and quite different, problems. It resulted, first of all, in a considerable strengthening of the authority of the Roman bishop. This is nowhere more clearly evident than in the letter of the African bishops, in which they subjected themselves to the authority of Pope Innocent I. It is true that the Council of Carthage in 418 prohibited all appeals to Rome. This did not annul the fact, however, that the authority of the Roman bishop had recently been recognized in an unprecedented way. Thus the Pelagian controversy is of importance for the development of the primacy of Rome in relation to the other churches.

Finally, the Pelagian controversy led to a further development of the concept of tradition. On the one hand, the primacy of Rome was promoted, at least temporarily, by the followers of Augustine for the sake of furthering their doctrine of grace. On the other hand, the formulation of the principle of tradition was undertaken to advance the interest of the semi-Pelagian opponents of Augustine. In spite of these differences, however, both the primacy of Rome and the newly formulated principle of tradition were soon united with each other. They were, of course, closely related from the beginning. Moreover, Augustine's total, unabridged doctrine of sin and grace was not acceptable to the church, and the joint opposition of primacy and tradition to the extremes of Augustine also had a unifying effect upon the two.

The semi-Pelagian controversy is an excellent example of the degree to which a given era may bring forth results which are not related to the topics that are being discussed at the time. It illustrates, too, how the secondary results of such an era may contain within themselves, or at least point toward, the basic themes of later epochs.

While the results of the Pelagian controversy do represent considerable progress with reference to the doctrine of sin and grace, there were many things which remained ambiguous, or at least not sufficiently clarified. This is true, for instance, of the concept of sin. To be sure, Augustine's understanding of sin as concupiscence did not find expression in the decisions of the councils. But this did not prevent the further development of the practical equation of sin and concupiscence. Such an equation is noticeable almost throughout the Middle Ages. To be sure, no major theologian of the Middle Ages believed that the concept of sin was exhausted in the concept of concupiscence. Yet the low estimate of the body, as well as the basically ascetic orientation of the whole Middle Ages, can hardly be understood apart from this Augustinian element. In this respect a deepening of the understanding of sin, perhaps even a new beginning, was necessary.

This, however, did not take place during the Middle Ages. It was Luther who first overcame the weaknesses of the Augustinian understanding of sin and who actually developed further the doctrine of sin. To be sure, Luther says upon occasion that the act of generation has been rendered sinful by lustful desire, and that sin perpetuates itself as a result of this act. As a rule, however, Luther's understanding of concupiscence included much more than simply sexual desire. In Luther's thought it had reference to the self-will of man, who wants to assert himself against God and thus to keep God from being God. Luther was fully aware of the difference between himself and Augustine at this important point. He saw quite clearly that in Augustine, as well as in Jerome and others, there was a strong tendency to equate sin with man's corporeality. He felt that this was the reason sin and grace were understood in the sense of the ancient dichotomy between body and spirit. In contradistinction to this understanding of sin, St. Paul, so Luther insisted, regards the whole man either as "flesh," or as "spiritual," depending upon whether or not he has been renewed by faith in God. On one occasion Luther wrote concerning the difference in the understanding of these important concepts: "Without such a grasp of these words [spirit and flesh], you will never understand this letter of St. Paul, nor any other book of Holy Scripture. Therefore beware of all teachers who use these words in a different sense, no matter who they are, even Origen, Ambrose, Augustine, Jerome, and others like them or even above them."[17] The ascetic characteristic which the conflict with sin had up to that time was vanquished only by Luther, who had a more total understanding of sin.

That such was possible is not merely the result of a new understanding of the concept of concupiscence, but of the new theology of Luther in general. To Luther sin was personal. It was something which man does with his whole being and which, therefore, in the last analysis has the same significance as lack of faith and a lack of trust in God. He says, "Sin, in the Scripture, means not only the outward works of the body but also all the activities that move men to do these works, namely, the inmost heart with all its powers."[18] Luther knew well that sinful desire is so deeply embedded in man that it may even use external humility to gain its end. "True humility, therefore, never knows that it is humble, as I have said; for if it knew this, it would turn proud from contemplation of so fine a virtue."[19] Given these premises Luther can no longer regard the end of the total process of sanctification as the climax of man's justification, since, in that case, self-will in the sublime form of an ascetic self-contemplation would not yet be overcome. On the contrary, it is the beginning of this process which Luther believes to be of decisive significance.

This new, Reformation understanding of sin which, on the one hand, is free from the mere historicizing of sin and, on the other, is not restricted to the area of the sexual, is excellently expressed in the *Augsburg Confession* (1530), which states "that since the fall of Adam all men who are born according to the course of nature are conceived and born in sin. That is, all men are full of evil lust and inclinations from their mothers' wombs and are unable by nature to have true fear of God and true faith in God. Moreover, this inborn sickness and hereditary sin is truly sin and

[17] Luther, *Preface to the Epistle of St. Paul to the Romans* (1546, 1522), *LW* 35, 372.

[18] *Ibid., LW* 35, 369.

[19] Luther, *The Magnificat* (1521), *PE* 3, 147.

condemns to the eternal wrath of God all those who are not born again through Baptism and the Holy Spirit."[20]

For the Catholic church also, the decisions made during the Pelagian and semi-Pelagian controversies were, and have always remained, of great significance. During the period of Scholasticism greater attention was given to Augustinian theology. This was especially true in the case of Peter Lombard (d. 1160) and Thomas Aquinas (d. 1274). In his concept of predestination Thomas actually came rather close to Augustine. On the other hand, semi-Pelagianism, and even Pelagianism, has raised its head in the Roman church at all times. This applies to the late Middle Ages almost as a whole. It is true of Erasmus, who in his later days was of the same opinion as Pelagius, namely, that man can attain salvation by his own efforts, without divine grace.[21] Subsequently too, however, semi-Pelagian tendencies emerged again and again, as they did, for instance, in the Spanish Jesuit Luis de Molina (d. 1600). In the controversy about Molinism, the Curia avoided a decision. Yet, the conciliar decisions during the Pelagian and semi-Pelagian controversies mean that a moderate Augustinianism is officially recognized also in the Roman church.

[20] *Augsburg Confession*, II, 1-2, *BC*, p. 29.

[21] K. H. Oelrich, *Der späte Erasmus und die Reformation* (Münster: Aschendorff, 1961), pp. 125 f.

5

Word and Sacrament

The Early Church

THE DECISIONS which have been discussed above in relation to the great controversies over the doctrine of the Trinity, Christology, and the doctrine of sin and grace, constitute a unity, insofar as they became binding both for the East and for the West. They thus represent a heritage which the Greek, the Roman, and the Protestant churches have in common. Even though there are certain differences in the understanding of these decisions (as in the case of the Pelagian controversy, which in another form was taken up once more during the century of the Reformation) the significance of this common heritage should not be underestimated.

The doctrinal developments which must be treated in this and the following chapters are no longer shared by the great communions in this way. It should be noted that the magnitude of that which is common to them and that which separates them is different in each case. Modern Roman Catholic dogmas have gained no acceptance either in Orthodoxy or in Protestantism. There are, on the other hand, many common elements in the doctrine of the sacraments. There are also a number of doctrinal decisions, though certainly not all, which are binding for at least the two great churches of the West, the Roman and the Protestant.

It is not by accident that the next great dogmatic task which the church faced had to do with the doctrine of the sacraments. In the ancient church there was, of course, no dearth of other problems which also needed clarification. And some decisions were made which led to new and binding declarations of the church with respect to one facet or another of the Christian faith. This is true especially of the controversy of the North African church with Donatism. The Donatists, named after their leader Donatus, had separated themselves from the rest of the church in the early days of the reign of Constantine the Great. Besides the personal differences which were involved, and which played a considerable role, there were those which had an objective reference. The Donatists held that, according to its nature, the church is a community which includes only men and women who have not committed mortal sins and that for this reason only a priest who is also free from mortal sins can administer the sacraments validly. In contradistinction to this opinion, the rest of the church held that the personal holiness of a priest, desirable though it might be, is not a precondition for the validity of the sacraments. The reason is that in the sacraments the decisive thing is Christ's institution of them, and his gift, not that of the priest. The decisions against the Donatists, which, primarily as a result of Augustine's profound treatment of this question, were made at the beginning of the fifth century, constitute an important step in the development of the doctrine of the church. The confessional writings of the Reformation refer explicitly to these decisions and, to a considerable degree, made them their own.

Still during the centuries following the Donatist controversy the doctrine of the church was not given the same attention as the doctrine of the sacraments. Work on the doctrine of the sacraments proceeded, even in its initial stages, and more especially in its later development, without the acute stimulation of great doctrinal controversies. It is true that there was no dearth of discussions concerning certain questions which had to do with the theology of the sacraments. But these were actually the result, not the cause, of the church's intensive interest in the doctrine of the sacraments.

How did this great interest in the doctrine of the sacraments originate? Several causes worked together. One is that for the man of antiquity there was an element in the sacraments which was especially appealing. Mysterious acts of consecration were found in various religions of the time. The holy acts of the church appeared to be on the same level as these. The Greek word for sacrament, *mysterion* ("mystery," "secret"), served to reinforce this view. Furthermore, for centuries to come the number of sacraments was not carefully delimited. Baptism and the Lord's Supper stood out, to be sure, so that when the sacraments were mentioned, there was the tendency always to think first of them. But besides these, there were a large number of other holy acts which today are no longer recognized as sacraments even in the Roman Catholic church.

It is quite possible that it was the Latin word *sacramentum* which had special significance for the development of the later interest in the theology of the sacraments. The New Testament did not use the inclusive concept "sacrament" for baptism and the Lord's Supper. It simply permitted these two symbolical, or parabolical, acts to stand alongside one another, each with its own distinctive character. There was no attempt to compare them in detail, let alone to draw a parallel. This raises a question regarding the entire subsequent development of the doctrine of the sacraments, namely, whether it was not too strongly influenced by the inclusive concept "sacrament" and whether the individual sacraments were seen within this larger perspective, instead of each of them being understood more expressly in its individuality. In contradistinction to this, Luther and the Lutheran confessions display a certain reserve—which from the point of view of Scripture is well founded—toward the concept "sacrament." However this may be, while the Greek concept "mysteries" may have placed the Christian sacraments on the same level with other "secrets," the Latin word *sacramentum*, which in itself contained a variety of meanings, focused attention on the distinctive character of the sacraments. For that reason its use was bound to lead to reflection on the meaning of the sacraments. The term *sacramentum* was chosen quite early as a designation for the sacraments. Tertullian, the first of the fathers to write in Latin, assumes that the term is known. From this it is concluded that the concept must have been in use before he employed it. The choice of this term must have been premeditated, since *mysterium* was in use in Latin as a loan-word from the Greek.

Of great significance for the later theological interest in the doctrine of the sacraments was, finally, the development of the understanding of the content of the sacraments. While this development can, basically, be observed in relation to all sacraments, it is most easily discerned in relation to the Lord's Supper. Briefly stated, it consists in the fact that soon after the New Testament period the Lord's Supper came to be designated as an "offering," and that this expression, which was at first meant figuratively, gradually came to be understood in an increasingly literal sense. According to Irenaeus, who lived in the second half of the second century, Christians bring an offering of bread and wine. Irenaeus does not think, however, that Christ himself is offered as an oblation. He holds, rather, that as a result of the words of institution bread and wine are regarded as the body and blood of Christ. His concept of an offering, then, is still a derived one: what is offered is bread and wine, though these are in a certain sense the body and blood of Christ at the same time. Still, even Irenaeus could already say that Christ had instituted "the new oblation of the new covenant," an oblation which the church received from the apostles, and which it now makes throughout the world.[1]

Cyprian, Bishop of Carthage until his death in 258, went considerably further. He was the first to spell out a concept already held here and there, namely, that the body and blood of Christ are sacrificial gifts offered by the priests. In the Eucharist, he said, the offering upon the cross is repeated: "That priest truly discharges the office of Christ, who imitates that which Christ did; and he then offers a true and full sacrifice in the Church to God the Father, when he proceeds to offer it according to what he sees Christ Himself to have offered."[2] It appears certain that not every word should be minutely analyzed here. Cyprian's words are not as carefully thought through as are the theories of the Mass propounded since the high Middle Ages. Still the difference between this concept of an offering and that of the New Testament is clearly apparent.

The thinking of the ancient church on the sacrament of the altar reached a certain terminus in Ambrose. His writings contain statements about the transmutation of the "elements" of

[1] Irenaeus, *Against Heresies*, Bk. IV, chap. 17, sec. 5. *ANF* 1, 484.

[2] Cyprian, *ANF* 5, 362, letter 63, par. 14.

bread and wine which follow certain assertions of Greek theology. The older theology of the West had paid no attention to these questions. The thoughts of Ambrose receive their clearest expression in his two writings *On the Mysteries* and *On the Sacraments.* For a long time the authenticity of these treatises, and especially of the second, was much debated; today, however, it may be regarded as having been established. While Ambrose did not know the later term "transubstantiation," his concept of the nature of the sacraments came very close to that of the Middle Ages. Bread and wine, he says, are changed, or transmuted, by the words of consecration into the flesh (or body) and blood of Christ. He writes: "But if the blessing of a man [namely, Elisha, 2 Kings 6:5-7] had such power as to change [*convertere*] nature, what are we to say of that divine consecration where the very words of the Lord and Savior operate? For that sacrament which you receive is made what it is by the word of Christ."[3] While here, too, many ideas about the process of change, which were later supplied by Scholasticism, are missing, yet the fact of change as such is given expression by Ambrose.

The medieval doctrine of the sacraments was influenced by this realism of Ambrose. But Augustine, too, had great influence on the doctrine of the sacraments, an influence which extended even beyond the Middle Ages to the sacramental teaching of the Reformation. Augustine differs from Ambrose not only in the emphases he places in the concept of the Lord's Supper, but in the fact that he was the first theologian to give serious thought to the nature of the sacraments. Without Augustine's work on the sacraments, the whole medieval teaching concerning the sacraments would be wholly unintelligible. In this respect, too, the Middle Ages, as well as the church in general, are indebted to Augustine for basic impulses.

Word and Sacrament in Augustine

Augustine still held to the broad concept of sacrament which was prevalent throughout the ancient church. Not only could he designate certain rites, such as the various exorcisms which preceded baptism, as sacraments, but upon occasion he even called

[3] Ambrose, *On the Mysteries,* chap. 9, sec. 52. *NPNF*[2] 10, 324.

the great events of the church year sacraments.

In spite of this inclusive terminology, Augustine was the first to define precisely what a sacrament is. The definition reads: "The word is added to the element, and there results the Sacrament, as if itself also a kind of visible word."[4] Word and element thus necessarily belong to the sacrament. The accent in this case lies upon the word. This is already apparent in the fact that for him the sacrament is a "visible word." It is especially evident, however, in the following observation: "Take away the word, and the water is neither more nor less than water."[5]

In speaking of the sacraments Augustine also differentiates between sign and thing signified. Over against the realism of the older theologians, Augustine sees a certain distance between the sacrament as such and the gift which it is meant to communicate. Basically the sacraments point toward the invisible grace of which they are signs, and they are to be honored because of the grace which is invisible presently in them. Upon occasion Augustine expressed himself more in line with Ambrose's realistic view of the sacraments. But his actual understanding was that the sacraments are signs.

A third basic feature of the Augustinian teaching on the sacraments is of considerable importance for the concept of the church as well: Augustine differentiates clearly between the mere use of the sacraments and their efficacy. The administration of the sacraments by the various heretical and schismatic groups made it a burning question for the church how these sacraments were to be regarded. The problem became acute when someone who had been baptized in another "communion" joined the Catholic church. Was his baptism, if performed in the name of the triune God, to be recognized, or was he to be baptized again, his first baptism being considered invalid. Augustine did not doubt that heretics and schismatics (he had reference here especially to the Donatists) really possess the sacraments and administer them validly. He would only insist that sacraments which are administered by schismatics and heretics do not have the "effect of a sacrament," since their churches are

[4] Augustine, *Homilies on the Gospel of John,* tractate 80, sec. 3. *NPNF*[1] 7, 344.

[5] *Ibid.*

separated from the communion of the Holy Spirit and of love. Only when a heretic, or schismatic, becomes a member of the Catholic church does the sacrament have an effect.

Through these careful distinctions Augustine not only precisely defined the sacraments in a way that has been basic for almost all subsequent theology. In addition, his third distinction in particular made it possible for him to restrict materially the rather pronounced magical element which the concept of the sacrament had previously possessed. The emphasis was now no longer merely upon the prescribed procedure in the administration of the sacrament, but also upon the inner acceptance of the grace offered in the sacrament. Augustine succeeded in expressing this more clearly than the older theology. This insight enabled him to develop further the doctrine of baptism. This does not mean that Augustine preached the Reformation understanding of baptism. To him it was not faith, but sanctification, which signified the right use of baptism. Yet it was a sanctification which could take place in considerable independence of the act of baptism. Thus the connection between the sacrament of baptism and the Christian life, which is present in Augustine's thought in a rudimentary way, is again dissipated.

The significance of Augustine's basic theology of the sacraments is seen clearly in his conception of the Lord's Supper. Here we find the most important points of contact between his theology and later theology.

It is self-evident, first of all, that the words of institution are to Augustine the "word" in his own definition of sacrament, while bread and wine are "elements." Above all, however, there is evident in Augustine's doctrine of the Lord's Supper his symbolic understanding of the sacraments. Frequently he says that bread is only a "sign" of the body of Christ. "The Lord did not hesitate to say, 'This is my body,' when he gave a sign [*signum*] of his body."[6] Sometimes he emphasizes that either the bread or the wine is a *figura* (image) of the body or the blood of Christ.[7]

In speaking of the Lord's Supper, Augustine differentiates be-

[6] Augustine, *Contra Adimantum Manichaei discipulum,* Bk. I, chap. 12, sec. 3. *MPL* 42, col. 144.

[7] Augustine, *Expositions on the Book of Psalms,* Psalm 3, sec. 1. *NPNF*[1] 8, 5.

tween the mere sacrament and its effect: ". . . the sacrament is one thing, the virtue of the sacrament another."[8] In this case the power of the sacrament is a twofold one. It bears, first, upon a person's remaining in Christ, and, second, on his connection with the church. On this basis Augustine's concept of the Lord's Supper becomes almost a purely symbolical one. "All this," he says, "that the Lord spoke concerning His flesh and blood;–and in the grace of that distribution He promised us eternal life, and that He meant those that eat His flesh and drink His blood to be understood, from the fact of their abiding in Him and He in them; . . . let all this, then, avail us to this end, most beloved, that we eat not the flesh and blood of Christ merely in the sacrament, as many evil men do, but that we eat and drink to the participation of the Spirit, that we abide as members in the Lord's body, to be quickened by His Spirit, and that we be not offended, even if many do now with us eat and drink the sacraments in a temporal manner, who shall in the end have eternal torments."[9] Sometimes the words of Augustine create the impression that the spiritual eating of the sacraments can be basically independent of the physical reception of the Lord's Supper. The Lord's Supper is actually a symbol of the one body of Christ, and whoever belongs to the body of Christ eats his body and blood.

At this point Augustine makes an important distinction (and here, too, later theology followed him) between baptism and the Lord's Supper. On the basis of the distinction mentioned above between the mere use of the sacrament and its effect, Augustine could say that the effect of baptism performed by a heretic is static until he joins the Catholic church. For the lasting effect which baptism has upon man Augustine coined the word "character." Baptism is an indelible seal by which a person is marked as belonging to Christ. According to Augustine ordination, too, conveys such a character. For that reason there can be no question of repeating baptism and ordination. Later theology took over this concept of Augustine, modifying it only by speaking of "indelible character" (*character indelebilis*), which baptism was thought to impart. In the thinking of Augustine the Lord's Sup-

[8] Augustine, *Homilies on the Gospel of St. John,* tractate 26, sec. 11. *NPNF*[1] 7, 171.

[9] *Ibid.,* tractate 27, sec. 11. *NPNF*[1] 7, 177-178.

per, on the other hand, does not bestow such a character, which could lie dormant for a season. The heretic or schismatic eats to his own condemnation. For Augustine this was a necessary conclusion, since for him the gift of the Lord's Supper and remaining in communion with the church are equivalent. That is, it is necessary to be a member of the body of Christ if the gift of communion with Christ and with the church is to be received in the Lord's Supper.

Alongside these ideas, however, Augustine could frequently give expression to others which move more definitely within the framework of sacramental realism. Thus he can say, for instance, that converted Jews drink the same blood they once spilled; or he may simply speak of eating and drinking the body and blood of Christ. Most such passages, however, are uttered either under the influence of liturgical language, or they have reference to John 6:51-58. Basically Augustine never gave up his symbolical understanding of the Lord's Supper. The relation of realism and symbolism in his thinking is especially evident in the statement he makes in a letter in which symbolism is again dominant. He writes, "If the sacraments had not some points of real resemblance to the things of which they are the sacraments [i.e., signs], they would not be sacraments at all. In most cases, moreover, they do in virtue of this likeness bear the names of the realities which they resemble." It is interesting to note his application: "As, therefore, in a certain manner the sacrament of Christ's body is Christ's body, and the sacrament of Christ's blood is Christ's blood, in the same manner the sacrament of faith is faith."[10]

That Augustine could, on the one hand, cling to the traditional terminology and, on the other, maintain his own understanding is apparent, finally, in his interpretation of the idea that the Lord's Supper is an offering. This idea was not unknown to Augustine. He himself used it often, although he always gave it his own interpretation. From the very beginning, however, Augustine tries to avoid the impression that the Lord's Supper can be a repetition of the sacrifice of Jesus Christ made once upon the cross. It is true that the church makes a sacrifice, but its sacrifice has the purpose of maintaining the memory of the one sacrifice of Christ. The church is to perpetuate the memory

[10] Augustine, *NPNF*[1] 1, 410, letter 98, sec. 9.

of a sacrifice already made. Here as elsewhere Augustine attempts to broaden traditional concepts, in this case the idea of sacrifice. He likes to emphasize that the church offers itself to God, and that it does so through its high priest, Christ. This self-offering takes place as the church spends itself in a life of deeds, in the consummation of the church's communion of love. Thus again, Augustine's idea of sacrifice, very much like his general understanding of the sacraments, is placed into a context which is broad enough to reach beyond the administration of the sacrament and to embrace the entire Christian life.

Accordingly, Augustine's theology of the sacraments is filled with tensions, which for him, however, never become contradictions, but always form a living whole. Yet, the element in Augustine's understanding of the sacraments that became especially influential in history was his symbolism, which constituted a counterpoise to the realism of Ambrose.

Eucharistic Controversies during the Middle Ages

The differences in the understanding of the Lord's Supper which obtained between Ambrose and Augustine had an influence upon liturgy. The older Gallic and Spanish liturgies betray the influence of Ambrose. In them one encounters concepts which clearly express the idea of transmutation, or change of the elements, as the result of the consecration of the priests. In the Roman liturgy, on the other hand, Augustinian influence is evident. This comes to the fore especially in the use of such words as "to consecrate" or "to dedicate" or "to bless," which are more restrained than the realistic terms of Ambrose. Toward the end of the eighth century the Roman liturgy penetrated the empire of the Franks. The result was a more pronounced consciousness of the tensions between the ideas of Ambrose and Augustine. This created the task of developing the doctrine of the Lord's Supper in one direction or another.

For the moment, then, the situation was this, that in theology the symbolical view of Augustine preponderated, while in the realm of ecclesiastical practice the realism of Ambrose was dominant. The notion of sacrifice, especially, was apt to strengthen realism. It had been part of the understanding of the Lord's Supper for a long time. Even Augustine had accepted it and, in spite of his symbolical interpretation, occasionally gave it decided emphasis. It shows itself especially in the fact that Augustine shared the opinion, which was prevalent before his day, that the sacrifice of the altar can and should be offered also for the dead. If this sacrifice is made for Christians who have died, it means that it is a thankoffering for those who lived very good lives, and a propitiatory offering for those who lived lives not so very bad; for the latter it provides some alleviation of their condition. To the very bad the sacrifice offers no help, to be sure, though their loved ones may gain consolation from it.[11] Thus the proponents of the idea of sacrifice could find a point of contact with their view even in Augustine. It was the piety of the people, frequently accompanied by a crude faith in miracles, which led to an intensification of realism. In the Carolingian age it had become generally accepted that bread and wine are somehow changed into the body and blood of Christ as the result of the priestly consecration.

The first controversy concerning the Lord's Supper ensued as a result of a book by Paschasius Radbertus (*ca.* 790-856 or 859), a monk of the convent of Corbie in France. About 843 Radbertus had become abbot of his convent. A whole series of theological works had brought him prominence. Upon the request of his abbot he had written a treatise on the Lord's Supper (*ca.* 831 to 833), which he entitled *Concerning the Body and Blood of the Lord.* It was the first extensive treatment of the Lord's Supper which had appeared. In itself the treatise does not contain any original thoughts. Most of what Radbertus says could have been said earlier, either in the same or in a similar way. The new element consists of his attempt to combine Augustine's symbolical understanding of the Lord's Supper with the widely prevalent view that a change occurred in the elements. It is noteworthy, of course, that Radbertus should even set himself the task of thoroughly reworking the traditional doctrine of the Lord's Supper in the first place.

Augustine's symbolical understanding of the sacraments appears to show itself in Radbertus' opinion that Christ and his flesh do not constitute a bodily meal, but a spiritual and divine repast. Like Augustine, Radbertus could say that the eating of the flesh of the Lord, and the drinking of his blood, signifies

[11] Augustine, *Enchiridion,* chap. 110. *NPNF*[1] 3, 273.

nothing else but that the Christian remains in Christ and that Christ is in him. On the other hand, only he can remain in Christ who eats his flesh and drinks his blood. In a way similar to Augustine, Radbertus also differentiates between the visible and the invisible in the sacrament.

Yet, alongside this symbolical understanding of the Lord's Supper, a realistic view is also evident in Radbertus. In the Lord's Supper the believer actually receives the body of Christ which was born of Mary, suffered upon the cross, and rose from the dead. Nor does Radbertus have reference here only to the "power of the flesh and blood" of Christ, as he specifically emphasizes, but truly to the body and blood of the Lord. Here Radbertus uses the concept of transmutation. Bread and wine are changed into the body and blood of Christ. In this process the form, the color, and the taste of the elements remain the same, but the substance is "inwardly" changed. Radbertus emphasizes that this is a miracle which is performed against the order of nature. The transmutation is an act of the Creator which takes place as a result of Christ's words of institution. The priest cannot speak these words by virtue of his own strength; but through the Son he asks the Father to perform this miracle.

But how can these two emphases be reconciled? In the first place, Radbertus emphasizes that the body of Christ cannot be perceived with the senses. Nor is it necessary that it be visibly present. Such sensible perception would not intensify the reality of his presence; moreover, the literal eating of Christ's flesh would provide an unnecessary offense. Then too, a perceivable miracle would contradict the nature of a sacrament, which always veils the actual content. Finally, Radbertus emphasizes that only believers actually eat and drink the body and blood of Christ. Receiving the Lord's Supper frees them from their daily wrongdoings, strengthens their faith, and, in fact, makes them corporeally one with Christ. From unbelievers, on the other hand, the sacrament withholds its power.

Radbertus soon found opponents in Rhabanus Maurus and Ratramnus. Rhabanus (780-856), who had long been abbot of Fulda, was made Archbishop of Mainz in 847. The most prolific writer during the days of the Carolingians, he based his eucharistic argument in the main upon the position of Augustine.

Hence he emphasized more strongly that bread and wine are symbols. The assertion of Radbertus that the bread which has been changed into the body of Christ is identical with the flesh which Christ had during the days of his flesh seemed especially obnoxious to him. Rhabanus did not deny that as a result of the consecration a change does take place, but he felt that bread and wine become Christ's body and blood "mystically" or "sacramentally."

In similar fashion Ratramnus, too, opposed Radbertus. Ratramnus (d. after 868), who was also a monk of Corbie and also defended the Augustinian theology with reference to problems such as that of predestination, now wrote a treatise with the same title as that of Radbertus: *Concerning the Body and Blood of the Lord.* In it he tries to answer two questions: first, whether or not the Lord's Supper contains a mystery which can only be perceived with the eyes of faith; and, second, whether or not the elements are identical with the body of the earthly Jesus as a result of their transmutation. The way these questions are put already indicates that Ratramnus does not place the accent upon the sacrifice of the Mass. In a way similar to that of Rhabanus, Ratramnus too denies the identity of the elements with the body of the earthly Jesus. He then asserts that in the Supper bread and wine remain what they are. It is true that he does not deny the idea of change in the sacrament, but it is a spiritual or symbolical change. It is not the body and blood of Christ which, as Radbertus thought, are hidden under the form of bread and wine, but only "Christ's spiritual body and spiritual blood." The sacrifice of the Mass is meant solely to perpetuate the memory of Christ's sacrifice upon the cross. Bread and wine are "images," that is, signs of remembrance. Accordingly, what the believer receives is, on the one hand, not merely Christ's' true body and blood, or, on the other hand, merely bread and wine. In the Supper something more exalted, more heavenly and divine is received, which can only be perceived and consumed by the believing soul. On the basis of these considerations Ratramnus could answer yes to the question whether or not the Lord's Supper contains a mystery which can be perceived only with the eyes of faith.

For the first time in the history of the church the various points of view relative to the theology of the Lord's Supper had now been precisely formulated. There was, on the one side, the realistic doctrine of transmutation, though it contained certain Augustinian ideas and, on the other, the symbolic interpretation. Central to the latter was the idea that elements are basically signs, as well as the idea of spiritual communion with Christ. The controversy between Radbertus, on the one side, and Rhabanus and Ratramnus, on the other, did not come to an end at the time. But that the various points of view had been so precisely expressed was already quite an achievement. During the controversy the two basic interpretations of the Supper which are actually possible had been thought through and clearly articulated. Even the Reformation could not go beyond the two leading motifs, namely, realism and symbolism. This does not mean, of course, that the doctrine of the Supper was not developed further, or that, indeed, it did not have to be developed further. In the course of this further development it was clear from the beginning that the future would belong to the realistic interpretation of Paschasius Radbertus. The piety of the masses was on his side.

The development of the doctrine of the Lord's Supper during the Middle Ages was furthered especially by a second controversy, which arose over the teaching of Berengar (d. 1088), one of the most famous theologians and scholars of the eleventh century. Head of the school at Tours from about 1040 on, he brought to the doctrine of the Lord's Supper a thoroughgoing application of the dialectical method, which had recently been introduced into the area of theology. Criticism was directed, above all, at Berengar himself. His critics were not concerned with this or that opinion which he espoused, but with the way he approached his task as a theologian. He created the impression that his inquisitive mind desired to penetrate even that which is not amenable to human comprehension.

Berengar's doctrine of the Lord's Supper may be called an antirealistic symbolism. He continued to maintain, to be sure, that as a result of the priest's consecration bread and wine become the body and blood of Christ. But he felt that this did not mean a change of substance, for it is impossible for a thing to lose its substance or that which is peculiar to it. If after the consecration the appearance of the elements is still the same, then their substance must also be the same. But how is it possible to rhyme the assertion that as a result of the consecration bread and wine are changed into the body and blood of Christ with the observation that the substance of the elements remains the same? In answer to this question Berengar adduces the following considerations. Through the consecration no change is wrought in the elements. Yet something new—invisible but nevertheless real—is added to the elements, namely, the whole, heavenly Christ. To be sure, Christ's body remains in heaven. It would be unworthy, Berengar thought, to try to bring down to earth, through the consecration, the body of Christ which is exalted in heaven. Such consecration, however, does add to the elements, as it were, the saving power of the death of Christ and his spiritual presence.

At least as important as the position he himself espoused was Berengar's criticism of the position of Radbertus. The opinion of his opponent seemed to Berengar to be not only contrary to reason, but it appeared to lead to the conclusion that the body of Christ is fragmented. He felt that Radbertus and his followers have only "little pieces" of Christ upon the altar, while he himself was concerned about the whole body of Christ. Lastly, Berengar saw in the view of his opponents a duplication of the flesh of Christ, since they differentiated between the heavenly and the sacramental body of the Lord.

On the other hand, Berengar's teaching led to the conclusion that the body and blood of Christ is given only to believers, since only they believe in the presence of Christ, and since the appropriation of Christ's suffering and death is possible only through faith. Strictly speaking, therefore, bread and wine are merely signs, and only in the figurative sense of being a pledge of salvation can they be called body and blood of Christ. But even in this figurative sense they are body and blood of Christ only for believers.

There was a great deal of opposition to Berengar's theology of the Lord's Supper. In spite of well-meant warnings from others, Berengar not only published his opinions, but decided to attack. Probably in the spring of 1050 he wrote a letter to Lanfranc. The latter was a monk at the convent of Bec in Normandy, which was famous for its learning. In the year 1070 he became Archbishop of Canterbury. Lanfranc had not said anything as yet against Berengar's doctrine of the Lord's Supper. It is possible, therefore, that the latter hoped to win the famous theologian, more conservative though he might be, for his cause. In his letter Berengar condemned Radbertus' doctrine of the Supper. The letter served to crystallize the opposition to Berengar. At the time the letter arrived in Bec, Lanfranc was in Rome. It was forwarded to him and reached him there, but only after various other people had read it. The result was that a considerable number of them became acquainted with Berengar's teachings. A synod convened in the same year, 1050, condemned his teachings and excommunicated him.

During the following years Berengar's doctrine of the Lord's Supper was repeatedly the subject of reconsideration. The result was that he was again condemned. Of special importance is the fact that in the year 1059 he signed a formula which was laid before him at a synod in Rome. The formula, which strongly contradicted his earlier opinion, asserted "that bread and wine which are laid upon the altar are, after the consecration, not only a sacrament, but they are also the true body and blood of our Lord Jesus Christ, and they are not merely sacramentally, but sensibly and in truth held by the hands of the priest, and thus they are broken by the faithful and masticated with their teeth."[12]

The signing of this formula obviously signified a profound humiliation for Berengar. It proved impossible for him to come to terms with the formula, and he therefore renewed his opposition later. It is not sufficient, however, to see in this formula, provocative though it might be, only the triumph of Berengar's opponents. Neither is it sufficient to note that the view which asserted the change of the elements into the body and blood of Christ now prevailed. What is important is the background for, and the actual sense of, this formula. It came from the pen of Cardinal Humbert. It was Humbert (d. 1061) who was chiefly instrumental in guiding and furthering the reformation of the Catholic church which had previously been initiated. He was not only a theologian with a keen mind but had long been, as it were, the gray eminence of the Curia. It was he who in 1054, as representative of the pope, uttered the anathema of excom-

[12] J. D. Mansi (ed.), *Sacrorum conciliorum nova et amplissima collectio* (Florence and Venice, 1758 ff.; reprinted, Graz, 1960-61), vol. 19, col. 900A.

munication against the Greek church at Constantinople. Perhaps he is also the author of the decretal of 1059 regulating the election of popes, making it independent of the influence of the German kings as well as of the parties of the Roman nobility.

As is made evident from the formula which Berengar signed in 1059, Humbert's doctrine of the Lord's Supper very decidedly supported the idea of a change in the sacramental elements. According to recent research[13] Humbert went beyond the older theology by regarding the Supper strictly in a christocentric perspective. In the Greek East, as well as in the Latin West, the older theology had taught that for the communicant grace is imparted to the elements of the Lord's Supper only upon the saving operation of the Holy Spirit. In opposition to this, Humbert declared in his discussions with eastern theologians that the Supper is nothing other than the unique body of the incarnate Son of God, and that the Holy Trinity has no other part in the sacrament but that of bringing about the presence of this body, which happens when the whole Trinity is invoked. For Humbert this position is grounded in the idea that it was only the incarnate Son of God who died for us, and that nothing but his substitutionary death is the basis for the celebration of the Lord's Supper.

Humbert's more strongly christocentric view brought about a change in the theology of the Lord's Supper. His lead was followed by Frederick of Lorraine (the later Pope Stephen IX) and by many other theologians who took part in the eucharistic controversy with the Greeks as well as with Berengar. The results of this change reached still further, however. For one thing, Humbert's view created the theological foundation for the adoration of the host apart from Communion, a practice which now became general, even though its beginnings reach back into antiquity. Furthermore, Christocentricity obviously had the most far-reaching significance for the whole of the subsequent theological treatment of the doctrine of the Lord's Supper. No matter how great may be the differences between the Reformers and the theologians of the eleventh century, Luther, Zwingli, and Calvin still adopted the christocentric interpretation of the

[13] A. Michel, "Die folgenschweren Ideen des Kardinals Humbert und ihr Einfluss auf Gregor VII," in G. B. Borino (ed.), *Studi Gregoriani,* 1 (1947), 65-92.

Lord's Supper. This they did in spite of their denial of the doctrine of transmutation.

These circumstances must be taken into consideration if the formula of 1059 is to be appreciated properly. It must also be remembered that Berengar was as slippery as an eel and that Humbert was moved to his harsh formulation partly because of this fact.

As has been mentioned, Berengar had not really accepted the formula he had signed. Toward the end of the sixties he attacked the view of his opponents once more. Lanfranc replied, and upon his reply Berengar answered in a treatise which was lost until Lessing found it in the library at Wolfenbüttel and saw to its publication. In the year 1079 another synod met at Rome, which again forced Berengar to sign a formula. This one stated that "the bread and wine, which are placed on the altar, through the mystery of the sacred prayer and the words of our Redeemer are substantially changed into the true, proper, and life-giving flesh and blood of our Lord Jesus Christ."[14] In content this formula was very similar to that of 1059, though it was somewhat milder in its wording. Although he had now, for the second time, signed a formula which was considered orthodox, it need hardly be supposed that Berengar had changed his mind. He continued to hold firmly that the body of Christ is exalted in heaven and may not be brought down every time the elements are consecrated. In 1088, however, he died in the peace of the Catholic church.

In summarizing the results of this second eucharistic controversy it should be said, first, that the notion of the change of the elements into the body and blood of Christ was now firmly established, though the concept of "transubstantiation" was still lacking. Second, the idea now prevailed that Christ was present in every host. This has a number of important consequences, among them the idea of ubiquity, or the belief that, because of his omnipotence, Christ, even in his exalted human nature, can be omnipresent wherever and whenever he wills. A further consequence is the belief that the unworthy, too, receive the body of Christ, though naturally not to their salvation. Third, theology after Radbertus accepted the view that while the appear-

[14] Denzinger, par. 355. *TCT*, par. 712. The translations from *TCT* are used with the permission of the publisher, B. Herder Book Co.

ance of the elements of the Lord's Supper is not altered as a result of the consecration, the substance is changed. Finally, the sacrificial character of the Supper was emphasized to a greater degree. The realistic tendency had now won out over the symbolical one. While the Christocentricity which has dominated the doctrine of the Supper since Humbert is to be welcomed, it also needs to be said that the idea of sacrifice and the theory of change in the sacramental elements represent a dogmatizing of doctrines which are alien to the New Testament. Nor are they consequences which necessarily follow from the affirmations of the New Testament, as do the doctrine of the Trinity and Christology.

Further Development of the Doctrine of the Sacraments

The decisions which grew out of the second eucharistic controversy established only a few basic ideas concerning the doctrine of the sacraments in general and the doctrine of the Lord's Supper in particular. There were still many points which theology had to continue to ponder and which would require dogmatic clarification.

The most important question had to do with the number of sacraments. Down into the twelfth century there was still considerable uncertainty on this point. Such an important ascetic and theologian of reform as Peter Damiani (d. 1072) counted no less than twelve sacraments: baptism, confirmation, anointing of the sick, consecration of bishops, anointing of kings, consecration of churches, confession, consecration of canonists, of monks, hermits, and nuns, and marriage. In this enumeration, the Eucharist, repentance, and certain other sacraments of the Roman Catholic church are even missing. To be sure, his summary should be understood not so much in the sense of a firm delimitation as in that of mystical contemplation. Still it is significant that monasticism is here included among the sacraments. This throws much light upon the ascetic ideal of the Middle Ages and upon the higher estimate placed on celibacy as over against marriage.

With the rise of a theology which made use of a scientific methodology, however, the problem of the number of the sacraments was progressively illuminated. In theologians like Hugo of St. Victor (d. 1141) and Peter Abelard (d. 1142), we already find a systematic treatment of the doctrine of the sacraments, though uncertainty still prevails with regard to their number. The fixing of the number of sacraments at seven, the number still accepted by the Roman church today, is found first in Peter Lombard. He was active for a long time as teacher of theology at the cathedral school of Notre Dame, until in 1159 he was elevated to the position of Bishop of Paris, only to die the following year. His *Sentences,* a theological text in four books, was basic to all subsequent theology in the Middle Ages. The work treated, in order, the doctrine of God, creation, redemption, the sacraments, and the last things. Here the seven sacraments are clearly delineated: baptism, confirmation, the Lord's Supper, repentance, extreme unction, ordination of priests, and marriage. Where and when the number of sacraments was first set at seven is a matter of dispute. Peter Lombard simply assumes it without further elucidation. There is the distinct possibility, therefore, that he took the number from someone else. To the present day the question of the origin of the number seven as applied to the sacraments has not been satisfactorily answered. Certain it is that this number soon prevailed. Only occasionally, and only for a short time, are there references in the late twelfth century to older enumerations.

Not only with regard to the number of sacraments was there progress during the twelfth century; attention was devoted also to the definition of the nature of the sacraments. It was especially Hugo of St. Victor and Peter Lombard who took over older ideas, notably those of Augustine, and reformulated them. According to Hugo the sacrament is "a corporeal or material element set before the senses without, representing by similitude and signifying by institution and containing by sanctification some invisible and spiritual grace."[15] Here it is emphasized more strongly than in Augustine that the sacrament "contains" grace, that grace is tied to the sacrament. Peter Lombard gave a shorter but very similar definition: The sacrament is a sign of God's grace and the form of invisible grace.[16] Since Peter did not include the idea of a visible element in his definition of a

[15] Hugo of St. Victor, *On the Sacraments of the Christian Faith,* trans. Roy J. Deferrari (Cambridge, Mass.: The Mediaeval Academy of America, 1951), p. 155.

[16] Peter Lombard, *Sententiarum libri quatuor,* Bk. IV, dist. 1, sec. 2, *MPL* 192, col. 839.

sacrament, he could, without difficulty, designate as sacraments such acts as repentance and marriage, in which no "element" is present. In this connection high Scholasticism, especially Thomas Aquinas (1225-1274), substituted the Aristotelian concepts of "matter" and "form" for the earlier differentiation between "element" and "Word." Matter was said to receive spatial definition only through form. Furthermore, a distinction is made between that which actually bestows grace, namely the Word, and that which is only a means toward it, namely, matter.

As to the efficacy of the sacraments, the development of high Scholasticism continued to strengthen the tendency to tie grace wholly to the sacraments. The idea that the sacraments contain grace is broadened to mean that they alone can mediate grace. Augustine's symbolical interpretation, according to which the efficacy of grace is not restricted to the administration of the sacraments, is discarded in favor of a realistic understanding of both the "change" in the elements and the efficacy of the sacraments. For Peter Lombard, the sacraments are not only signs which point to invisible grace; they are also efficacious signs of grace. "Every sign of the new covenant," he says, "accomplishes that which it signifies."[17] While many differences can be observed relative to the understanding of the sacraments among the theologians of the various schools, notably those of the Dominicans and the Franciscans, they all held that the sacraments are necessary to salvation and that they are efficacious simply because they are administered (*ex opere operato*). There are some preconditions, of course. The first is that the administrant must have the intention of doing what Christ and the church want to do, that is, he must administer the sacrament according to its institution. Second, the recipient must not be aware of being guilty of mortal sin, nor must he inwardly resist the administration of the sacrament. In the language of theology, he must not "interpose an obstacle [*obex*]." Yet, fullness of saving faith is not considered to be a precondition for the reception of the sacraments.

While theology thus continued to develop the doctrine of the sacraments in the direction indicated by the two eucharistic controversies, further doctrinal decisions were being made by councils. Only the most important may be mentioned here. The

[17] *Ibid.*, Bk. IV, dist. 22, sec. 3. *MPL* 192, col. 898 f.

doctrine of the Lord's Supper, which had long been the object of special attention, was considered at the Fourth Lateran Council of 1215 and the idea of transmutation given dogmatic status. According to the decision of this council the "body and blood [of Christ] are truly contained in the Sacrament of the Altar under the species of bread and wine, transubstantiated by the divine power—the bread into his body and the wine into his blood [namely, when the words of consecration are spoken]."[18] Here the concept of "transubstantiation," which had already appeared in the theology of the first half of the twelfth century, is used to describe the change in the elements. This term actually renders more accurately than the words used hitherto what had been the conviction of most theologians since Ambrose.

The next decision concerning the doctrine of the sacraments, and one which was very important, came in 1439 at the Council of Florence. This council met to restore the unity of East and West. The Greeks, who were sorely threatened by the Turks (Constantinople fell in the year 1453), were ready for concessions greater than those they had been prepared to make heretofore. Thus the circumstances for the removal of the schism, which had now lasted for four hundred years, seemed more propitious than before. A decree of union, which was accepted by both sides, was actually produced. However, the representatives of the Roman church, taking advantage of the difficulties of the Greeks, had forced upon them the acknowledgment of papal primacy. The Greek people objected strenuously to this requirement, and the proposed union was never consummated. Yet this council is of great significance because of its definition of the Catholic doctrine of the sacraments. It was in this council, in the *Decree for the Armenians,* that the number seven as applied to the sacraments, which had long since been accepted in theology, was officially recognized. In addition there are detailed explanations of the nature and peculiarity of each of the seven sacraments; matter, form, and effect are carefully differentiated, and it is also established who is permitted to administer the sacraments. Most of them are to be administered by the priest, while confirmation and the ordination of priests are reserved for the bishop; baptism may, in cases of necessity, be administered by laymen.

[18] Denzinger, par. 430. *TCT*, par. 659.

It was the Council of Trent (1545-1563) which gave extensive explanations concerning the sacraments, establishing at the same time a line of demarcation between its doctrine of the sacraments and that of the Reformation. Basically, however, the definitions of Trent do not, as a whole, go beyond past decisions, though new explanations are given with reference to a number of points around which controversies had raged in the meantime.

The Reformation was not able to accept all the results of the development of the doctrine of the sacraments. Still, much of that which was accomplished during the Middle Ages in the way of clarifying the doctrine of the sacraments cannot be surrendered by the major Protestant communions. For example, there is the recognition that the validity of the administration of the sacraments is not dependent upon the holiness or sinfulness of the pastor, but upon Christ's institution of the sacraments. Another example is the christocentric orientation which is evident in the eleventh-century understanding of the doctrine of the Lord's Supper and which was a presupposition for all the Reformers, though they may not have admitted this to themselves explicitly. As reinterpreted by the Reformation, this Christocentricity became the basis of a thorough rethinking of the whole doctrine of the sacraments; this new theology of the sacraments became the common property of the Reformation, irrespective of the differences between Lutherans and Reformed. Finally, the differentiation between matter and form was also taken over by the Reformation, though the term "Word" was preferred to the term "form."

There are a number of ideas, however, which the Reformation did not take over. For one thing, it gave up the idea of seven sacraments. One reason for this was the consideration that, according to the Gospel accounts, only baptism and the Lord's Supper were instituted by Jesus himself; another had to do with the Reformers' attempt to rethink the meaning of the terms "Word" and "element," an attempt which led to the conclusion that in the traditional sacraments "matter" was associated only with baptism and the Lord's Supper. Furthermore, as a result of a new biblical orientation, the idea that the sacraments "contain" grace was displaced by the idea that with the sacrament a promise is given, which consists in the word of institution. This promise, which is the chief thing in the receiving of the sacrament, cannot be claimed simply by not "interposing an obstacle." It must be claimed by faith which truly believes that this promise is meant also "for *me*." In the Reformation the objective categories of the Catholic doctrine of the sacraments were replaced by personal ones.[19]

Finally, the Reformation rejected emphatically the idea that the Lord's Supper is a sacrifice offered by the church. It is true that on this point many theologians of the late Middle Ages expressed themselves more one-sidedly and extremely than either Thomas Aquinas or more recent Roman Catholic theology, thus giving the impression that the sacrifice of Jesus Christ is actually made once more by the church. Here the Council of Trent was generally more restrained in its formulations, thus blunting some of the reproaches made by the Reformation. Still, the idea that the Lord's Supper is actually a propitiatory sacrifice was not discarded. The decrees of Trent state that the most holy sacrifice of the Mass is not only an offering of praise and thanksgiving, and not only a reminder of the offering which was made upon the cross, but, in truth, a propitiatory sacrifice through which God is reconciled and rendered gracious toward us.[20] Such a declaration endangers the uniqueness and inclusiveness of the saving significance of the sacrifice of Jesus Christ upon the cross.

[19] Luther was the first to employ such categories. See *The Babylonian Captivity of the Church* (1520), *LW* 36.

[20] "Doctrine Concerning the Sacrifice of the Mass," chap. 2; see also can. 3. *Canons and Decrees of the Council of Trent,* ed. H. J. Schroeder, O.P. (St. Louis: Herder, 1941), pp. 145-146, 149. Cf. Regin Prenter, "Das Augsburgische Bekenntnis und die römisch-katholische Messopferlehre," *Kerygma und Dogma,* 1 (1955), 42-58.

6

Justification

Distinguishing Characteristics of the Reformation Era

At the beginning of the preceding chapter we noted that only the most basic dogmatic decisions of the ancient church have become the common property of East and West, and that even the doctrine of the sacraments developed differently in East and West, with the development no longer being shared by all of Christendom. This process of splitting and fragmentation of the history of dogma was considerably accelerated during the period of the Reformation. Henceforth it is no longer possible to treat as a single entity the doctrinal development of the church as a whole. It must, rather, be portrayed separately for each of the large communions. Still, even in the modern era there are certain common features in the historical development of doctrine. Closer examination reveals that at least the questions and problems confronting the churches are often the same. The reason is that, in spite of their differences and antitheses, the various communions share the common heritage of the first centuries of the church and have been basically molded by it.

It is true that at the time of the Reformation this heritage was embroiled in conflict far worse than any in the history of the Christian church heretofore. There is hardly an important segment of Christian dogmatics about which there was no dissension between Luther and Rome, but also between Luther and Zwingli, and later between the Lutherans and Calvin. Even though Luther acknowledged and accepted the decisions resulting from the trinitarian and christological controversies, his emphases were different at many points and, as a result of his own reflections, he even contributed some entirely new perspectives. This is especially true of his Christology, which, as a result of his altercation with Zwingli, he sharpened most markedly with his so-called doctrine of ubiquity. That Luther did not simply accept without question the ancient church's doctrine of the sacraments has already been mentioned. His reduction of the number of sacraments from seven to two shows how very subject to dispute the ancient heritage was. But even with the doctrine of sin and grace Luther did not simply take up where the ancient church had left off. He embraced, of course, the decisions that came out of the Pelagian controversy. Yet his own conception of sin and grace differs in a number of details both from Augustine and from the decrees of the councils. It is not only more radical but, because of the Pauline influence upon his understanding of the nature of sin and grace, quite differently constituted.

Where, then, in relation to the history of dogma is the center of gravity for the Reformation era? Very different answers have been given to this question. From the Roman Catholic side the Reformation has frequently been presented as merely an apostasy from the true church, and hence also from inherited dogma. In that perspective Luther emerges as the one who destroyed the unity of the church and thus brought great misfortune not only upon all Christendom but also upon the West as a whole. Such an answer, however, smacks of historical dilettantism. The ideal of the one, undivided church has hardly ever been a reality. Within primitive Christianity there were already divisions. A movement such as Donatism would today be called a church or a denomination. And of course the schism between the Greek and the Latin churches, which occurred hundreds of years before Luther, must not be forgotten.

We have already mentioned that in his *History of Dogma* Adolf von Harnack answered the question under discussion by saying that the Reformation basically put an end to dogma. If dogma is defined in Harnack's sense, namely, as an inerrant doctrinal proposition, it would be difficult to find fault with his argumentation. If, on the other hand, dogmas are regarded as confessions, Harnack's judgment cannot be sustained. Even with such a definition, however, it will still not be easy to assign the Reformation its proper place in the history of dogma.

Ernst Troeltsch maintained the position that in many respects the Reformation must be regarded as medieval, insofar as it continued to believe that in religion man is confronted by an objective reality. To be sure, this reality was no longer the same as it was during the Middle Ages. Nevertheless, said Troeltsch, while the Middle Ages possessed its objective reality in its dogmas and sacraments, the Reformation had its objective reality in the Word of God and the Bible. Hence, the modern era does not begin with the Reformation. Indeed, he maintains that it would be more correct to say that the Reformation delayed for some time the dawn of the modern era.

Troeltsch's position, too, does not provide a satisfactory answer to the question of how the Reformation fits into the history of dogma. Though it is true that Luther reduced the number of objective realities confronting man, this reduction can be understood only within the context of the presuppositions that led to it. These presuppositions are nothing other than his new experience of justification and the doctrine of law and gospel, which is intimately related to that experience. It is here that we have the central theme of the age of the Reformation with respect to the history of dogma. The many other problems that were reconsidered in the Reformation era must be seen within the perspective provided by this theme. It must also provide the basis for answering the question whether or not and in what sense the Reformation constitutes the beginning of the modern era. The answer given will certainly vary, depending upon one's attitude toward the central theme of the age of Reformation. If this theme is regarded as merely another form of objectification, similar to those with which Troeltsch charged the Middle Ages, one kind of answer will be given; if, on the other hand, it is regarded as embodying the whole of the Christian faith, the answer will be different.

If the doctrine of justification is the central theme of the Reformation era, we see again what we have already frequently observed, namely, that in the history of dogma the center of gravity shifts constantly, but that with each new shift the whole of the Christian faith is debated once again. In the course of history it apparently happens again and again that the church, or at least a good part of it, is orthodox with regard to doctrinal decisions made in the past but is daunted by newly emerging problems. If it is apparent anywhere it is apparent in the history of the Reformation that the affirmations of the Christian faith are not a *depositum fidei* entrusted to the church, but that in each new instance they demand a total commitment.

It is not enough, therefore, to see in the Reformation only a reaction against certain abuses and certain instances of decadence in the church of the later Middle Ages. No matter how bad the corruption at the court of the Renaissance popes, and no matter how ghastly the deception of men through the multiplication of indulgences, relics, and the like, these things in themselves would not have led to the Reformation. As far as the general decadence is concerned, it had many causes that may be disregarded here. It is important to note in this context, however, that superstition, the system of indulgences, pilgrimages, and the rest are in the last analysis the result of a deficiency in the theology of Scholasticism and of the entire medieval church. The church was unable to satisfy man's desire for genuine assurance of salvation. The church taught that the certainty of salvation results only from a special revelation imparted by God to the individual. But even to seek such a special revelation from God was regarded as improper. The average Christian could hope for God's gracious acceptance if he regularly received the sacraments of the Catholic church and committed no mortal sin. No provision was made, however, either in the church's teaching or in its practice, for the person who was not satisfied with being an ecclesiastically approved, "average" Christian and, instead, took seriously God's demand in all its radicality. According to Catholic teaching then and now, man's justification depends in part on a righteousness to be found in man, and for this righteousness works are of great significance. There is no doubt that Thomas Aquinas had a great deal more to say about the question of the certainty of salvation than was known and taught in late medieval and Tridentine Catholicism. We shall have more to say about this later. In Luther's day, however, a man who was troubled by his sinfulness was simply told that he should set his hope on God. Certainty of salvation was unknown, and to long for such would have been regarded as presumptuous. The aim was to establish a balance between fear and hope.

Man before God

Though many men during the fifteenth and sixteenth centuries had a profound desire for the certainty of salvation, there was none who sought God's grace as earnestly as did Martin Luther. He took literally the church's demand that before confession he must search his heart and then bring forth an act of repentance commensurate with the sin involved. To say this differently, even during his early years as a monk Luther did not see man in the state in which he is acceptable in the eyes of an average priest, but in the condition in which he stands before God. As a result he was caught up in severe trials. Whenever Luther tried to feel real repentance, he always found that he did not shun sin as such, solely for God's sake, but merely because of its consequences, or out of self-interest. True repentance, so he had been taught, includes love for God; in fact, this love is the precondition of such repentance. But how can man generate love for God in himself? Can love be produced under the compulsion of the will? Luther felt that, while it was possible for him to fear God, he did not succeed in loving him for his own sake. Selfishness intruded ever and again into the inmost desires of the heart. Every human deed, he found, even every motion of man's inner life, is accompanied by self-will and, therefore, immediately loses its worth before God. This meant, however, that Luther could not meet the preconditions which, according to Catholic doctrine, are required if one is to receive absolution. The result was that his struggles became ever more severe, culminating in the question: "How can I get a gracious God?" [*Wie kriege ich einen gnädigen Gott?*]

Luther's inner difficulties were further intensified when his theological studies directed his attention to the doctrine of predestination. Having concluded, on the basis of a radical self-examination, that he could not be in a state of grace before God, he could come to no other conclusion but that he must be damned. His fellow monks did not have the same difficulties as he; his confessors did not understand him, and felt that he was overly scrupulous. In Luther, however, the fear of being damned led to the desire that God might not exist. Within him there grew up a hatred against this God who expects the impossible of man, and who ties his grace to the condition of accomplishing the impossible. Occamistic theology, in which Luther had been instructed at Erfurt, taught that if man does what he can God will not withhold his grace from him. This proposition, however, did not satisfy Luther either theologically or practically. He felt that theologically it detracted from the holy majesty of God, since the criterion by which man is judged must be in God, not man. On the practical level it proved impossible for Luther "to do what he could."

The Bible, too, which Luther knew as have few men in the history of the church offered him little help at first. Wherever in the New Testament he found the word "righteousness" he interpreted it as a judging righteousness. It was in this sense that Luther interpreted also Romans 1:17 at first: "For in it [the Gospel] the righteousness of God is revealed through faith for faith." Luther then made the discovery—probably in the fall of 1514 while he was working on the interpretation of Psalm 71:2 ("In thy righteousness deliver me")—that the righteousness here meant is not that which God himself possesses, but that which he bestows upon others. Luther himself later said about this discovery, "There I began to understand that the righteousness of God is that by which the righteous lives by a gift of God, namely by faith. And this is the meaning: the righteousness of God is revealed by the gospel, namely, the passive righteousness with which merciful God justifies us by faith, as it is written, 'He who through faith is righteous shall live.' Here I felt that I was altogether born again and had entered paradise itself through open gates. There a totally other face of the entire Scripture showed itself to me. Thereupon I ran through the Scriptures from memory. I also found in other terms an analogy, as, the work of God, that is, what God does in us, the power of God, with which he makes us strong, the wisdom of God, with which he makes us wise, the strength of God, the salvation of God, the glory of God."[1]

This righteousness, then, is pure gift, independent of any precondition that must be fulfilled by man. According to the apostle Paul (Rom. 4:5), it is God who justifies godless man. It is not man who seeks God; but it is God who in sheer grace comes to man. Toward God man can only be passive. Before Him he cannot point to any merits; he can do nothing more than to permit himself to be a recipient. In Christ, God is not Judge, but Father. Man has nothing to do but gratefully to receive God's gift. Precisely this is faith. To have faith means

[1] Luther, *Preface to the Complete Edition of Luther's Latin Writings* (1545), *LW* 34, 337.

not to trust in our own works, but humbly and gratefully to take the hand of God which reaches out to us. It means to trust and love God as a child its father. Such trust man can gain only if God graciously turns toward him in Christ.

It is a common misunderstanding to say that, while Luther set aside works as a precondition for receiving forgiveness of sins, he put faith in the place occupied by merits in Roman Catholic doctrine. In that case faith would be the precondition of justification and would thus still be a work undertaken by man. If Luther had held this opinion he would have been substituting a cheap, presumably evangelical grace for the costly Catholic grace. For him faith is not the condition of justification, however, but its realization, and even this realization, namely, faith, is the gift of God. Nor is Luther's concern here with a psychological judgment, but with a theological one. From the psychological point of view faith undoubtedly falls within the sphere of man's psychic life, and consists of certain acts which can be described in psychological terms. Yet, seen theologically, faith is still God's work. In his explanation of the third article of the creed, in the *Small Catechism*, Luther writes: "I believe that by my own reason or strength I cannot believe in Jesus Christ, my Lord, or come to him. But the Holy Spirit has called me through the Gospel, enlightened me with his gifts, and sanctified and preserved me in true faith." Luther knew from his own experience that such faith cannot be gained through one's own decisions—one's eyes must first be opened to it.

But does this conception of justification not leave man in a state of passivity? How is it possible to base a Christian ethic upon Luther's understanding of justification? In the sixteenth century Catholics repeatedly raised this question with reference to Luther's doctrine of justification, and in the literature discussing Protestant-Catholic differences it is still found today. Actually this objection rests upon a misunderstanding of the Lutheran doctrine of justification. Luther nowhere developed his ethical concept as briefly and strikingly as in his tract *The Freedom of a Christian* (1520). Here he set up two acutely formulated theses:

"A Christian is a perfectly free lord of all, subject to none.

"A Christian is a perfectly dutiful servant of all, subject to all."[2]

[2] Luther, *The Freedom of a Christian, LW* 31, 344.

Luther explains this paradox by saying that every man has a dual nature: according to his soul or inner man, his is a spiritual nature, but according to his old and external man, his is a corporeal nature. In the light of Holy Scripture these are as much opposed to each other as are freedom and servitude.

As far as his spiritual nature is concerned Luther holds that it is not works but faith alone which makes man pious, free, and blessed. "One thing and only one thing, is necessary for Christian life, righteousness, and freedom. That one thing is the most holy Word of God, the gospel of Christ. . . . Let us consider it certain and firmly established that the soul can do without anything except the Word of God and that where the Word of God is missing there is no help at all for the soul. If it has the Word of God it is rich and lacks nothing since it is the Word of life, truth, light, peace, righteousness, salvation, joy, liberty, wisdom, power, grace, glory, and every incalculable blessing."[3] When man stands before God there is no room for accomplishment, but only for faith and trust.

Man is not only spiritual, however, but also corporeal. If he were entirely spiritual no further efforts would be required of him. As long as man remains on earth, however, the new righteousness, which has been imputed to him fully, according to his spiritual nature, is never present in final form, but always in an incipient and incomplete state. "Here the works begin," writes Luther, "here a man cannot enjoy leisure; here he must indeed take care to discipline his body by fastings, watchings, labors, and other reasonable discipline and to subject it to the Spirit so that it will obey and conform to the inner man and faith and not revolt against faith and hinder the inner man, as it is the nature of the body to do if it is not held in check."[4] These works are not to be done with the idea that through them man becomes righteous and pious in God's sight. Rather, they are to be done out of love, freely and graciously. Good and pious works never make a good and pious man, but a good and pious man does good and pious works. For his relation to his fellows this means, however, that a Christian, precisely because of his freedom, must make himself the servant of all.

Thus Luther does not base his ethic merely upon an appeal

[3] *Ibid.*, p. 345.

[4] *Ibid.*, pp. 358-359.

to man. It is intimately connected with his understanding of justification and its spiritual significance. Within this perspective Luther developed an entirely new concept of vocation. "Vocation" to him is no longer the call to the monastic life, an estate higher than that of life in the world. It is now an effort expended for the benefit of mankind in general. The modern concept of vocation goes back to Luther.

Luther's Reformation discovery in itself had to do only with God's righteousness and the justification of man. But actually it contained the makings of a comprehensive new theology. During the years after 1514 Luther continued to draw from this basic insight inferences which extended almost to all areas of theology and of ecclesiology. The doctrine of the church was reshaped, and in the process the emphasis was placed upon the preaching and right hearing of the gospel. In the sacraments Luther could no longer see a new quality which is objectively infused into man and acquired by everyone who does not "interpose an obstacle"—a quality which was supposed to enable man to live a life better and more acceptable to God as well as to contribute toward his own justification (in the sense of making him righteous). Thus, with respect to the sacraments also, Luther's concern was the divine promise, to be claimed in faith. Here, too, personal categories took the place of objective ones. Even the hierarchical system of Catholicism and the concept of ecclesiastical law had to fall, though in practice Luther at first meant to proceed so as to preserve as much as possible.

From the point of view of the history of dogma, however, one thing was to gain special importance, namely the Reformation's new understanding of confession.

The Twofold Nature of Confession

It is obvious that the church has always known itself to be entrusted with the task of confessing. St. Augustine gave profound expression to the subject in his *Confessions*. And yet, in Luther confessing assumed a new character. The reason is that for him confession, too, is intimately connected with his new Reformation insight. St. Augustine's *Confessions* had the twofold purpose of confessing sins as well as the praise of God. As he indicates, he tells others of his own life in order "that I and all who read them [his *Confessions*] may understand what depths there are from which we are to cry unto thee. For what is more surely heard in thy ear than a confessing heart and a faithful life?"[5] This understanding of confession was considerably deepened in Luther as a result of his experience of anguish [*Anfechtungserfahrung*] and his Reformation discovery.

In his first series of lectures on the Psalms, Luther had already said that to be pious does not mean insisting upon one's own righteousness, nor does it mean to justify oneself. It does mean subjecting oneself to God's righteousness, taking upon oneself the task of confession: in principle, accusing oneself, judging oneself, acknowledging that God is right after all.[6] Here the confession of one's own sinfulness is as radical as possible. Only he who knows and confesses his own nothingness and unworthiness will be justified. For that reason the confession of one's own sinfulness is indissolubly connected with justification. Insofar as man confesses himself to be wholly God's debtor he acknowledges that God is right in his judgments. This confession, however, is at the same time the true praise of God. "We cannot praise God better than by confessing our sins."[7] Thus confession of sin and confession in praise of God are only two sides of the same thing. In his lectures on the Epistle to the Romans, Luther says, "For confession is the principal work of faith: Man denies himself and confesses God and he does this to such an extent that he will deny even his life and everything else before affirming himself. For by confessing God and denying himself, he dies. And how can he better deny himself than by dying in order to confess God? For then he forsakes himself in order that God and the confession to him may stand."[8]

This confession, however, is not made only before God. The Christian addresses his confession also to his fellow men. In the preface to the 1522 edition of Luther's translation of the New Testament there are these magnificent words: "Truly, if faith is there, he [the believer] cannot hold back; he proves himself, breaks out into good works, confesses and teaches this gospel before the people, and stakes his life on it. Everything that he

[5] Augustine, *Confessions*, Bk. II, chap. 3, sec. 5, *LCC* 7, 52.

[6] Luther, *Dictata super Psalterium* (1513-1516), *WA* 3, 26, ll. 22-25.

[7] Luther, *ibid.*, *WA* 3, 378, ll. 24 f.

[8] Luther, *Lectures on the Epistle to the Romans* (1515-1516), *LCC* 15, 294.

lives and does is directed to his neighbor's profit, in order to help him—not only to the attainment of this grace, but also in body, property, and honor. Seeing that Christ has done this for him, he thus follows Christ's example. . . . For where works and love do not break forth, there faith is not right, the gospel does not yet take hold, and Christ is not rightly known."[9]

In view of all this, it is only natural that Luther and the other Reformers found the courage and the strength to formulate new confessions. These new confessions were not originally called forth by certain external circumstances, as can be said of the *Augsburg Confession.* They developed out of the urge to express the faith in a new way. The first new confession, which was formulated by Luther, is found at the end of his tract *Confession Concerning Christ's Supper* (1528). This treatise was intended by Luther to be his final statement in the eucharistic controversy with Zwingli. At the end Luther formulates his faith, to which he expects to cling to his death, and he does so in order that everyone might have a clear idea of what he believed. He discusses, in order, faith in God the Father, in the Trinity, in Jesus Christ, in the Holy Spirit, and in the Christian church. Thereafter he takes up a series of individual questions such as indulgences, prayers for the dead, the invocation of saints, the Mass, and others. At the end comes his confession concerning the resurrection of the dead. The arrangement is such that upon the explanation of the basic articles of faith there follows the confrontation with Rome concerning the various abuses of the Roman church in doctrine and practice, and, finally, a discussion of eschatology. The confrontation with Rome does not, however, come only in the middle section of the confession. Luther has, in fact, already dealt with various disputed questions in the first articles. This is most clearly apparent in the second section, which deals with Christ.

In this section Luther takes up, first of all, the ancient church's two-nature doctrine, which he expresses in his own words. But he is not content merely to expound the christological dogma of Chalcedon. Rather, it is characteristic of this section that the entire doctrine of redemption is subsumed under Christology. He writes: "I believe also that this Son of God and of Mary, our Lord Jesus Christ, suffered for us poor sinners, was crucified,

[9] Luther, *Preface to the New Testament* (1546, 1522), *LW* 35, 361.

dead, and buried, in order that he might redeem us from sin, death, and the eternal wrath of God by his innocent blood."[10] In the same section Luther also condemns Pelagius' doctrine of free will, as well as the neo-Pelagians, who see in sin only a defect or an error. As if that were not enough, Luther includes a rejection of religious orders and monasteries, because the monks believe they can be justified before God if they observe the evangelical counsels of the Roman church. Luther admits, to be sure, that there have also been saints in the monasteries who did not trust in their works but in God's grace. In this connection he says that the only holy orders and true institutions which God himself appointed are the office of the priesthood, the estate of matrimony, and the civil government (or the secular vocations). He who lives in these estates does works that are altogether holy.

In his other confessions Luther tied Christology and soteriology together in a similar way. This is true, for instance, of his two catechisms, but especially of his *Smalcald Articles* of 1537. There he states "that Jesus Christ, our God and Lord, 'was put to death for our trespasses and raised again for our justification' (Rom. 4:25). . . . Inasmuch as this must be believed and cannot be obtained or apprehended by any work, law or merit, it is clear and certain that such faith alone justifies us. . . . Nothing in this article can be given up or compromised, even if heaven and earth and things temporal should be destroyed. . . . On this article rests all that we teach and practice against the pope, the devil, and the world. Therefore, we must be quite certain and have no doubts about it. Otherwise all is lost, and the pope, the devil, and all our adversaries will gain the victory."[11]

It is evident from these excerpts that Luther readily acknowledged the dogmas of the ancient church and made them his own. A basic critique of the doctrinal decisions of the ancient church was wholly foreign to his outlook. Only where his study of Scripture had led him to other conclusions did he attack such doctrines. In his day, however, this procedure would hardly touch the defined dogmas. Luther accepted the decisions of the councils in the trinitarian and christological controversies, as well as those which had to do with the Pelagian controversy, even

[10] Luther, *Confession Concerning Christ's Supper* (1528), *LW* 37, 362.
[11] *Smalcald Articles* (1537), II, 1, *BC*, p. 292.

though at certain points he sharpened the emphasis. Of course, Luther rejected the doctrine of transubstantiation, which had been given dogmatic status at the Fourth Lateran Council. But his criticism was directed not so much against the concept of change as such, as it was against a certain rationalism implicit in the fact that the dogma attempts to give a binding explanation of the mystery of the presence of Christ in the sacrament. In the last analysis this was really the only dogma which Luther attacked. One could argue about how much doctrinal weight was officially attached to certain bulls and decisions of popes concerning such matters as indulgences. Surely Luther was not simply wrong when in 1517 he insisted that in reference to the doctrine of indulgences nothing had been settled and that hence one might dispute about it openly. A dogma concerning the papacy did not yet exist, neither had anything been defined in connection with Mariology. Therefore, Luther could rightfully claim that he and his party truly represented the ancient church, and that they adhered to the doctrine of that church.

Of course Luther criticized many decisions of the ancient church. Even the decisions of councils were not spared his criticism. At the Leipzig disputation in 1519 he attacked openly the decision of the Council of Constance regarding John Huss. Still, it is worth noting that, generally, Luther accepted the dogmatic decisions of the ancient church. It must also be remembered that the theory concerning the infallibility of councils was still relatively new. In the form in which this theory was used against Luther by Catholic theologians, it had been unknown to the ancient church as a whole, and had really come into being only during the period of high Scholasticism. It is true that St. Augustine believed in the infallibility of the church, but he had drawn from this belief no inferences with respect to canon law. Also in Vincent of Lérins, who was the first to think through all aspects of the concept of tradition, one finds nothing as yet which could be regarded as similar to the late medieval theory of the authority of councils. Hence Luther could lay great emphasis upon the ecclesiastical continuity represented in the evangelical party.

Two limitations must of course be noted here. Though Luther fully acknowledged the authority of the conciliar decisions of the ancient church, he did not view them uncritically. He finds the doctrine of the Trinity clearly expressed in Scripture. Yet, he has an aversion to the concept of "threefoldness," because in deity there is the highest unity. Still, Luther holds to the idea that this unity is at the same time the threeness of differentiated persons. Luther even coined a new word in this connection when he says, "Call it a triplicity [*Gedritts*], I cannot give it a name."[12] The concept of "person," too, seemed questionable to him. Finally, Luther had some misgivings even about St. Augustine's interpretation of the word "person" in relational terms, although he fully appreciated the legitimate intent of this interpretation.

Even more important is the second limitation. It is not that Luther accepted the authority of the conciliar decisions of the ancient church simply in order to add to them a new doctrine of justification. On the contrary, he saw the old decisions in the light of his Reformation discovery and he made them his own from that point of view. For instance, Luther found his own understanding of salvation expressed in the Christology of the ancient church, i.e., it was easily possible to read this into the old dogma, and rightly so. In Luther, Christology and soteriology are intimately connected with each other, as they are in Athanasius, or Cyril of Alexandria, except that Luther makes the connection much more explicit. Christology is realized in the doctrine of justification, and the doctrine of justification is nothing else but a summary of Christology in soteriological perspective.

Controversy concerning the Lord's Supper

Confession, which in Luther had regained a place of primary importance, led not only to new confessional formulations which had meaning for himself, but to certain doctrinal demarcations setting his position off from other points of view. Even within the various streams of the Reformation movement, decisions and divisions were inevitable. In one such demarcation—against the so-called enthusiasts—Luther had been engaged ever since the early 1520's. Of special importance for the history of dogma, however, was the controversy over the Lord's Supper, for here various segments of previously established doctrine, as regards both Christology and the sacraments, were reconsidered. In the

[12] Luther, *Predigten des Jahres 1538, WA* 46, 436, ll. 7-12.

main, the controversy involved Luther and Zwingli. To discuss it the basic positions of the two main contestants must first be sketched.

Luther's doctrine of the Lord's Supper underwent several changes, the significance of which is variously assessed by scholars. It may be said that, even today, the differences in the understanding of the Lord's Supper which are found within the Lutheran church derive in no small part from the various stages which Luther's doctrine of the Lord's Supper passed through. In Germany, for instance, the various stances which Lutherans have taken in recent discussions of the Lord's Supper, or the positions they have adopted toward the so-called *Arnoldshain Theses* (1957) on the Supper, can at least partially be explained on this basis.

In his early sermons (1519) Luther made a threefold distinction in his doctrine of the sacraments. He spoke of the sacrament or sign, of the meaning of the sacrament, and of faith. This is still based upon the Scholastic distinction between the sacrament as such and the "matter" in which it consists, though it is noteworthy that Luther, in effect, includes faith in the definition of the sacraments, since faith brings to the fore the inner meaning of the external gift and thus represents the connecting link between the sacrament and its meaning. In the year 1520 Luther first began to emphasize the centrality of the words of institution for the interpretation of the Lord's Supper. This is most noticeable in his treatise *The Babylonian Captivity of the Church* (1520). Here he understands the Lord's Supper primarily as divine promise, which the Christian must accept in faith. God deals with man in no other way but through the word of his promise. Hence no more and no less is required of man than faith. It is true that Luther distinguishes between two entities in the divine promise, namely, *verbum* and *signum,* the promising word and the accompanying sign. But his interest was wholly concentrated upon the word, so that it is possible for Luther to assert pointedly that, if necessary, man could appropriate the word even without the sign. He admitted subsequently that at this time he flirted with the symbolic understanding of the words of institution.

The third stage in the development of Luther's doctrine of the Lord's Supper begins around 1524. Even in 1523 he had said upon one occasion that the word "brings with it everything of which it speaks, namely, Christ with his flesh and blood and everything that he is and has."[13] The idea of the real presence now gained in importance for him. While he certainly had not denied the real presence before, it had been pushed entirely into the background. Though the idea of the forgiveness of sins retained its centrality in his thought, Luther at times insisted almost exclusively upon the "is": "This *is* my body." This intensified emphasis upon the "is" is to be traced to the fact that certain theologians were denying the bodily presence of Christ in the sacrament. In his sermon on *The Sacrament of the Body and Blood of Christ—Against the Fanatics* (1526) Luther differentiates between the *objectum fidei*, meaning the work or thing which one believes or to which one is to adhere, and faith, meaning the right use of the sacrament. Then he says, "Up to now I have not preached very much about the first part. But because the first part is now being assailed by many . . . the times demand that I say something on this subject also."[14] To the denial of the bodily presence of Christ was added the fact that some of the enthusiasts severed the connection between the work of the Spirit and the word of Scripture, a connection which had decisive significance for Luther.

Zwingli, too, underwent a significant development in his doctrine of the Lord's Supper, though it proceeded in a direction opposite to that of Luther. Until 1524 Zwingli's understanding of the Supper was very similar to that of Luther. At this time there is no trace of his later symbolical interpretation. To the contrary, Zwingli taught that under the bread the believer really receives Christ, who otherwise sits at the right hand of God; or, that in the Lord's Supper, Christ himself descends to earth. With the question how Christ unites himself with the elements he did not concern himself further at this time. In this union of Christ with the elements he saw a miracle, the secret of which is not to be unraveled, and which actually need not worry the believer since he is certain of his faith.

Zwingli came to his symbolic understanding of the Lord's Supper only after he became acquainted with a letter written

[13] Luther, *The Adoration of the Sacrament* (1523), *LW* 36, 278.

[14] Luther, *The Sacrament of the Body and Blood of Christ—Against the Fanatics* (1526), *LW* 36, 385.

by the Dutch humanist Cornelius Hoen (Honius) in the spring of 1521. Zwingli read this letter in 1524. In it Hoen had interpreted the word "is" of the words of institution in the sense of "to signify" (*significat*). This interpretation seemed illuminating to Zwingli. At the same time Luther's decided tendency to emphasize the real presence moved Zwingli to rethink the problem. In doing so he arrived at a result quite different from that of Luther. The Supper was for him only a reminder of Jesus' suffering and death. At the same time, however, it is also an occasion of confession, it being a sign by means of which those who put their trust in Christ's death and in his blood confess their faith in the presence of their brethren. This position was bound to drive Zwingli into opposition to Luther. In fact, it was Zwingli who commenced the attack upon his opponent.

If the controversy had been mainly about the right exegesis of the words of institution it would certainly not have been waged with such acrimony and might even have been laid aside. In actuality, however, many other theological problems were involved in the varying interpretations of the words of institution. They had to do with Christology, with the understanding of the incarnation of the divine Word, and especially with the gift offered in the Lord's Supper. Under the circumstances the controversy was concerned, in the last analysis, with the central problem of the Reformation era.

What Luther was especially concerned about was the simple meaning of the words of institution. They promise and give man forgiveness of sin. This Luther found expressed in the words "for you," and from it he was not to be turned aside. However, such forgiveness has as its premise that not only bread and wine are contained in the sacrament of the Supper, but also Christ himself, with his body and blood. Luther says in one passage, "Thus the words first connect the bread and cup to the sacrament; bread and cup embrace the body and blood of Christ; body and blood of Christ embrace the new testament; the new testament embraces the forgiveness of sins; forgiveness of sins embraces eternal life and salvation."[15] This is in truth a stringent argument from which nothing can be deleted if the true gift of forgiveness of sin is to remain.

Luther, of course, could not be satisfied with simply asserting

[15] Luther, *Confession Concerning Christ's Supper* (1528), *LW* 36, 338.

this opinion. His opponents' objections forced him to give a more detailed account of Christ's presence in the Supper. Zwingli noted that the idea of eating Christ bodily contradicts the statement in John 6:63: "The flesh is of no avail." This passage constituted one of the main points of contention between Luther and Zwingli. Zwingli interpreted these words to mean that the flesh is of no avail, only the Spirit. The Lord's Supper, he felt, has to do with spiritual things, and these have an effect on the spirit of man. How can a bodily eating of Christ have any effect on the spirit of man? Such reasoning, based on John, chap. 6, forced Zwingli into a symbolical understanding of the Supper. In opposing this view Luther contended that Zwingli's understanding of "flesh" differed from that of the Bible—his understanding of corporeality was derived instead from the world of antiquity. For Luther the distinction between spirit and flesh was not the same as that between spiritualism and realism; it was, rather, the distinction between the divine Spirit and human sinfulness. Therefore, bodily eating, if it is done in faith, may indeed be spiritual eating. This being the case, furthermore, the flesh of Christ is not carnal, but spiritual; it comes from the Spirit. To eat spiritually does not mean to partake of something that is of the nature of spirit, but to receive that which comes from the Holy Spirit. Moreover, Luther denied that John, chap. 6, had anything at all to do with the Lord's Supper.

Finally, under the pressure of this controversy Luther continued to develop his Christology. In it Luther had always given centrality to the thought that God confronts us only and exclusively in Christ, that in him, however, all of God is revealed. Accordingly it is indeed necessary to differentiate between that which is divine and that which is human in the person of Christ, but these still constitute an inseparable unity. It is not possible, therefore, to separate Christ's body from his spirit. This is true also of the time after his ascension. Nowhere is Christ only spiritually present. If he is present, he must also be present bodily, otherwise his presence would have no saving effect. Christ's risen and exalted body is always his crucified body, and it is his crucified body which is exalted. On the basis of the so-called *communicatio idiomatum,* or the mutual communication of the properties of one nature of Christ to the other, this body is present in the sacrament. This is the so-called doctrine of ubiquity. It has its apex in the assertion of the omnipresence even of the human nature of Christ. Luther was unwilling to conceive Christ's sitting at the right hand of God in local terms and, hence, to develop a celestial geography. God, he held, is the will which moves and penetrates all; hence his "right hand" is everywhere. With this conception Luther remained within the framework of Alexandrian Christology, though he sharpened the emphases considerably.

Of course Zwingli, too, had his reasons. Even though he did not understand the distinction between spirit and flesh in the biblical sense, but in that of antiquity, he must not simply be accused of rationalism. His concern, too, was basically theological, namely, to safeguard the pure spirituality of faith. Above all, he wanted to preserve the character of faith as pure trust. Faith cannot and must not be dependent upon that which is created, otherwise it would no longer be faith. He says, "Our substantive faith rests upon the one God who was crucified bodily, not eaten bodily."[16] For Zwingli, too, Christ is present in the Supper, but it is a presence only "for the contemplation of faith," hence not a true, bodily presence. Spiritual presence has meaning only for faith; and whatever faith receives, it partakes of spiritually. Christ, Zwingli held, is present in the Supper insofar as one trusts him in faith.

In Christology, Zwingli did not follow the Alexandrians, but the Antiochenes, so that he drew a sharp distinction between Christ's divinity and his humanity. He thought of the body of the exalted Christ as being confined to a given space in heaven. Christ's bodily nature, being creaturely, is not infinite after the ascension and hence cannot be omnipresent. If, in spite of this, Scripture asserts of the one nature what belongs to the other, this is a matter of *alloiosis* (mutual exchange), that is, of a nonliteral form of speech, which changes nothing with regard to the uniqueness of essence and operation of each of the two natures of Christ. If, then, it is said of Christ that he is at the right hand of God, this refers only to his divine nature. At the same time it must be said that Zwingli was thoroughly faithful to the doctrinal decisions of the ancient church with regard to the unity of the person of Christ. He did not succeed, however, in explaining this

[16] Cited from W. Köhler, *Dogmengeschichte als Geschichte des christlichen Selbstbewusstseins,* 2 (Zurich: Niehans, 1951), 317 f.

unity as convincingly as did Luther. On the other hand, it must be admitted that at times Luther is in danger of abridging the human nature of Christ in favor of his divine nature.

After Luther and Zwingli, each supported by a number of other theologians, had engaged in years of literary struggle with each other, a meeting of the two was finally brought about in October of 1529. This conversation, known as the Marburg Colloquy, had been arranged by Philip, landgrave of Hesse. Its purpose was to create a greater degree of theological understanding between the Reformation in German Switzerland and in Germany as the precondition of a comprehensive alliance of Protestants against the continued threat of the Catholic emperor and the estates of the empire. Unfortunately it must be said that this plan suffered shipwreck before it could even be developed. The differences between Luther and Zwingli were too weighty to be dispelled by a brief conversation. Neither side was willing to give up any segment of its basic convictions. Thus full ecclesiastical unity between Zwingli and Luther could not be achieved, and the bold plan for an alliance fell by the wayside.

Even so, the degree to which Luther and Zwingli agreed at Marburg is amazing. Fifteen articles were put forward. With reference to the first fourteen, which treated of the Trinity, of Jesus Christ, of original sin, of the Word of God, of baptism, etc., complete unanimity prevailed. The fifteenth article had to do with the controversial doctrine of the Lord's Supper. It states:

> Fifteenth, we all believe and hold concerning the Supper of our dear Lord Jesus Christ that both forms should be used as instituted by Christ; also that the mass is not a work whereby one obtains grace for another, dead or living; also that the sacrament of the altar is a sacrament of the true body and blood of Jesus Christ, and that the spiritual partaking of this body and blood is especially necessary for every Christian. In like manner that the use of the sacrament has been given and ordained by God, as was the Word of God Almighty, in order that weak consciences might be moved to faith by the Holy Spirit. And that, although we are at this time not agreed as to whether or not the true body of Christ is corporeally present in the bread and in the wine, each party should still show Christian love toward the other, insofar as consciences will permit, and both parties should pray diligently to God that by his Spirit he might confirm to us the true understanding.[17]

[17] Quoted in *Die Bekenntnisschriften der evangelisch-lutherischen Kirche* (2nd. rev. ed.; Göttingen: Vandenhoeck und Ruprecht, 1952), p. 65, ll. 15-26.

Even in this article, agreement between Luther and Zwingli has been noted at several points. Aside from the anti-Roman polemics, in which there was agreement, Zwingli here admitted that the Supper is a sacrament of the true body and blood of Jesus Christ; he made room, furthermore, for a special benefit bestowed by the sacrament. Luther, too, by acceding to the formulation "spiritual partaking," revealed a certain readiness to make compromises. In these respects the Marburg Colloquy did bring a *rapprochement* between Luther and Zwingli.

Unfortunately this was not taken into consideration in subsequent Lutheran confessional writings. In the very next year Melanchthon, who had participated in the Marburg Colloquy and who also had signed the articles, used formulations in the *Augsburg Confession* which again widened the gulf between Wittenberg and Zurich, and which contradict both the wording and the spirit of the *Marburg Articles*. Article 10 of the *Augsburg Confession* states: "Our churches teach that the body and blood of Christ are truly present and are distributed to those who eat in the Supper of the Lord. They disapprove of those who teach otherwise."[18] This condemnation of those who teach otherwise was, beyond the shadow of a doubt, directed primarily against Zwingli and a few enthusiasts such as Carlstadt and Schwenckfeld. At the same time Melanchthon said nothing here about the distinction between this and the Roman doctrine of the Lord's Supper, as he often did in reference to other matters. Unfortunately this was not the last time that Lutherans showed themselves less willing to meet and less ready to understand their opponents than the Reformed. Later on Calvin, at any rate, was subjected to experiences similar to those of Zwingli.

The Confessional Treatises of Lutheranism

The new understanding of confession not only led to certain doctrinal demarcations, such as were discussed in the previous section, but also to comprehensive confessional treatises. Various causes contributed to this development. Basically there was the wish simply to confess the evangelical faith. In that sense the first common evangelical confession may be said to have been made at the Diet of Speyer in 1526 when the followers of the two evangelical princes, the landgrave of Hesse and the elector of

[18] *Augsburg Confession*, X, *BC*, p. 34 (Latin text).

Saxony, carried inscribed on the sleeves of their coats the words, *Verbum Dei manet in aeternum*—"The word of God abides forever" (see Isa. 40:8). However, there were other external factors which led to the writing of the confessional treatises. This is especially true of the *Augsburg Confession,* which was written with the religious discussions of the Diet of Augsburg (1530) in view. Other reasons, quite different from those already mentioned, account for the writing of confessional treatises. The two catechisms of Luther were written to further instruction in the evangelical faith and, originally, were not even intended as confessional treatises. Later on, however, they gained entrance to the confessional corpus because of their wide distribution and their significance for preaching and doctrine. The *Smalcald Articles* were originally intended to be the basis for discussion at a council which was called to meet at Mantua in 1537, but which did not actually convene until 1545 at Trent. Other confessional treatises were meant to decide certain doctrinal controversies within the church itself. In the Lutheran church this is true especially of the *Formula of Concord.*

The confessional treatises of the Reformation differ at certain points from the confessions of the ancient church, as well as from the dogmatic decisions of the Middle Ages. From an external point of view the differences are apparent in this, that the confessions of the ancient church were used in the services of worship, but that not a single treatise of the Reformation has ever been so used. According to their very nature they are not suitable for such use. Even so, the purely external character of Luther's confession of 1528 is similar to that of the confessions of the ancient church, inasmuch as it speaks in the first person. Furthermore, Luther's explanation of the creed in his *Small Catechism* has often been used in Lutheran services of worship. The difference between the confessions of the ancient church and the confessional treatises of the Reformation, however, becomes more apparent if one examines the content. The older confessions are succinctly formulated statements concerning certain items of the content of the Christian faith. The confessional treatises, on the other hand, offer long and even discursive discussions concerning many questions which have to do with the evangelical faith and the differences between Roman Catholic and Protestant theology. They are theological explanations which extend over much territory and which, according to both form and content, only occasionally give the impression of being true confessions.

Still there can be no doubt that, in the last analysis, the confessional treatises of the Reformation also seek to do nothing else but confess the faith. The special character of these treatises is determined by the fact that they speak out of a situation totally different from that in which earlier confessions were formulated.

The *Augsburg Confession* is regarded as the first Lutheran confessional treatise. It was the intention of the emperor, Charles V, to mediate between the two contending parties at a diet which had been called to meet at Augsburg in 1530. Previously the Diet of Worms (1521) had put Luther under the ban and had decreed the suppression of the evangelical movement. Yet, the message of the Reformation had spread so rapidly that there could be no thought of a quick, forcible solution to the problem. Then, too, ever since the Diet of Worms Charles V had been forced into incessant wars and for years had been absent from the territory of the empire. This explains the remarkably mild tone of the imperial announcement convoking the Diet of 1530. Charles wanted to hear everyone's "appraisal, opinion, and point of view." The evangelical party, therefore, had to be prepared to give an account of itself. For this purpose the theologians of Wittenberg set forth in March of 1530, at Torgau, the so-called *Torgau Articles.* These dealt primarily with practical questions of church reform. Upon arriving in Augsburg, the evangelical party quickly discovered that the climate of discussion was much more rigorous than might have been surmised on the basis of the imperial announcement. For that reason the doctrinal questions had to be considered in detail. Since Luther had the status of an outlaw and could not appear before the emperor at Augsburg, Melanchthon took this task upon himself. For the doctrinal questions he drew upon the *Marburg Articles* of October, 1529, as well as upon the so-called *Schwabach Articles* of the summer of 1529. The latter had been set forth by the theologians of Wittenberg and had themselves served as a basis for the *Marburg Articles.* For his treatment of practical questions Melanchthon used the *Torgau Articles.* Yet these earlier articles were always given a new form by Melanchthon;

furthermore, they were altered in many places, so that the *Augsburg Confession* represents an entirely new confession. Though he was assisted by other members of the evangelical party, most of the formulations derive from Melanchthon himself. On June 25, 1530, the solemn reading of the German text of the *Augsburg Confession* took place before the Diet and in the presence of the emperor. It exists in both a Latin and a German edition. These texts differ somewhat in a few places, even in some passages of theological importance. The present discussion is based upon the Latin text.

The manner in which the *Augsburg Confession* originated is also reflected in its structure. It contains two parts. The first of these, comprising articles 1-21, discusses the "Chief Articles of Faith"; the second, containing articles 22-28, treats of "Articles in Which an Account is Given of the Abuses Which Have Been Corrected." Even the headings of these two parts indicate that the *Augsburg Confession* seeks to create the impression that it is not the actual questions of doctrine which are controversial, but only certain abuses. At the end of the first part Melanchthon actually says, "This is about the sum of our teaching. As can be seen, there is nothing here that departs from the Scriptures or the catholic church or the church of Rome, insofar as the ancient church is known to us from its writers. Since this is so, those who insist that our teachers are to be regarded as heretics judge too harshly. The whole dissension is concerned with a certain few abuses which have crept into the churches without proper authority."[19] This was a decided weakening of the existing differences, and was the less convincing since Melanchthon said nothing in the confession about questions such as the papacy or indulgences. On the other hand, doctrinal matters which had to do with justification, with preaching, and with the church were considered in the first part—regarding these there were presumably no differences of opinion! Melanchthon could hardly have made such statements with a clear conscience. He knew too well the depth of the gulf between Catholics and Protestants. The reason for his attempt to make things appear harmless is to be found in the very seriously threatened situation of the Protestants. Melanchthon wanted to do everything he could to conciliate the Catholics. On the other hand, he did not want to

[19] *Augsburg Confession*, summary of first part, *BC*, p. 47 (Latin text).

give up articles central to the evangelical faith.

The first articles treat of God, of original sin, and of the Son of God. Melanchthon here makes use of the decisions of the councils of the ancient church. He does so, however, without bringing about the close connection with soteriology which is found in Luther's confessions. The fourth article explains justification:

> Our churches also teach that men cannot be justified before God by their own strength, merits, or works but are freely justified for Christ's sake through faith when they believe that they are received into favor and that their sins are forgiven on account of Christ, who by his death made satisfaction for our sins. This faith God imputes for righteousness in his sight.[20]

With this sentence Melanchthon gave succinct and pointed doctrinal expression to the evangelical understanding of justification. At the same time, it is true that one does not find here the full depth of Luther's understanding of this doctrine. This is not so much because the famous word "alone" is missing in the wording of this formula, but rather because its content gives evidence of several changes of emphasis. For instance, the words "for Christ's sake through faith" can easily be misunderstood here as a rationalization, as though faith were to take the place which merits occupy in the Catholic scheme. Melanchthon certainly did not want this article to be understood in that way. Yet, the formula does give evidence that it was not something discovered in the midst of severe inner trials. In fact, at a later date a change which had serious consequences does become noticeable in Melanchthon's doctrine of justification. He sees man as possessing the ability to render himself receptive to God's grace; conversion he regards as having three co-efficient causes, namely, the Word, the Holy Spirit, and the will, the latter not being passive, but resisting its own weakness.

That Melanchthon did not reproduce here Luther's full concept of justification is also apparent, and especially so, in the sixth article, which speaks of obedience. It states:

> Our churches also teach that this faith is bound to bring forth good fruits and that it is necessary to do the good works commanded by God. We must do so because it is God's will and not because we rely on such works to merit justification before God.[21]

[20] *Augsburg Confession,* IV, *BC,* p. 30 (Latin text).

[21] *Augsburg Confession,* VI, *BC,* pp. 31-32 (Latin text).

Luther never said that the doing of good works involves a "must" which places an obligation on faith. Melanchthon did not reproduce at this point Luther's comprehensive and profound understanding of faith. Here, too, a difference in accentuation is apparent, a difference which indeed was hardly noticed at first, but which later was to lead to developments fraught with consequences.

Concerning the ministry, the fifth article says:

> In order that we may obtain this faith the ministry of teaching the Gospel and administering the sacraments was instituted. For through the Word and the sacraments, as through instruments, the Holy Spirit is given, and the Holy Spirit produces faith, where and when it pleases God, in those who hear the Gospel.[22]

It is significant that here the gift of the Holy Spirit is tied to word and sacrament. With that the notion of the enthusiasts, to the effect that it is possible to possess the Spirit apart from preaching and the sacraments, was warded off.

Word and sacrament also define the church. The seventh article states:

> Our churches also teach that one holy church is to continue forever. The church is the assembly of saints in which the Gospel is taught purely and the sacraments are administered rightly. For the true unity of the church it is enough to agree concerning the teaching of the Gospel and the administration of the sacraments. It is not necessary that human traditions or rights and ceremonies, instituted by men, should be alike everywhere.[23]

Here the new evangelical understanding of the church is evident. On the one hand, there is exclusive concentration upon preaching and sacrament. Nothing has been subtracted from the faith that is necessary to salvation; it is not enough simply to refrain from "interposing an obstacle." On the other hand, the evangelical understanding of the church manifests ecumenical breadth. External factors are not decisive for the existence of the church. The Reformers did not deny that the church includes the Roman church. Luther found that Rome, too, in spite of its distortion of the Christian message, possesses the Scripture, the sacraments, and, in a certain sense, also the faith. Luther's accusation against Rome was that it mixes together that which is divine and that which is human, and that matters of secondary importance are declared to be necessary to salvation. In Luther's

[22] *Augsburg Confession,* V, *BC,* p. 31 (Latin text).

[23] *Augsburg Confession,* VII, *BC,* p. 32 (Latin text).

opinion these matters may be tolerated as long as they remain of secondary importance. This freedom provides the basis from which the Lutheran church approaches, for instance, the problem of apostolic succession.

Of course, the doctrine of the sacraments as taught by the *Augsburg Confession* is not without problems. This is true, first, with respect to the question of the number of the sacraments. Melanchthon does not treat this question directly. Indirectly, however, his conception is clearly evident. Since he considers in succession baptism, the Lord's Supper, and confession and repentance, and since thereafter he speaks of "the use of the sacraments" (articles 9-13), it is quite certain that repentance, or confession, is also understood as a sacrament. In his *Loci communes* of 1521, however, Melanchthon, had already accepted Luther's idea that only baptism and the Lord's Supper are sacraments, since to them alone external signs are added. Yet in this passage of the *Augsburg Confession* Melanchthon again permitted himself to be guided by his frequently excessive readiness to compromise. In the *Apology* he specifically conceded three actual sacraments: baptism, the Lord's Supper, and repentance. If need be he was even ready to regard ordination as a sacrament. Here the basic confession of the Lutheran church is given to a certain lack of clarity which later confessional treatises, too, did not remove.

Among the other confessional treatises of the Lutheran church —the catechisms and the *Smalcald Articles* of Luther have already been referred to—the *Apology* and the *Formula of Concord* must still be mentioned.

After the *Augsburg Confession* was read and presented to the emperor the Catholics proceeded to draft a reply. According to the imperial announcement they, too, should have given an exposition of their doctrine. Initially, however, they had refused to present a confessional document, and they had done so with the excuse that it was not they but the Protestants who had departed from the inherited teaching, and that hence it was the latter who were obligated to defend themselves. Now, however, a few Catholic theologians, notably Eck, wrote a reply, the so-called *Confutation.* It takes up the *Augsburg Confession* point by point and seeks to refute it. As a reply to the *Confutation* Melanchthon then drafted the *Apology* of the *Augsburg Con-*

fession. The emperor, by the way, had refused to give the evangelical party a copy of the *Confutation* after it was read on August 3, 1530. In drafting his *Apology,* therefore, Melanchthon was dependent upon a few notes which some of the Protestants had secretly made during the reading of the *Confutation.*

The structure of the *Apology* adheres strictly to that of the *Augsburg Confession.* Most important in the former is the fourth article, which treats in detail the doctrine of justification, citing proofs from the fathers of the church to indicate that the evangelical doctrine of justification does not represent something wholly new. With respect to content, it is especially significant to note Melanchthon's repeated emphasis that justification refers not only to the imputation of the grace of another, namely, Christ, but also to making the unrighteous man righteous. At this point the discussions in the *Apology* constitute an important supplement to those in the *Augsburg Confession.*

Between the drafting of the *Augsburg Confession* and of the *Apology,* on the one hand, and of the *Formula of Concord,* on the other, five decades intervened. The latter originated in its present form in the year 1577. During those decades both Lutheran theology and the Lutheran church underwent a significant change, one which had many consequences. Luther died in 1546. After his death a series of serious doctrinal controversies erupted within the Lutheran church. These were brought about in part by the transformation which Melanchthon's theology had undergone beginning with the middle of the 1530's and which, in the course of time, became increasingly noticeable. Some wanted to re-emphasize the true heritage of Luther, others, Melanchthon among them, were striving to establish an irenical line, while still others found themselves somewhere between these two groups. Luther himself had ignored the theological differences between himself and Melanchthon, which during his last years had become evident. He must have been aware of them, since they were specifically pointed out to him by various parties. Yet, because of his magnanimous disposition, he did not take them seriously except in a few instances. It was precisely this refusal of Luther to take a position here which made it so difficult for later theologians to make a decision. None of the contending parties were, in fact, fully justified in appealing to Luther. That Melanchthon had departed from him at important points was clear. But even the "Gnesio-Lutherans" ("genuine Lutherans") were more in possession of Luther's formulas than of his spirit. The development of orthodoxy now began on a broad front. The confessional church became a doctrinal church. Yet, there can be no doubt that the position taken in the *Formula of Concord* on the various questions at issue is nearer to the theology of Luther than are the opinions which the *Formula* rejects.

The controversies, into which it is not possible to enter fully here, had to do, among other things, with various problems related to justification. Among them was Melanchthon's "synergism," i.e., the assertion of the joint operation of divine grace and human will. Beyond this there were questions pertaining to the doctrine of the Lord's Supper and to certain problems of Christology, as well as questions relative to the doctrine of law and gospel. Extensive efforts and lengthy discussions were required before the *Formula of Concord* was finally adopted by a large number of Lutheran princes and theologians. Still it never achieved total acceptance within Lutheranism. The *Augsburg Confession* continued to remain the basic confession of Lutherans, a position it has retained to the present day.

The new Luther research has at many points clearly set forth the differences between Luther and Melanchthon, as well as those between Luther and the *Formula of Concord.* For that reason the question arises whether, in instances where the two conflict, the Lutheran church should follow Luther or its confessional writings. Both answers which can be given to this question have their own special difficulties. The decision that the confessional treatises, especially the Augsburg Confession, are normative, has the advantage of not relying upon the words of one single master. Yet this requires giving up of some of Luther's basic insights, the sacrifice of which has repeatedly had serious consequences in the past. If, on the other hand, Luther's theology is elevated above the authority of the confessions, a single theologian is made the judge of later developments, some of which have proceeded from an entirely new situation. The advantage in choosing Luther, of course, is that one then has a theology which, in depth and integrity, is perhaps without equal in the history of the church and in the history of dogma.

It is a good thing that the Lutheran church need not answer this question either in the one way or the other. If it would be true to the content of the gospel, it must not attempt to reach a final solution to this problem. Neither the theology of Luther nor the statements of the Lutheran confessions constitutes an ultimate. Nor were they, in fact, intended to be such. The intention which they do embody is that of leading to a deeper and better understanding of Holy Scripture. For that reason the claim to infallible authority is purposely not made by the confessions. They are meant to be subject to the authority of Scripture. Consequently the Lutheran church possesses evangelical freedom both with regard to Luther's theology and with regard to the confessions. This freedom does not imply either arbitrariness or individualism, for the fathers of the Lutheran church made their confessional statements on the basis of a scrupulous study of the Scriptures and, not infrequently, at the risk of their existence. In these statements the church has found a witness to the right understanding of the gospel.

Calvin and the Reformed Church

No single, uniform Protestant church resulted from the Reformation movement, but rather two great, Protestant church types, namely, the Lutheran and the Reformed, each of which is still further subdivided. How did this happen, and what is the meaning of this fact from the point of view of the history of dogma?

The answer to this question appears to be more simple than it really is. Naturally, the Reformed churches stem from Calvin, even as the Lutheran churches go back to Luther. However, the question about the internal reasons which led to the origin of two Reformation churches cannot be answered so readily. Neither can the question about their uniqueness within the context of the history of dogma. In both instances various factors have been operative.

First, it must be pointed out that Luther, as well as the other Reformers, did not intend to found a new church. Their intention was, rather, to reform the whole church, to cleanse it from "papistical" additions, and to reshape it according to the Word of God. During the sixteenth century this attempt was made at various points. As a whole it was unsuccessful, insofar as the Roman church rejected the Reformation. This is the reason Protestant churches came to be established. At the time, however, the task of bringing the various churches into unity was not yet recognized, nor was it undertaken in sufficient measure. The controversy with Rome, as well as the various political complications in which the Reformation became embroiled, prevented the many attempts to achieve a unified Protestant church from coming to fruition. Or else these attempts were brought to a standstill at midpoint. Even though it had come to a break between Luther and Zwingli, a closer fellowship at other points between the various Protestant churches which took shape should have been possible in principle.

It needs to be said, however, that the inner development of the Lutheran Reformation after Luther's death was such as to make a closer fellowship with other Protestant churches essentially impossible. The compacting of Lutheran theology into a Gnesio-Lutheran orthodoxy, which in itself was significantly conditioned by Melanchthon's sacrifice of a number of Luther's central concerns, led especially to an estrangement between the Lutheran church and the Reformation of Calvin. As a result, the seeds of unity which had been sown were allowed to lie dormant. Calvin never wanted to found a Reformed church. He did not regard the adherents of the *Augsburg Confession* as members of another church. In fact, Calvin himself signed the *Augsburg Confession,* though in its altered form of 1540, and he attempted to bring the various evangelical movements into closer proximity, but with no success. Protestantism to the present day has had to suffer the consequences of this development.

Recent research has made it increasingly evident that Luther and Calvin are close to each other in many things, particularly in the questions which matter most. Calvin himself was aware of his indebtedness to Luther. The first edition of his great work *Institutes of the Christian Religion* (1536) was modeled in its structure, as well as in many details, after Luther's *Small Catechism.* In a letter of November 25, 1544, Calvin wrote: "Although he [Luther] were to call me a devil, I should still not the less hold him in such honour that I must acknowledge him to be an illustrious servant of God. But while he is endued with rare and excellent virtues, he labours at the same time under serious faults."[24] In 1545 he even sent a letter to Luther, through Melanchthon, in which he testifies to his esteem. Calvin calls the Wittenberg Reformer his "highly esteemed father in Christ."[25] The timorous Melanchthon, however, did not deliver the letter to Luther. Thus this single attempt in the direction of establishing contact between Luther and Calvin came to nought.

As for Luther, he sometimes worried about the possibility that, with regard to the doctrine of the Lord's Supper, Calvin might be on the side of Zwingli. Yet he definitely knew how to differentiate between Zwingli and Calvin. In 1539, in a letter to Bucer, he asked that his greetings be extended to Calvin, because he said that he had read with special pleasure Calvin's Reformation treatise *Reply to Sadoleto.*[26] Even though later one no longer finds such a friendly remark by Luther, he never drew a line of demarcation between himself and Calvin. Until Luther's death the situation remained fluid. Subsequently, however, the relationship between Calvin and the Lutheran theologians quickly deteriorated.

Moving on from the personal relationships between Luther and Calvin to their theology, one notices that here, too, many promising beginnings were not further developed. It used to be common to regard Calvin's teaching of double predestination as one of his special peculiarities. Yet there can be no doubt that Luther, too, hewed a strict line with regard to predestination. At just this point both have in common an important feature. For both, the doctrine of predestination does not represent the focal point with reference to which all else is developed; rather, this doctrine is coordinated with the doctrine of justification and can be properly evaluated only within the framework of such coordination. Again, Calvin's fourfold division of offices has sometimes been designated as a special characteristic of the Reformed church: the offices of pastors, teachers, elders, and deacons are encountered on every hand. It is true that the Lutheran church does not have this division in the same way. Yet in making this division was not Calvin taking seriously and applying practically the idea of the universal priesthood, an idea which

[24] *Letters of Calvin,* ed. Jules Bonnet (Edinburgh: Thomas Constable and Co., 1855), 1, 409. *CR* 11, 774.

[25] *CR* 12, 7.

[26] Luther, *WA,* Br. 8, letter 3394, ll. 29-31.

Luther strongly emphasized theologically, though he did not give it ecclesiastical form in his reorganization of the church's practices? The same is true of many other items of doctrine which have been designated as a peculiarity of the one or the other. Differences in emphasis are of course evident throughout. If attention is given, however, to the individual differences between the two men, and above all to their situations, which developed along different lines as regards both external and internal aspects, most of these differences prove to be of secondary importance. It was Luther who began the Reformation; Calvin is already a man of the second generation. Out of concern for the weak, Luther moved slowly and circumspectly in carrying through his reform measures. Calvin, who lived at the beginning of the Counter-Reformation and faced a world filled with enemies, had to act more resolutely and incisively.

One peculiarity of the Protestantism which was shaped by Calvin is undoubtedly found in its special emphasis on the duty of confessing the faith. Calvin admonished the French Protestants in particular not to make any compromises with Catholicism. At the time, going to Mass was considered the touchstone of the faith. Many adherents of the Reformation had thought that in externals they could accede to the demands of Catholicism, while internally they would still be evangelical Christians. Calvin, however, was untiring in pointing out that one step would follow another once a person had begun to give in. Hence he strictly forbade participation in the Catholic Mass. He insisted that the consequences which might attend such courageous confessing must be trustfully left to God. He who truly casts his cares upon God, Calvin emphasized, will not be forsaken by him. In this way he imparted to his followers incomparable strength for action.

Over against Lutheranism this represents merely a sharp change of emphasis. In the doctrine of the Lord's Supper, however, real differences between Luther and Calvin may be observed, though their importance has often been overestimated. Calvin's doctrine of the Lord's Supper moves between that of Luther and that of Zwingli. Over against the latter, Calvin continued to hold that the Supper is more than a confession of the congregation. With Luther he maintained the real presence of Christ in the Supper. Yet he was not able to follow Luther in all respects. According to Calvin, Luther's strong emphasis on the real presence of Christ in the elements denies the ascension. Calvin maintains that after the ascension the body of Christ is located at a certain place in heaven. Hence it cannot of itself be omnipresent, not even on the basis of the *communicatio idiomatum.* To Calvin, Christ's presence in the Supper is mediated by the Holy Spirit. Our communion with the flesh and blood of Christ results from the power of the Holy Spirit. The secret power of the Holy Spirit, he taught, is our bond of union with Christ. The presence of Christ through the Holy Spirit, however, is given in reality. For that reason the eating of the body of Christ does not merely signify faith, but it is a true and special union with Christ which, to be sure, presupposes faith. The communion established with Christ in the Lord's Supper, then, is not only "spiritual," it is real. Bread and wine are not merely signs, but seals of the actual gift conveyed by the Supper. While man's body receives bread and wine, a spiritual nourishment of the soul takes place concurrently. It is mediated by the Holy Spirit for the purpose of the forgiveness of sins.

This doctrine of the Lord's Supper is undoubtedly closer to Luther than to Zwingli. Calvin himself declared Zwingli's doctrine to be "profane."[27] On the basic issue Luther and Calvin agree, namely, in their conception of union with Christ and of forgiveness of sins, as these gifts are given in the Supper. They differ only in the way they defined the presence of Christ. At this point Calvin was unable to share Luther's understanding of the omnipresence of Christ's glorified human nature.

It was just these endeavors of Calvin to bring about a closer fellowship among the various churches of the Reformation which, in connection with the differences about the doctrine of the Lord's Supper, were to lead to a sharpening of the differences between him and the Lutherans. In 1549 Calvin entered with Zurich into the so-called Consensus Tigurinus, which resulted in a far-reaching agreement between the two Swiss reformations. The formula on the Lord's Supper which was drawn up at the time as part of the Consensus was somewhat of a concession to the Zwinglians. Calvin himself, as is evident from several letters, had a number of reservations about the Consensus formula. On the Lutheran side the suspicion was reinforced that in his

[27] *CR* 11, 438.

doctrine of the Lord's Supper Calvin was basically on the side of Zwingli. The result was that Joachim Westphal, a pastor in Hamburg, immediately made a sharp attack upon Calvin. Calvin's reply to this attack was the more incisive in that he saw himself misunderstood at the point of his innermost concern, the unifying of Protestantism. A second eucharistic controversy now erupted, leading to a deeper cleavage between Lutherans and Calvinists.

Because Calvin did not have the desire to found his own Reformed church, the Reformed communion does not possess a well-defined corpus of confessions which is comparable to the Lutheran corpus. There are no Reformed confessions which are generally recognized as valid in all Reformed churches. Instead, a whole series of different confessions exist, which at certain points exhibit considerable differences. Of course, in the Reformed church, too, a development in the direction of orthodoxy soon arose. It was a development which in no way lagged behind the tendency within Lutheranism and Lutheran theology toward a congealment of doctrine.

Rome's Answer

The Roman church could not evade the questions which had been put to it by Luther and the Reformation. It had to go beyond the mere condemnation of "heretics" and give answers to the questions themselves. That the distinguishing characteristic of the history of doctrine in the sixteenth century is its concentration on the problem of justification and of the appropriation of salvation is unqualifiedly true of the Roman church as well. This theme was not merely dictated to it by the Reformers. Rome, in fact, had to admit that at this point basic problems had hitherto remained unclarified.

To the questions which were raised by the Reformation, Rome answered variously at the time. It first attempted to settle quietly the disturbance which Luther had created. Then Luther was put under the ban. When his work continued to gain adherents, however, an attempt at mediation was made. At last the council which had been repeatedly demanded by all sides convened at Trent in 1545 and met, with long interruptions, until 1563. Convoked for the purpose of giving Rome's definitive answer, nothing in that answer has been altered to the present day. This answer had reference primarily to three problems: the relation of Scripture and tradition, the doctrine of justification, and the question of the certainty of salvation.

Vincent of Lérins was the first to formulate the Catholic concept of tradition. During the Middle Ages the problem of the relation between Scripture and tradition received relatively little attention. The thoughts on the subject which are found in church fathers such as Irenaeus and Vincent remained valid. In general the question of Scripture and tradition posed no serious problem for Scholasticism. This observation needs to be qualified only insofar as the rediscovery of Aristotle caused theology to reflect on the nature and limits of revelation as opposed to the natural knowledge of man. In doing so it clarified an important presupposition for the treatment of the question of Scripture and tradition. To be sure, only a few critical theologians recognized the problem which was here awaiting a solution. It is the keen dialectical thinker Abelard (d. 1142) who needs to be mentioned first in this connection. In his treatise *Sic et non* ("Yes and No") he set contradictory statements of the fathers over against each other. Mention must also be made of the critical English theologian of reform, John Wycliffe (d. 1384), who began to question human institutions on the basis of Scripture. In Scripture, to be sure, he saw only the divine law, not the gospel.

When the Reformers appealed to Scripture, in contradistinction to tradition, the Catholic church had to clarify and state definitively its understanding of Scripture and tradition. The decisive factors had indeed long been present, beginning with the concept of conciliar authority and extending to the practical coordination of Scripture and tradition. But not until the Council of Trent was this opinion set forth in a precise formula. The fourth session spoke of saving truth and moral precept, proclaimed by Christ himself and preached by the apostles according to his will. It declared "that this truth and teaching are contained in written books [the Bible] and in the unwritten traditions that the apostles received from Christ himself or that were handed on, as it were from hand to hand, from the apostles under the inspiration of the Holy Spirit, and so have come down to us."[28] Immediately thereafter it is expressly specified that the church "with the same sense of devotion and reverence with

[28] Denzinger, par. 783. *TCT*, par. 95.

which it accepts and venerates all the books of the Old and New Testament, . . . also accepts and venerates traditions concerned with faith and morals . . . ." Herewith the oral, apostolic tradition is put on a par with Scripture, and this is done with reference to both divine inspiration and authority in the church. Some segments of recent Roman Catholic theology have held that this definition does not exclude the idea that the divine revelation is already contained in Scripture alone. While this may be true with reference to the wording of this decision, it does not alter the fact that the decision as such was meant to oppose the scriptural principle of the Reformation. Beyond this, the more recent Catholic dogmas are proof that oral tradition is actually accorded equal value with the Scripture. Furthermore, the apostolic character of this oral tradition has been understood in an ever broader sense, and no attempt has been made to set up objective criteria as to what may be regarded as apostolic tradition and what may not.

The decision of the Council of Trent concerning the relation of Scripture and tradition was directed against the foundation stone of the whole Reformation. The definition of the sixth session, concerning justification, contains the Roman answer to the conclusion the Reformation had drawn from its scriptural principle. The council fathers, to be sure, did not give sufficient attention to Luther's doctrine of justification. Their knowledge of it was slight. In fact, Luther's writings were for them largely *terra incognita.* All the more, then, were they concerned about mediating between the opposing views which had been present within the Catholic doctrine of justification ever since the days of Scholasticism. The result was actually a compromise, which, of course, excludes Luther and the Reformation, but which otherwise accepts the opinions of the various schools within the Roman church. The depth and precision of Augustine's concept of justification was certainly not recovered here.

Like Augustine and Thomas Aquinas, the Tridentine decree regards justification as a process in the course of which man is made righteous. It states: "In the preceding words a description is given of the justification of the unjust. Justification is a passing from the state in which man is born a son of the first Adam, to the state of grace and adoption as sons of God (*see Rom. 8:15*) through the second Adam, Jesus Christ, our Savior."[29] At the beginning of this process is the call (*vocatio*) effected by predisposing grace, there being no merits which lead to this call. Yet predisposing grace operates in such a way that it motivates man and helps him to "convert" himself to his justification. This takes place when man assents to grace and cooperates with it. "The result is that, when God touches the heart of man with the illumination of the Holy Spirit, the man who accepts that inspiration certainly does something, since he could reject it; on the other hand, by his own free will, without God's grace, he could not take one step towards justice in God's sight."[30] It is evident that the decision of the council tries to maintain a position exactly midway between two extremes—between ascribing everything to divine grace, on the one hand, and permitting man to gain justification by his own merits, on the other. The preparation as such is dependent upon faith and love. At the end of this process of renewal is the actual event of justification. It consists not merely in the forgiveness of sins, but at the same time in sanctification and in the renewal of the inner man. Man receives this justification through the sacraments, through which grace is infused, which then will lead to a new quality within him.

It is clear that this definition limits man's cooperation in his justification to a minimum. Basically man is capable only of either accepting God's grace or denying it his consent. In saying this the council materially reduced the differences between Luther's concept of justification and that of certain theologians of the late Middle Ages, who held to an absolute Pelagianism. Still there are important differences between the Lutheran and the Tridentine point of view. For one thing, since justification is here tied to the sacraments, grace loses its character as God's personal turning to man. Instead, it is understood as a thing, existing in itself. The result is that the necessity of a personal faith recedes into the background. Furthermore, though man's cooperation is severely limited, it is not removed from the picture entirely. This has most serious results for the question of the certainty of salvation, as will be shown presently.

[29] Council of Trent, session 6, chap. 4. Denzinger, par. 796. *TCT*, par. 560.

[30] *Ibid.*, chap. 5. Denzinger, par. 797. *TCT*, par. 561.

Finally, perhaps the most serious accusation which needs to be raised against the Tridentine decree on justification has to do with its complete orientation to the question of how justification proceeds psychologically. It does not concern itself with the theological question concerning the ultimate basis of man's justification and of his certainty of salvation. The psychological description of the process of justification and the theological question concerning the foundation of grace and certainty are not the same. Since the Council of Trent did not make this distinction, it could only regard Luther's opinion that the objective righteousness of Christ is imputed to sinful man, and that this righteousness can only be appropriated by faith, as nothing but idle self-trust.

As to the certainty of salvation, the Council of Trent actually denies it. In line with the anthropological and psychological orientation of its doctrine of justification, the council also sets down only a few general conclusions regarding the question of the certainty of salvation. These do not come to grips with the strictly theological issue. Sins are forgiven, to be sure, through grace, for Christ's sake. Yet, the sins of anyone who glories in the hope and certainty of forgiveness are not really forgiven. Beyond this we are told, "Furthermore it should not be asserted that they who are truly justified must unhesitatingly determine within themselves that they are justified."[31] Also rejected is the idea that the only sins which are truly forgiven are those of the person who believes firmly that God has forgiven him, or that justification may be obtained through faith alone. Actually, so it is said, he who does not believe this with such firmness need not therefore entertain doubts regarding the promises of God or regarding the power of the death and resurrection of Christ. "For no devout man should entertain doubts about God's mercy, Christ's merits, and the power and efficacy of the sacraments. Similarly, whoever reflects upon himself, his personal weakness, and his defective disposition may fear and tremble about his own grace, since no one can know with the certitude of faith, which cannot admit any error, that he has obtained God's grace."[32] Fear and hope, then, must be kept in balance.

We are not being too severe when we say that the authors

[31] *Ibid.*, chap. 9. Denzinger, par. 802. *TCT*, par. 566.
[32] *Ibid.*

of this decision did not understand at all the concern of Luther, who saw man as he stands before God. The difference between the way Luther understands justification and the way it was handled at Trent becomes especially apparent by comparison with the first sermon Luther preached at Wittenberg upon his return from the Wartburg. Delivered on Invocavit Sunday, March 9, 1522, it begins as follows: "The summons of death comes to us all, and no one can die for another. Every one must fight his own battle with death by himself, alone. We can shout into another's ears, but every one must himself be prepared for the time of death, for I will not be with you then, nor you with me. Therefore every one must himself know and be armed with the chief things which concern a Christian."[33]

Recent Roman Catholic theology, in Germany especially, has made an effort to be more just to Luther. Of course, he is still accused of subjectivism, an accusation which is beside the point. Recently, however, the Dominican theologian Stephanus Pfürtner has made a noteworthy contribution to the argument about the question of certainty.[34] Pfürtner demonstrates, above all, that the Tridentine decree falls considerably short of Thomas Aquinas' conception of the certainty of salvation. According to Pfürtner it is necessary to distinguish in Aquinas between the certainty of salvation and the certainty of hope. According to Aquinas, says Pfürtner, no true certainty of faith is obtainable, but only a "conjectured certainty." Yet both Catholic and Protestant research in Thomas Aquinas has hitherto overlooked the fact that Aquinas does teach a certainty of hope. The differences between Aquinas and Luther at this point are, in the main, of a formal nature. Luther regards trust as an element of faith; Aquinas, on the other hand, understands faith as knowledge and brings trust into conjunction with hope. In any case, the certainty of hope for Thomas Aquinas is not certainty without content, but confidence regarding one's own salvation. For that reason there can be no doubt that Aquinas actually taught the personal certainty of salvation. The fathers of Trent also lacked clarity in this matter. As Pfürtner emphasizes, they considered only the problem of the certainty of faith.

[33] Luther, *The Eight Wittenberg Sermons, LW* 51, 70.

[34] S. Pfürtner, *Luther und Thomas im Gespräch* (Heidelberg: F. H. Kerle, 1961).

This is a point, an especially important one, at which the two great communions may come closer to each other in our day. It would appear, at least, that the Roman Catholic church is capable of saying more and better things concerning the question of certainty than was said by the Council of Trent.

7

Dogma within Recent Catholicism

The Understanding of Dogma

THE REFORMATION marks the deepest cleavage in the history of dogma since the days of the ancient church. This is true not only because Christianity in the West has been split since that time, but also because the very nature of the problems which arise in the history of dogma has been basically altered since the Reformation. In any case, this is true of Roman Catholicism.

The Roman Catholic church is the only Christian communion which in modern times has declared certain propositions of faith to be absolutely binding dogma. It would seem, then, that for this reason, at least, Catholicism can make the claim that within its sphere the history of dogma has continued uninterruptedly. Yet the external impression of continuity might in this instance be deceptive. It is true that some of the recent decisions of the Roman church do not lack an integral connection with earlier doctrinal decrees to which they refer. Still there is a basic difference between the older conciliar decisions and the three recent dogmas defined by the Roman church in the nineteenth and twentieth centuries. The older dogmas, even those of the Middle Ages, remain in close proximity to the Scriptures and to the faith which the church basically possessed from the beginning. The three new dogmas, on the other hand, depart considerably from the New Testament as well as from the tradition of the early church, and they do so both with regard to their content and the themes they treat. All the recent dogmas of the Roman Catholic church have to do with problems which, as is conceded, were not known, even in embryonic form, either in the New Testament or in the early church. The proof of the antiquity of these dogmas by Catholics is for that reason extraordinarily difficult to muster. In fact, such proof has been waived in part, and the recent dogmas have been substantiated in a way that would have been unthinkable in the ancient church or even in the Middle Ages.

The stage was set for this new development by the decree of the Council of Trent concerning the relation of Scripture and tradition. Apart from this decree the history of dogma in recent Roman Catholicism remains incomprehensible. Only the coordination of the authority of the oral apostolic tradition with the authority of Scripture has made possible the recent Catholic development of dogma. In this respect it was especially the lack of clarity in the Tridentine statements concerning the apostolic character of the oral tradition which proved to be so consequential. The Council of Trent, therefore, is very significant for the course the history of dogma has taken in recent Catholicism. The last three dogmas may be said to be a continuation of the development which began at Trent, but not of the earlier history of dogma. For this reason the Roman Catholic church cannot simply claim the element of continuity for its development of doctrine, an element which it likes to deny to Protestant churches.

This does not mean, of course, that the problems involved in the history of dogma in recent Catholicism are not also of significance in some sense to other Christian communions. The Marian dogmas not only contain teaching concerning the Virgin Mary, but also an understanding of redeemed mankind and of the church. The dogma of papal infallibility not only has for its content the authority of the highest representative of the Roman hierarchy, but also the doctrine of the authority of the church. It is self-evident, therefore, that, if the Protestant church would remain faithful to the gospel, it cannot accept these decisions. Moreover, the attempt to compromise with Roman Catholics in such questions by use of equivocal formulas, which, though they have no basis in Scripture, might be acceptable to the Roman church, must also be strongly advised against. Though certain circles within Protestantism strive toward such compromises, nothing is gained by them. It is true, however, that precisely those questions which arise in conjunction with recent Catholic dogmas, without constituting their major theme, have meaning, though in a different form, also for the Protestant church. The evangelical origins of the Reformation cannot and must not be discarded. Still, with regard to many problems, the Reformation has not yet led to final solutions. From the point of view of the New Testament there is more to be said about the church, particularly about its unity, than is to be found in the *Augsburg Confession,* for example. This and other questions which constitute the content of recent Catholic dogmas might well be regarded by the Protestant church as an occasion to unfold the richness of Scripture, developing it not with Roman Catholic but with Protestant breadth. The mere denial of the recent Catholic dogmas is as inadequate as are questionable attempts at compromise.

The Immaculate Conception of Mary

Roman Catholics often insist that the church now finds itself in the Marian age. For Catholicism this is indeed true. Two of the three Catholic dogmas which were defined during the modern period have to do with Mariology. Beyond this, the veneration of Mary occupies a very prominent place in modern Catholicism. According to present-day Catholic doctrine four statements about Mary constitute items of faith necessary to salvation. These are that Mary gave birth to God, i.e., she is the mother of God; that she remained ever virgin, even in giving birth to Jesus; that she was immaculately conceived; and, finally, that she was bodily assumed into heaven. It is possible that the Roman Catholic church will define other dogmas concerning Mary.

Mariology went through a long development before the Marian dogmas came into being. Formally this development gives evidence of many connections with, and parallels to, christological dogma, though in content it is decidedly different from other dogmas of the church. The New Testament knows of no particular Marian piety and of no Mariology. Both Matthew and Luke report, to be sure, that Jesus was born of Mary, the virgin, with Joseph playing no part in the parentage. Yet the fact that Mark, John, and Paul do not once refer to this miracle indicates that it had by no means the central significance which the Roman Catholic church accords to it. The accounts in both Matthew and Luke are probably intended to emphasize only the uniqueness of Jesus. Whatever may be the facts concerning the virgin birth, however, no special prominence of Mary is deduced from this birth in the New Testament. Everything that Roman Catholic piety and theology attempt to find in the New Testament in this connection is read into it without exception, and cannot be exegetically substantiated in any way.

It is a fact that Marian piety already experienced an upswing toward the end of the second century. At the beginning it did so particularly within certain circles of ascetic Gnosticism. The so-called *Protevangelium of James,* which stems from the second half of the second century, is the first extant assertion of the perpetual virginity of Mary. The notion that the brothers of Jesus were not sons of Mary, but came from a former marriage of Joseph, and were hence only his stepbrothers, found entrance also into ecclesiastical circles. Jerome altered this theory by asserting that the "brothers" of Jesus were his cousins, and he attempted to find exegetical proof for this view. He felt that Joseph, too, remained virgin. It is clear that in all these ideas the wish to picture Mary as an example for the ascetics was father of the thought. Augustine contributed the theory that Mary was the first to take the vow of perpetual virginity. Yet, in spite of these proliferating notions concerning Mary's ascetic manner of life, a true veneration of Mary was as good as absent from the ancient church. Even the decision during the christological controversy to concede to Mary the predicate "mother of God" (*theotokos*) does not indicate a mariological, but a christological, interest.

Mariology was developed further during the Middle Ages. The veneration of Mary, which in the ancient church was found only on the periphery and only at a late date, also became more prevalent. To venerate Mary was to venerate the mother of sorrows, the queen of heaven, the mediatrix in all afflictions. Altars to Mary were set up. Many miracles were ascribed to the ever virgin one. It was not something unusual when John Paltz (d. 1511), Luther's teacher at Erfurt, praised the humility of Mary and held that by virtue of her humility she "pulled God down" from heaven, established the three vows of chastity, poverty, and obedience (Mary is now no longer, as in Augustine, connected only with the vow of virginity), and in fact, founded all cloisters, indeed, even the entire Christian faith.[1] If piety began to have such results, we need not be surprised to find that theology gradually followed suit. If it is true anywhere, it was true in Mariology, that piety prepared the way for dogmas. Involved in all this was primarily the question whether or not Mary was subject to original sin.

The ancient church, quite like the New Testament, knew nothing of a sinless Mary. There had been no hesitancy to speak about Mary's faults and weaknesses, and some passages in the Gospels give occasion to do so. Augustine did say that when sins are being mentioned he would not wish to permit any discussion of the Virgin Mary, but he emphasizes that he does this "out of honour to the Lord."[2] Even Anselm of Canterbury (d. 1109), the father of Scholasticism, was still able to say that Mary was conceived in sin and subject to original sin, only Christ himself having been sinless.[3] The heads of the two great theological schools of Scholasticism went further, however. Thomas Aquinas does not yet maintain the immaculate conception of Mary, but he does say that after her body had been given a soul, and before she was born, she was cleansed in such a way that she did not enter into personal sin. Upon this first sanctification, he continues, a second one followed at the time of the conception of Jesus, as a result of which Mary was freed from the residue of original sin. Duns Scotus (d. 1308), on the other hand, held the opinion that Mary was already cleansed from original sin in the body of her mother. When an extensive academic controversy arose about the question, Pope Sixtus IV (1483) forbade the practice of mutual anathematizing, on the ground that the Roman church and the apostolical chair had not yet decided this question.

The state which Marian piety had now reached is, in a certain sense, even reflected in Luther's view of Mary, although one also finds in Luther severe criticism of an exaggerated

[1] B. Lohse, *Mönchtum und Reformation: Luthers Auseinandersetzung mit dem Mönchsideal des Mittelalters* (Göttingen: Vandenhoeck und Ruprecht, 1963), pp. 160-171.

[2] Augustine, *On Nature and Grace,* chap 42. *NPNF*[1] 5, 135.

[3] Anselm, *Cur Deus Homo?* chap. 2, sec. 16; in S. W. Deane (trans.), *Saint Anselm: Basic Writings* (La Salle, Ill.: Open Court, 1962), p. 269.

veneration of Mary. On various occasions Luther expressed his opinion on the question of the immaculate conception of Mary. He is closer to the Thomist than to the Scotist postion. For him Mary occupies a position "midway between Christ and other men."[4] Occasionally, however, Luther speaks critically about the immaculate conception and refers it only to Christ, not to his mother. Nor does Luther simply take a critical position toward tradition with respect to other questions related to Mariology. He, too, affirms the perpetual virginity of Mary. He even approves of the belief in Mary's bodily assumption into heaven, a belief which was already rather widely held. It is true that he rejects every possible speculation as to how Mary got to heaven, but he is sure that Mary lives in Christ together with all the saints.[5]

The new tone Luther uses in his Mariology already becomes evident at this point. It is not his concern to contradict occasional pious opinions, as long as they do not degenerate into superstition. To Luther the question here is not one concerning the merits of Mary through which she was made worthy to become the mother of Christ, but one which concerns the grace of God. For that reason Luther can even say in a sermon, "I am not much concerned as to whether she was virgin or wife, even though God wanted her to be virgin."[6] With considerable emphasis, however, Luther warns against making her divine, as was done by popery, and against seeking, in addition to this, more grace from her than from Jesus Christ.[7] Since, in the Magnificat, Mary humbles herself and gives God the glory, Luther calls her our *rechte Päpstin.*[8] Rome, he felt, converted the true Marian piety into its opposite.

This freedom which Luther preserved in his Mariology is not to be found in the Roman Catholic church at any time. To the contrary, the prevailing tendencies developed further. In a bull issued in 1661 Pope Alexander VII called the immaculate conception of Mary an ancient belief of all Christendom.[9]

[4] Luther, *Festpostille* (1527), *WA* 17^2, 288, ll. 17 f.

[5] Luther, *Predigten des Jahres 1522,* no. 44, *WA* 10^3, 268, ll. 13-269, l. 1.

[6] Luther, *Predigten des Jahres 1524,* no. 1, *WA* 15, 411, ll. 22 f.

[7] Luther, *Hauspostille* (1544), *WA* 52, 627, ll. 16-24.

[8] Luther, *Predigten des Jahres 1529,* no. 51, *WA* 29, 454, l. 31.

[9] Pope Alexander VII, *Sollicitudo omnium.* Denzinger, par. 1100.

Theology and piety had adapted themselves to each other. The belief in the immaculate conception of Mary had now become ripe for elevation to the status of dogma. This was done in 1854 by Pope Pius IX in the bull *Ineffabilis Deus,* after the opinion of the Roman Catholic bishops concerning the projected dogma had first been canvassed.[10]

This bull, which follows closely the argumentation of Alexander VII, states that "the most Blessed Virgin Mary in the first instant of her conception, by a unique grace and privilege of the omnipotent God and in consideration of the merits of Christ Jesus the Savior of the human race, was preserved free from all stain of original sin, . . ."[11] It is stated that this proposition has been "revealed by God and therefore must be firmly and constantly held by all the faithful." This decision means that the Scotist doctrine was victorious over the Thomist doctrine.

The significance of this decision is not, however, exhausted in the immediate content of the decision. It extends beyond this to the question of papal infallibility, as well as to the problem whether or not, and in what sense, proof of antiquity is needed to give dogmatic status to a proposition of faith.

With respect to the notion of papal infallibility, it is possible to see in this decision a direct preparation for the dogma of infallibility. As has been mentioned, Pius IX had sent an inquiry to the Roman Catholic bishops, requesting them to take a position on the projected elevation of the immaculate conception of Mary to the status of dogma. Not a few answers were negative. The German and Austrian bishops, especially, warned against the plan. The majority of the bishops, however, assented to it. The plan was also supported by a commission which had been set up by the pope. Pius IX did not consider the calling of a formal council for the purpose of discussing this question. He preferred to promulgate this dogma by virtue of his papal authority. He was supported in this by the opinion of those bishops and cardinals who were present in Rome and who believed in papal infallibility. Thus for the first time in the history of the church a dogma was promulgated without its having previously been considered by a council. It is self-evident

[10] Pope Pius IX, *Ineffabilis Deus.* Denzinger, par. 1641. *TCT,* par. 510.
[11] *Ibid.*

that the promulgation of a dogma asserting the infallibility of the pope was bound to follow sooner or later.

The dogma of the immaculate conception represents a novelty also with respect to proof from tradition. Formerly it had been understood that the content of a dogma had to be contained in Scripture. During the trinitarian controversy the Arians had pointed out, among other things, that the concept of *homoousia* is not found in the New Testament and should for that reason be rejected. With this argument Athanasius had no end of trouble. Vincent of Lérins, though he accepted other criteria for the establishment of items of Catholic belief, was very much concerned about the antiquity of true doctrine. Now, however, the commission Pius IX had called together declared that neither proof from Scripture nor proof from a broad and ancient stream of tradition was required to promulgate the dogma of the immaculate conception of Mary. It insisted, further, that the authority of the church today is quite sufficient to define this dogma, and that this authority even at that time, i.e., before the First Vatican Council, had its concrete expression in the pope alone. Pius IX readily accepted the opinion of his commission and hence waived every proof of antiquity in setting forth this dogma. Actually, therefore, the infallibility of the pope and of the teaching church was dogmatically asserted along with it.

The Infallibility of the Pope

Basically it is even more difficult to find proof from tradition for the dogmatic assertion of the infallibility of the pope than it is for the doctrine of the immaculate conception of Mary. In fact, in the history of the church there are not a few events which stand in opposition to any infallibility of the pope. Thus there were many obstacles which made the promulgation of the dogma of infallibility difficult. But the pope and the Curia surmounted these obstacles in the same way in which they surmounted them in connection with the first Marian dogma. They waived scriptural proofs.

In order to appreciate properly the significance of the promulgation of the dogma of infallibility it is necessary to distinguish carefully between the primacy of Rome and papal infallibility as defined by the First Vatican Council. Whatever may be the meaning of the commission given to Peter in Matthew 16:18-19, nothing is said there of any infallibility of Peter, let alone of his successors. The strong opposition which later developed between Paul and Peter, of which we read in Galatians, chap. 2, precludes any such idea with reference to apostolic times. It is true, however, that from an early date the Roman church enjoyed a certain pre-eminence in relation to other churches. This pre-eminence was based upon the fact that Peter and Paul had suffered martyrdom there. Also the size of the congregation, located in the capital of the empire, as well as its exemplary charitable work, contributed to the special honor accorded Roman Christendom. Rome, however, possessed no doctrinal authority during the days of the ancient church. Questions of doctrine were considered and decided upon by councils. The Council of Chalcedon (451) decided upon the equality of the Bishop of Constantinople with the Bishop of Rome. It is true that the representative of Rome was not present when this decision was made, and Rome has never acknowledged the decision.

During the Middle Ages it was possible for the popes to strengthen their position in all directions. In the long conflict with the emperors they emerged as victors. In the famous bull of 1302, *Unam sanctam,* Pope Boniface VIII formulated most sharply the papal claim to power: both "swords," the temporal as well as the spiritual, are said to be in the hands of the church. The latter is to be wielded by the church, the former is to be wielded for the church. The bull insists that to be saved it is necessary to subject oneself to the Roman pontiff.[12] The doctrinal authority of the pope, as well as his jurisdictional power, was increasingly emphasized during the Middle Ages. In 1075, in his *Dictatus papae,* Gregory VII stated that the Roman pope alone possesses the universal episcopate, that in the plenitude of his own power he may make and depose bishops, and that no synod may claim the rank of a general council unless it is called by the pope. The notion of the infallibility of the pope in doctrinal matters gained widespread acceptance during the days of high Scholasticism. It was maintained especially by Thomas Aquinas.

Of course, criticism of this development was not lacking dur-

[12] Denzinger, par. 469. *TCT,* par. 154.

ing the Middle Ages. The infallibility of the pope was by no means universally accepted. Even if the serious charges against exaggerated claims to papal power, made by reform theologians like John Wycliffe, are disregarded, it is still true that it was especially the councils which were opposed to the infallibility of the pope. The Council of Constance (1414-1418) declared that "as a general council rightfully convened in the Holy Spirit, representing the Catholic Church, it has its authority immediately from Christ," and that its decrees are to be obeyed by everyone in the church, even the pope.[13] The pope, then, is unquestionably subject to the authority of an ecumenical council. The popes have not acknowledged this decree. At first, however, they were unable to assert their claims over against the council. Even at the Council of Trent (1545-1563) it would still have been impossible to achieve a dogmatic statement of the infallibility of the pope. Opposition would have been too great, though the council was united in its rejection of Luther's criticism of the papacy.

As to Luther's criticism of the papacy, it was not in itself directed against the presence of a supreme authority in the church. What Luther did was to charge the papacy with putting itself into the place of Christ by proclaiming or suppressing the Word of God according to its own judgment, and, in doing so, with publishing its own human decisions falsely under the name of divine law. Referring to the withdrawal of the cup from the laity, Luther asked by what authority the church may introduce an alteration of the clear, unambiguous institution of the Lord's Supper by Christ. This question the Roman church has never answered. At least during the first years of the Reformation, Luther was willing to recognize the pope as a human authority. While Melanchthon gave evidence of such a willingness throughout his life, Luther's criticism grew increasingly harsh as he saw there was no longer any hope that the papacy might tolerate the preaching of the gospel.

Luther's attack on the papacy had no influence upon the further development of papal theories within the Roman church. On the contrary, during the modern period various factors led to a sharpening of the points of view concerning the power

[13] Carl Mirbt, *Quellen zur Geschichte des Papsttums und des römischen Katholizismus* (5th ed.; Tübingen: Mohr, 1934), no. 392, p. 228, ll. 5-16.

of the pope. Theology continued to develop further the doctrine of the infallibility of the pope. Cardinal Bellarmine (d. 1621) had already taught that the bishops do not derive their authority directly from Christ, as was the case with the apostles other than Peter, but only from the pope. For that reason, he said, only the pope as the supreme head of the church has the right to make binding decisions with respect to faith and morals. Such decisions are infallible. Even though this position met with criticism, the political reaction after the wars of liberation during the nineteenth century, as well as the Romantic movement, led to the strengthening of papal authority. In view of a multitude of new intellectual and physical distresses, which caused convulsions and revolutions in all areas of life, it seemed advisable to many to return to the wings of an idealized ecclesiastical authority. The Middle Ages were glorified as the time of intellectual and ecclesiastical unity. This is especially apparent in Novalis' treatise of 1799, *Die Christenheit oder Europa.* Last but not least, the firm, ultramontane policies of the papacy fostered the growth of papal authority. Because of these factors, it was possible for the definition of the dogma of papal infallibility to appear to many Roman Catholics as an important task of the day.

In the year 1869 Pius IX convened the Vatican Council which was to proclaim as dogma the infallibility of the pope. During the preparations for the council it had become evident that a large number of Roman Catholic church leaders meant to raise the infallibility doctrine to the status of dogma. It was pointed out that the Council of Trent had not developed further the doctrine of the church and that hence there was uncertainty among the faithful with respect to this important item of doctrine. Opposition to these plans was not lacking, to be sure. Even during the discussions in the council there were severe differences of opinion. A sizable minority wanted to block the attempt to define infallibility as a dogma. It was constituted, significantly enough, of representatives of the German, the Austrian, and the French episcopates. Of the seventeen German bishops present in Rome thirteen were in opposition; the majority of the Austrians, and about a third of the French representatives opposed the move. While there is always an opposing minority with reference to conciliar decisions, some of the reasons cited by the opponents of infallibility are of special interest.

It was emphasized, for instance, that the formulation of a dogma of infallibility was not opportune, since this would be offensive to many Christians of a different persuasion, and since, on that account, the reunion of separated churches would be made more difficult. It was also said that infallibility was not yet universally accepted and hence was not ripe for definition. More important was the objection that giving papal infallibility dogmatic status would undermine the status and significance of bishops. The objection was made, furthermore, that councils would no longer have any function. Hence, the whole constitution of the church would be basically altered. The most important argument, however, was historical in nature. During the Monothelite controversy Pope Honorius I had propagated the idea that Christ had only one will. This opinion was condemned by the Sixth Ecumenical Council at Constantinople in 681. At the same time the anathema was pronounced upon the adherents of Monothelitism, including Honorius I. Pope Leo II (682-683) confirmed this decision. While it became part of the confession of faith which every newly elected pope had to take at his enthronement, it appears to have been speedily forgotten. During the later Middle Ages it is hardly referred to anymore. In more recent times theologians like Bellarmine attempted to picture the condemnation of the pope as a mistake on the part of the council. Yet, when the infallibility of the pope was to be given dogmatic status, the opposition, and especially Bishop K. J. von Hefele of Rottenburg, the well-known historian of the councils, pointed emphatically to the conciliar decision, which actually mocks the assertion of papal infallibility.

But the pope and the adherents of infallibility cared no more for the facts of history than they did for the witness of Scripture or of the ancient church. The following episode is characteristic. When Cardinal Giudi, Archbishop of Bologna, emphasized that with regard to decisions of faith the pope is dependent upon the previously ascertained advice of the bishops, Pius IX ordered him into his presence and told him, "I am tradition." Against such a conception, of course, arguments were of no avail. The movement to give dogmatic definition to the doctrine of papal infallibility could no longer be stopped.

Concerning infallibility the decision of the council, rendered on July 18, 1870, asserts:

> And so, faithfully keeping to the tradition received from the beginning of the Christian faith, for the glory of God our Savior, for the exaltation of the Catholic religion, and for the salvation of the Christian peoples, We, with the approval of the sacred council, teach and define that it is a divinely revealed dogma: that the Roman pontiff, when he speaks ex cathedra, that is, when, acting in the office of shepherd and teacher of all Christians, he defines, by virtue of his supreme apostolic authority, doctrine concerning faith or morals to be held by the universal Church, possesses through the divine assistance promised to him in the person of St. Peter, the infallibility with which the divine Redeemer willed his Church to be endowed in defining doctrine concerning faith or morals; and that such definitions of the Roman Pontiff are therefore irreformable because of their nature, but not because of the agreement of the Church.[14]

In order to understand rightly the significance of this decision a number of things must be kept in mind. First, infallibility as here defined has no reference to the person of the pope, but to his office. It is not stated that the pope is free from personal errors or sins. Infallibility, then, is objectively limited by the following conditions: a decision must be made *ex cathedra,* its content must consist in doctrine concerning faith or morals, and, finally, it must be intended for the whole church. It is also important that the decree of infallibility is prefaced by the statement that the Holy Spirit was not promised to the successors of Peter so that by his revelation they might disclose new doctrine, but that by his help they might exercise sacred guardianship of the revelation transmitted through the apostles and of the *depositum fidei,* and might faithfully expound it.[15] Of course the credibility of this assurance is not exactly strengthened by the dogmatic assertion of infallibility. Historical reality contradicts that claim, and not even the most solemn formulations can hide the fact.

Added to these misgivings concerning the content of the dogma of infallibility must be the fact that, despite all the debates and discussions concerning the wording, certain basic points in the dogma remained ambiguous. The decision does not

[14] Denzinger, par. 1839. *TCT,* par. 219.

[15] *Dogmatic Constitution I on the Church of Christ.* Denzinger, par. 1836. *TCT,* par. 216.

indicate, for instance, just when the pope speaks *ex cathedra*. He surely must do so when he expressly makes such a claim, possibly in the defining of another dogma. But what is the status of the various other bulls, encyclicals, etc., which he issues. Since the time under discussion all important statements of the pope concerning faith and morals have actually been surrounded in the eyes of many Roman Catholics by an aura of infallibility. Furthermore, it is not clear whether or not the infallibility which is here claimed for the pope is identical with that infallibility which, according to the Roman Catholic conception, is possessed by the whole church. To say it differently, Is the pope, so to speak, the representative of an infallibility in the perception of truth which in itself is possessed by the whole church? Or is he infallible as head of the church by virtue of the special assistance promised to him by God? Roman Catholics believe that in doubtful cases that opinion is valid which does not attribute any more to a decision than what is absolutely contained therein. However, in the history of the Catholic church only too often the most radical opinion has finally prevailed.

The First Vatican Council gave dogmatic status not only to the infallibility of the pope but to his universal episcopate as well. The authority of bishops and councils with respect to canon law was thus considerably limited in favor of the authority of the pope. The most important decree states:

> And so, if anyone says that the Roman Pontiff has only the office of inspection or direction, but not the full and supreme power of jurisdiction over the whole Church, not only in matters that pertain to faith and morals, but also in matters that pertain to the discipline and government of the Church throughout the whole world; or if anyone says that he has only a more important part, and not the complete fullness of this supreme power; or if anyone says that this power is not ordinary and immediate either over each and every church or over each and every shepherd and faithful member: let him be anathema.[16]

The pope is "the true vicar of Christ, the head of the whole Church, the father and teacher of all Christians."[17] Under these circumstances it is no exaggeration to say that the pope is the real bishop of every diocese and the bishops are only his representatives. The council emphasized, to be sure, that "this power

[16] *Ibid.* Denzinger, par. 1831. *TCT*, par. 211.

[17] *Ibid.* Denzinger, par. 1826. *TCT*, par. 206.

of the Supreme Pontiff is far from standing in the way of the power of ordinary and immediate episcopal jurisdiction by which the bishops who, under appointment of the Holy Spirit, succeeded in the place of the apostles, feed and rule individually, as true shepherds, the particular flock assigned to them."[18] An appeal is then made to the statement of Gregory the Great which says, "My honor is the honor of the whole Church. My honor is the solid strength of my brothers. I am truly honored when due honor is paid to each and every one." Here, too, the fact is, however, that this assurance, no matter how honestly the council fathers may have meant it, does not alter the decrees concerning the universal episcopate of the pope, which had so many consequences. All the appeals to tradition cannot alter the fact that nowhere does tradition count for less than it does in the Roman church.

The Bodily Assumption of Mary

The validity of the fear, voiced in many circles, that the dogmatic definition of papal infallibility might lead to a superabundance of dogmas in the Roman Catholic church cannot be substantiated. Since the First Vatican Council only one new dogma has been defined, namely, the bodily assumption of Mary into heaven. It is precisely this dogma, however, which indicates that the Roman Catholic church continues resolutely on the path that begins at the Council of Trent. For certain reasons this dogma deserves even more severe criticism than the dogmatic definition of the immaculate conception of Mary.

There was extensive preparation also for this most recent dogma. In papal encyclicals and other publications the significance of Mary has been systematically underscored in recent decades. Many Catholic church leaders, as well as many simple believers, had for years been expressing the wish that the bodily assumption might be proclaimed as dogma. Once again voices of warning were not lacking within the Roman church, but the warnings went unheeded.

The dogma proclaimed by Pius XII on November 1, 1950, in the bull *Munificentissimus Deus,* has the following wording:

> We, therefore, after humbly and repeatedly praying to God, and calling upon the light of the Spirit of Truth, for the glory of

[18] *Ibid.* Denzinger, par. 1828. *TCT*, par. 208.

> almighty God, who has shown great and particular love for the Virgin Mary, for the honor of his Son, the king of immortal ages and the conqueror of sin and death, for the increase of the glory of his great mother, for the joy and exultation of the whole Church, by the authority of our Lord Jesus Christ, of the Blessed Apostles Peter and Paul, and by our own autohrity, do pronounce, declare, and define as a divinely revealed dogma: The Immaculate Mother of God, Mary ever Virgin, after her life on earth, was assumed, body and soul, to the glory of heaven.[19]

Here, too, as in the other two dogmas of recent Catholicism, it is pointed out that this is a "divinely revealed dogma."

By no means unimportant are a number of other ideas set forth in the bull. Pius XII praises the privileges of grace with which the Virgin Mary is said to be endowed. He states that by His death Christ broke the power of sin and death. Yet, the faithful are not thereby saved from death. Only at the last day will the victory of Christ come to its full fruition. The most blessed Virgin Mary, however, is excepted from this general law. "She has gained the victory over sin through a special privilege of grace, through her immaculate conception, was for that reason not subject to the law of the corruption of the grave, and did not need to wait to the end of time for the redemption of her body."

These details are worth noting because they render invalid the attempts of certain Roman Catholic theologians to weaken this dogma by interpreting it. Karl Rahner has tried to take away the sting of this new dogma, which is felt even by many Catholics, by pointing to Matthew 27:52-53, where, within the framework of the passion story of Jesus, the author speaks of the resurrection of various people.[20] Rahner comes to the conclusion that if such special grace has been given even to other people, something similar may be asserted of Mary. This interpretation does not take into consideration, however, that the papal bull insists upon an exception from the general law in the case of Mary. It would seem, then, that this interpretation does not render truly the sense of this dogma.

The objections which must be raised against this dogma are

[19] Pope Pius XII, *Munificentissimus Deus.* Denzinger, par. 2333. *TCT,* par. 520.

[20] K. Rahner, *Das "neue" Dogma* (Vienna: Herder, 1951). Cited in Walther von Loewenich, *Modern Catholicism,* trans. Reginald H. Fuller (New York: St. Martin's, 1959), p. 210.

so many in number that only two of them can be mentioned here. The proof of this dogma on the basis of Scripture and tradition is even more difficult to muster than for any earlier Catholic dogma. To say it more bluntly, both Scripture and tradition univocally contradict this dogma. The first four hundred years of the history of the church do not contain a thing about any bodily assumption of Mary into heaven. Such a conception occurs for the first time in the fifth century, in the apocryphal treatise *The Passing of the Virgin Mary.* The treatise is so replete with fantastic legends that it would be difficult to imagine a worse foundation for a dogma than its assertion of Mary's assumption into heaven. Not until the beginning of the sixth century did theologians begin to accept the idea of a bodily assumption of Mary. The leading motive in this connection was the notion that such an assumption would be "fitting." On this basis, of course, a multitude of things can be proved.

Roman Catholics answer the objection regarding the age of the tradition by saying that to give a proposition dogmatic status proof from Scripture and tradition is not necessary. The living consciousness of the now existing church of Christ, it is asserted, is fully sufficient. This, the argument continues, finds its visible expression in the teaching office (magisterium) of the pope, and he in turn speaks infallibly in such a case. Against this kind of argumentation it can only be pointed out again and again that the contemporary Roman Catholic church, as long as it continues to think that way, has forsaken the foundations which for more than a thousand years determined the faith and doctrine of the church.

Another serious objection, however, needs to be made. The dogma of the immaculate conception of Mary still has a somewhat evangelical ring to it insofar as it emphasizes that Mary was made worthy of that special grace "in view of the merits of Jesus Christ." There is no such reference in the dogma of the bodily assumpion. This could hardly be an accident. The reason for this difference is found in the fact that within the new Catholicism, Mary has been steadily gaining a significance of her own alongside Christ. Pointing to older opinions, Pius XI, before he became pope, had already declared it to be a praiseworthy custom to designate Mary as "co-redemptrix."[21] In subsequent

[21] Denzinger, par. 1978*a*, note 2.

statements of the Roman Catholic teaching office similar opinions have been expressed repeatedly.

Indeed, signs are not lacking that some day the Roman church will give dogmatic status to the assertion that Mary is co-redemptrix. In this respect the Marian dogmas accord with the Catholic doctrine about the coordinate operation of divine grace and human nature. Ever more frequently the proposition is heard that the veneration of the Virgin Mary is the only way to Christ. Mary is even brought into relation to the Eucharist.[22] Not infrequently she is mentioned as the lady of the most holy sacraments. "Christ and Mary" is substituted for "Christ alone." Mariology, therefore, represents a barrier between the Protestant and Roman Catholic communions which is especially difficult to overcome. If with respect to many other problems they have today drawn closer together than they were at the time of the Reformation, this is more than offset by the estrangement on questions of Mariology.

[22] See G. Maron, "Maria und die Eucharistie," *Evangelische Theologie*, 22 (1962), 394-410.

8

Dogma within Protestantism

Is There a History of Dogma within Protestantism?

It is incomparably more difficult to write a history of dogma for Protestantism than it is for recent Catholicism. Even though in the Roman church both the understanding of dogma and the character of dogma have changed considerably, it cannot be denied that, at least since the Council of Trent, there has been a certain continuity in the development of the official doctrinal decisions of Rome. The same cannot be maintained for Protestantism. The difficulties which obstruct the attempt to write a history of doctrine with reference to Protestantism are many in number as well as in kind. The most important of them should be mentioned here.

First, there is the difficulty that Protestantism in general presents anything but a unified picture. It is fragmented into a great number of different confessions and denominations. In their teaching all of these emphasize different segments of the dogmas of the ancient church and of the decisions of the Reformation. Because of this there has been no unified development of doctrine within Protestantism. There are many other differences, however, which were shaped by certain political and intellectual changes and revolutions, and which have exerted considerable influence upon the various Protestant churches. The Church of England, for instance, was formed not only by the particular course which the history of the Reformation took in England, but also by the close contiguity of church and state which has existed there for centuries. The English Nonconformists, on the other hand, never maintained the radical enmity against the state which on the Continent was found among many enthusiasts. For that reason they generally possess what may be regarded as the characteristics of a major communion. The Lutheran and Reformed state churches, which existed for a while and still do exist in some countries, also followed paths of doctrinal development which were different from those, let us say, in Bohemia and Moravia, where the evangelical congregations were permanently shaped, not only by their opposition to the Roman Catholic monarchy of Austria, but also by John Huss and the Bohemian Brethren. The question now is, In writing a history of doctrine for Protestantism, what points of view should determine the selection of materials that must inevitably be made?

Even disregarding the nontheological factors does not make it easier to treat the doctrinal development of Protestantism, for this development is itself anything but uniform. In the recent history of the Church of England, for instance, the doctrine of apostolic succession plays an important role. The Lutheran bishops of Sweden, on the other hand, are also in apostolic succession, though the Swedish church attributes no doctrinal significance to this fact. The Lutheran churches of the Continent, which do not possess this tradition, also do not regard it as essential. Furthermore, the Reformed churches of the Continent, whose doctrine has affinities with the basic doctrinal document of the Anglican church, the Thirty-nine Articles, see in the doctrine of apostolic succession a falsification of the Christian faith and a denial of the message of the Reformation. Thus it is that precisely at the one point in the history of Protestantism where a significant body of doctrine did develop the writing of a unified history of doctrine for Protestantism is impossible. The same is even more true of certain special doctrines which here and there were placed into the center of interest by certain smaller Protestant denominations.

Even if dogmas are regarded as confessions, the task confronting us cannot easily be accomplished. There is not a single confession in the history of Protestantism which could be remotely compared in its significance with the dogmas of the ancient church or with the confessional writings of the Reformation. Basically this is true also of the *Barmen Declaration.* Admittedly this declaration was important during the days of the German church's struggle with National Socialism, and it is significant insofar as it represents an attempt to confess the Christian faith in a new way. Yet, not even the Protestant churches of Germany have all made it part of their doctrinal foundation or of the confessional obligation of their pastors. Much less was this declaration accepted as binding by all of Protestantism.

For these reasons it actually seems best that for Protestantism the history of dogma should be regarded as coming to an end at the time of the Reformation. The history of doctrine within modern Protestantism could then be treated, as it is in the Protestant theological faculties in Germany, either within the framework of modern church history or as part of the history of theology.

Still such a solution is not satisfactory. The history of Protestantism indicates, to be sure, that dogma has entered a crisis, even as, in its own way, does the history of recent Catholicism. This dogmatic crisis has many causes. Within Protestantism these causes must, in part, be sought in the change which theology underwent during the age of Orthodoxy. From the point of view of the history of thought, the development of historical thinking is also responsible for the crisis of dogma. This constitutes a development which in the last analysis was unavoidable and with which Protestantism has to come to terms. Yet that this crisis of dogma does not also spell the end of dogma became evident, significantly enough, during the last decades of the history of Protestantism. The significance of the *Barmen Declaration* reaches far beyond the official reception which it has been given in Protestant churches. From a certain point of view the ecumenical movement, too, is part of Protestantism's history of dogma. Of course the contours of a history of dogma for Protestantism are discernible only in broad outline at this point. For that reason the following can only represent an attempt to break new ground.

The Age of Orthodoxy

The epoch between the Reformation and the Enlightenment is rightly called the confessional age. Theologically this period is notable for the primacy of Orthodoxy, or of pure doctrine, which in the great classical dogmatic systems was set forth on the foundation provided by the Reformation. The beginnings of the age of Orthodoxy reach back to the middle of the sixteenth century. Upon completion of the *Formula of Concord* (1577) the formation of Reformation doctrine within Lutheranism was basically ended. Within the Reformed churches the Synod of Dort (1618-1619) occupies a similar place by virtue of the rigid stand it took on predestination over against the attempted softening of that doctrine by Jacob Arminius (1560-1609) of Leiden and by the Arminians. In both of these great churches of the Reformation a new scholasticism now took rise. It was a scholasticism which, in the rigidity of its systems, compares with that of the Middle Ages.

If in our day a theologian is said to be orthodox, this is usually not intended as a compliment. In present-day usage, the concept of orthodoxy generally denotes something that is ossified, fossilized, even dead. On the other hand, we praise the "openness" of those who do not cling to the old, but who take seriously the questions of our day. The Orthodoxy of the Lutheran and the Reformed churches is not without blame for the fact that the concept of orthodoxy has come to have this negative connotation. In practically all areas of theology Orthodoxy substituted something static for the dynamic of the Reformation. The boundaries between the confessions gradually hardened. In every church the primary concern was purity of doctrine.

It would be wrong, of course, to think of Orthodoxy as hollow. In spite of their overemphasis upon doctrine the men of that day were still basically concerned about the faith. Men like Paul Gerhard or John Sebastian Bach were not men who stood outside the church; they supported the concerns of the church with their whole heart. In those days the question of truth was not taken lightly. For that reason a hasty judgment of Orthodoxy must not be made.

From the point of view of the history of dogma, in what does the uniqueness of Orthodoxy consist? In the nature of the case, several answers may be given to this question. With reference to systematic theology the epoch of Orthodoxy has been exceptionally fruitful, for example, in connection with the definition of the relation between reason and revelation. In addition to this, the age of Orthodoxy led to many new attempts to define doctrine authoritatively, though none of these new confessions gained general acceptance. If the theological work of Orthodoxy is compared with the earlier development of doctrine in the church, and if the subsequent epoch of the Enlightenment and of critical thinking is also kept in mind, it would appear that Orthodoxy's uniqueness in the history of dogma lies in the doctrine of Holy Scripture. Neither before nor after was the doctrine of Scripture as central as it was within Orthodoxy. This does not mean, of course, that other epochs did not not also give much thought to the authority of Scripture. Yet it was Orthodoxy that gave priority to this question. The way in which Orthodoxy developed this doctrine helped, at the same time, to prepare indirectly for the later epoch of the Enlightenment.

It is significant that the older confessional writings of Lutheranism do not contain a section on the doctrine of Scripture. That both Luther and Melanchthon held to the principle of "Scripture alone" (*sola scriptura*) is self-evident. It was felt, however, and for good reasons, that it was not necessary to secure this principle in a confession. For Luther the authority of Scripture was never a formal one. It was always located in its center, which means in Jesus Christ. This being the case, it was possible for Luther, on the one hand, to be very critical of a certain book of the canon, as he was of the Letter of James or the Book of Revelation. On the other hand, he could assign almost canonical authority to later Christian confessions, as long as they witnessed to Christ in the right way.

The first doctrinal allusion to Scripture is found in the *Formula of Concord* of 1577 and bears this title: "The Comprehensive Summary, Rule, and Norm according to which all Doctrines should be Judged and the Errors which Intruded should be Explained and Decided in a Christian Way." It then states:

> We believe, teach, and confess that the prophetic and apostolic writings of the Old and New Testaments are the only rule and norm according to which all doctrines and teachers alike must be appraised and judged. . . . Other writings of ancient and modern teachers, whatever their names, should not be put on a par with Holy Scripture. Every single one of them should be subordinated to the Scriptures and should be received in no other way and no further than as witnesses to the fashion in which the

doctrine of the prophets and apostles was preserved in post-apostolic times.[1]

In itself this principle coincided entirely with the theology of Luther. And yet we find here the first traces of that development which sought to find in Scripture merely proofs for a comprehensive system of doctrine and which, at the same time, used Scripture as a law book for the purpose of deciding controversial issues.

When the fathers of the *Formula of Concord* penned these sentences, the doctrine of the divine inspiration of Scripture was already beginning to be developed here and there by dogmaticians. The idea that the authors of the canonical books were inspired by God was, of course, not new in itself. It goes back to the earliest days of the church, and certain traces of it are already found in the New Testament (cf. 2 Tim. 3:16; 2 Pet. 1:21). It was in Hellenistic Judaism, especially, that one found a well-developed doctrine of inspiration which the ancient church drew upon in its own thinking. In general, however, the church did not understand inspiration to mean that the personality of the biblical author was totally eliminated from the process of writing. According to Origen inspiration does not consist in the blotting out of the writer's consciousness, but rather in the illumination of his consciousness and in the good judgment he displayed. Of course, occasionally theories were already being advanced about the dictation of Scripture by the Holy Spirit. In general, however, the doctrine of inspiration was not developed to its final state of acuteness either in the ancient church or during the Middle Ages. One reason was that the authority of the church guaranteed at the same time the authority of Scripture. There was therefore no necessity to develop further the doctrine of Scripture.

When at the Council of Trent the Roman church developed its doctrine in comprehensive fashion, the doctrine of Scripture had to be given greater weight within Protestantism. The Roman concept of the inspiration of Scripture and tradition required that the Protestants take the position that Scripture alone is inspired. Protestantism, however, went beyond the older conception and attempted to fix the inspiration of Scripture objec-

[1] *Formula of Concord,* Pt. I: Epitome, "Rule and Norm," 1, *BC,* pp. 464-465.

tively. This was done in order to obtain a bastion which would be safe from attack by the Roman church. To achieve this goal not even the most curious theories were disdained.

The theological controversialist of the sixteenth century, Matthias Flacius Illyricus (1520-1575), already held a distinctive form of the doctrine of inspiration. Not only is the wording of the canonical books inspired, said Flacius, but so are the Hebrew vowel points given below the consonants in the text of the Old Testament. Flacius asked, If the churches permit the devil to throw doubt upon this hypothesis, will not all Scripture lose its authority for us completely? He emphasizes, too, that the Holy Spirit would hardly present us with a doctrine of God which is obscurely and indistinctly recorded in the Scriptures. It is rather God's intention, so he continues, that everything is to be understood by the church, so that it will know how to honor God and to find the way to its blessed destiny. Thus the Holy Spirit is the author of Scripture and, at the same time, its interpreter.[2]

Flacius' successors developed this conception further. In doing so they followed Scholastic distinctions, differentiating between the efficient cause of Scripture and the less important (*minus principalis*) cause. The former is the Holy Spirit, the latter consists in holy men who, under the impulsion of the Holy Spirit, wrote down word for word what was given to them. The authors of the canonical Scriptures were nothing more than the stylus employed by the Holy Spirit. For that reason the individuality of the biblical authors played no role in the composition of the Scriptures.

The Orthodox dogmaticians even drew up a series of criteria by which inspiration was to be recognized. In his dogmatics David Hollaz (1648-1713) differentiates between external and internal criteria. Among the external criteria are the age of the writing, the special light possessed by the holy "writing aids" (i.e., the writers), their striving for insight and truth, the glory of the miracles by which the heavenly doctrine of Scripture is supported, the unanimous testimony to the divinity of Scripture by a church that encompasses the earth, the steadfastness of the martyrs, and the severe punishments which came upon those

[2] Matthias Flacius Illyricus, *Clavis scripturae sacrae* (Basel, 1567), vol. 2, tractate 1, *Regulae cognoscendi sacras literas*, par. 3. Cited in E. Hirsch, *Hilfsbuch zum Studium der Dogmatik* (3rd printing; Berlin: Walter de Gruyter, 1958), p. 314.

who scorned and persecuted the divine Word. In referring to the internal criteria Hollaz thinks, for example, of the majesty of God who witnesses to himself in the Holy Book, of the exalted nature and the gravity of the style of the canonical books, of the truth of all biblical assertions, and of the sufficiency of Holy Scripture for eternal salvation.[3]

At the beginning of the seventeenth century the doctrine of scriptural inspiration was the subject of a lively controversy. While Hermann Rahtmann (1585-1628), a pastor in Danzig, did not deny the doctrine of inspiration as such, he did modify it by asserting that the supernatural element which the inspired Scripture possesses is not present except in its use; it is added only when the Word is proclaimed. Rahtmann emphasized that God did not reveal Scripture for the purpose of letting it stand on paper as a dead letter, but in order that through the Spirit and through faith it might come to life within us and make of us new creatures. His opponents charged, and not without some justification, that his position was determined by the distinction between Scripture and Spirit, which had been made by Schwenckfeld and others, and that therefore he must be numbered among the enthusiasts. Rahtmann's opponents, on the other hand, became involved in very problematical assertions. The demurrer which the theological faculty of Jena issued in 1626 concerning the teaching of Rahtmann objects, to be sure, to the opinion that a magical or supernatural power of illumination is to be ascribed to the words of Scripture. Thereupon, however, the Jena theologians assert, not only that "the word which is heard, read, and reflected upon will work faith in the hearts of those who will read it, hear it, and reflect upon it," but also that the divine power which works faith is always present in the sense and understanding of Scripture as the "internal form of the Word," and that for this reason Scripture possesses its internal power, even if it is not being used.[4]

For the present, then, Rahtmann's view was rejected. Nevertheless, it represents the first attempt to mitigate a doctrine of scriptural inspiration which had been pushed to extremes. Other

[3] David Hollaz, *Examen theologicum acroamaticum* (1707), Prolegomenon, part III, questions 29-30. Hirsch, *op. cit.*, p. 316.

[4] From the statement of the Jena theologians, George Major, John Gerhard, and John Himmel. Cited in Hirsch, *op. cit.*, pp. 319-321, from John Musaeus, *Introductio in theologiam* (Jena, 1679).

attempts soon were to follow this first one. They were undertaken much more insistently, and finally succeeded in calling into question the whole Orthodox doctrine of Scripture. It must be considered fortunate that the doctrine of Scripture was not set forth at this time in a manner which was binding upon the Evangelical church. Instead, there was a disposition to be satisfied with decisions which occupy a position clearly less authoritative than the dogmas of the ancient church or the confessional writings of the Reformation. That the proponents of Orthodoxy did not attempt to make their formulations binding is not to be attributed to their insight into the problems in their own position nor to their embarrassment at having to formulate a new confession. The reason is to be found, rather, in an overemphasis upon the authority of the confessional writings, to which one would not dare to add anything. The truth is that Orthodoxy, in spite of the greatness which must be attributed to much of its theological work, never satisfactorily solved the problem of the development of the doctrine of Holy Scripture, though this was a problem which had been peculiarly its own. It was for this reason that the crisis in which this dogma soon found itself was bound to become so serious and so radical.

The Rise of Historical Thinking

While Orthodoxy was still in process of pursuing its doctrine of verbal inspiration to its remotest consequences, a sharp attack was already being launched against it from various sides. In historical sequence it was Pietism which first opposed Orthodoxy, only to be soon followed by a much more far-reaching movement.

In its criticism of the Orthodox doctrine of inspiration Pietism did not begin with the scientific untenability of the doctrine. It was concerned, rather, with the practical use to which this doctrine was put in the church. One could hardly say that there was actual polemic within Pietism against Orhodoxy's doctrine of inspiration. Still, for Pietism this doctrine was a house in which it could not feel at home. The tendency was, therefore, to acknowledge fully the doctrine of inspiration and to let it rest upon its own evidence. Beyond this, however, the emphasis was made that the doctrine of inspiration and its acknowledgment is not of decisive significance, but that the important thing is living faith and the inner experience of that to which Scripture witnesses. The mere knowledge of Scripture, and the external acknowledgment of its authority, is not sufficient, for these do not bring one beyond a dead, historical faith. What is necessary is that the truth of the scriptural assertions be personally experienced. Man must feel in his own life the power of sin and the saving power of grace. For that reason the problem of the total content of the faith is less important than constant self-examination as to whether or not one really believes.

With respect to this basic concern the various intellectual leaders of Pietism, whether Philipp Jacob Spener (1635-1705), the "father of Pietism," or August Hermann Francke (1663-1727), or Count Nikolaus Ludwig von Zinzendorf (1700-1760), are agreed. Considered individually, certain marked differences existed between them. Spener emphasized more than those who came after him his agreement with Orthodoxy, though he was drawn into severe controversy with it. Francke departed further from Orthodoxy by emphasizing personal striving for salvation [*Busskampf*]. From his congregation of brethren Zinzendorf finally formed his own church, which simply ignored the confessional divisions of an earlier day and thus represents one of the first church unions: the confessions of the churches no longer possessed final authority but were replaced and relativized by the experience of faith and the confession of Christ.

Orthodox theologians quickly perceived that, in spite of Pietism's professed loyalty to the church's doctrine, a new spirit was at work here. Even though the controversy between Orthodoxy and Pietism was often very severe and petty, some of the theologians of that day were able to appreciate its significance. A man such as Valentine Ernest Löscher (1673-1749), one of the last and best representatives of Orthodoxy, warned with great anxiety and much earnestness against the danger of subordinating the content of faith to a religiosity that is subjective and psychological. It cannot be gainsaid that there was some justification to this criticism. Quite frequently, though by no means always, Pietism had a disintegrating influence upon the authority of Scripture and of the confessions. On the other hand, there can be no doubt that Pietism brought to life motives which had been important for Luther. What in the Reformation had constituted a unity was now separated into two parties, Orthodoxy and Pietism. For Luther the authority of the Word was founded in the fact that it witnessed to Jesus Christ; at the same time, however, it showed itself to be the truth that bound and freed his conscience. In the meantime Orthodoxy had succeeded only in holding to the formalized and historicized truth of Scripture, while Pietism was in danger of making subjective experience the criterion for the objective validity of the affirmations of faith.

In the controversy between Orthodoxy and Pietism there are occasional traces of a new problem which was to occupy both the theology and the church in the modern era as has hardly another, namely, the problem of historical thinking, with all of its consequences for the faith and doctrine of the church. It is true that in the controversy between Orthodoxy and Pietism the problem of history was never central. This does not obviate the fact, however, that unbeknown to the contending parties, the problem of history and of historical relativity formed the background to the controversy. The Pietist criticism of the Orthodox doctrine of inspiration must, to say the least, be understood in part with this in mind.

Modern historical thinking, beginning in the eighteenth century and slowly but increasingly penetrating all areas, has various roots and causes which, in part, reach far back. By historical thinking we do not mean only the Enlightenment. On the other hand, historical thinking and the Enlightenment cannot be separated from each other, since there are innumerable connections between the two. Still, in a summary of the history of Protestant doctrine, it may be well to keep the two apart. That the Enlightenment and historical thinking are not simply identical becomes evident in two prominent men, namely, Semler and Lessing. Both of them were more than representatives of the Enlightenment, and both contributed to the victory of historical thinking in the realm of theology. It is certain that the Enlightenment was in part responsible for the rise of historical thinking. Without the secularization of education, and without a point of view critical of the traditional teaching of the church, it would have been impossible to regard history critically. Historical thinking, however, developed very quickly into a method of doing scientific and theological investigation which was decidedly independent of the philosophical and theological systems of the theologians of the Enlightenment, all of which were conditioned by their time. For that reason it was a method which was to outlast the collapse of the world view of the Enlightenment in the period of Idealism and Romanticism. It was a method, furthermore, which was to help generate movements such as the historicism of the nineteenth century, while at the same time it could separate itself from those movements in order to celebrate its real triumph only in our own day. The rise of historical thinking is one of the greatest movements in the intellectual history of mankind.

Should contemporary historical thinking be included in a history of dogma? Within the framework of a history of dogma, would it not be better to speak of the various theological-philosophical systems of the Enlightenment and of their theological exponents? It is undoubtedly true that a history of theology must regard the treatment of the ideas of the theology of the Enlightenment as one of its primary tasks. Yet if by the history of dogma we mean the history of the church's confession, or of its doctrinal confession, and if our concern is not merely with the past formulation of certain affirmations of faith but also with their new appropriation and interpretation, then the historically conditioned and long since superseded systems of the theologians of the Enlightenment are of much less importance than is historical thinking itself. For it was as a result of the latter that the traditional teaching of the church in its entirety, as well as the biblical canon, became problematical in an unprecedented way. At the same time, however, it becomes clear that in the presence of historical thinking it is not enough to formulate this or that confession, but that theology had to permit itself to be drawn into this movement. Only thus could it participate in the general intellectual development and keep from becoming a victim of fossilization.

There can be no doubt that at first, and for some time to come, the effect of historical thinking on theology and the church was largely destructive and corrosive. The canon, the dogmas, and the confessions of the church were much more sharply attacked and more fully corroded by historical criticism than they had been by any heresy prior to the eighteenth century. It is possible, therefore, to write the history of dogma as the criticism of dogma; and it is possible to see in the attempt to keep the old confessions nothing more than a hysterical clinging to superseded forms as well as content. On the other hand, historical thinking has made it possible for theology to value the meaning of dogmas and confessions in an entirely new way. The understanding that they are historically conditioned and contingent does not detract from the importance either of the canon or of dogmas. Perhaps it is true that, as a result of such thinking, much of the luster of the doctrinal assertions of the church has been lost. Yet only in this way has it become radically clear that faith is not founded upon metaphysically demonstrable truths, but that it is ever and again called to decision; that, in fact, it can be faith only if it dispenses with external means of certainty. In this sense historical thinking has appropriated motifs which were already present in Luther's theology, though in different form. Above all, however, historical thinking has made it possible for theology to see clearly the uniqueness of biblical religion, which is, of course, specifically historical. The phenomenon of history was first recognized by ancient Israel. It is no accident, therefore, that historical thinking arose upon the soil of the Christian West.

The founder of the historical-critical method in theology was Johann Salomo Semler (1725-1791), professor of theology at Halle. In numerous studies he demonstrated the gradual development of the biblical canon, and in doing so undermined the Orthodox doctrine of the verbal inspiration of Scripture. For him the canon was no longer a dogmatic but a historical concept. Furthermore, Semler showed that the Orthodox doctrine of Scripture rests upon certain assumptions, which have nothing to do with the content of the Christian faith. In this way it was possible for Semler to refute the Orthodox doctrine of verbal inspiration, showing it to be a hypothesis which is scientifically untenable.

It has frequently been asserted that Semler was guided in his criticism by rationalistic considerations which actually left no more room for revelation. In contradistinction to this, it should be pointed out that in spite of the dated quality of many aspects of Semler's thought, he was not a devotee of rationalism. Though critical of the Orthodox doctrine of Scripture, he did not really surrender the concept of inspiration as such. The content of Holy Scripture does indeed derive from an infusion, said Semler. This, however, must not be understood as verbal inspiration but, rather, as real inspiration; i.e., Scripture and Word for Semler are not identical, but the Word of God is, first of all, Christ himself, and then it is also the apostolic witness to Christ. In similar fashion Semler could no longer recognize uncritically and without question the authority of dogmas. He pointed to the historical contingency of given doctrinal formulations and felt that theology had the task of examining the agreement of dogmas and confessions with Scripture.

It is understandable that at the time such a point of view was bound to have a corroding effect at first. The Orthodox theologians thought that failing to maintain the literal authority of Scripture would cause the very foundations to shake. At the same time the obligation of the pastors to be faithful to the confessions necessarily became a problem. Can one be obligated to a confession the historical contingency of which is clear? Thus for the first time questions were asked which during the nineteenth and twentieth centuries were to lead to heated controversies, but concerning which surprisingly little is heard in our own day. Semler held that it was possible to obligate a person to doctrine but not to faith. Though such a distinction may in some ways be justified, it does not really solve the problem which is involved here.

It was Gotthold Ephraim Lessing (1729-1781) who questioned the traditional view of doctrine much more radically than Semler. Lessing himself undertook extensive historical studies, including some in the area of church history, all of which materially aided theological research. In this way he came to the quite correct conclusion that Christianity is older than the Bible. He held that originally the source and norm of both the proclamation and the doctrine of the church was not the canon of the New Testament, but the rule of faith. In saying this Lessing was the first to accord proper recognition to the great importance which must be attributed to the rule of faith during the early days of the church.

Yet more important than Lessing's historical contributions to certain problems are his basic insights concerning the nature of the Christian faith as a specifically historical religion. In his very important treatise *Ueber den Beweis des Geistes und der Kraft* ("On the Proof of the Spirit and of Power") there is the well-known dictum, "Accidental truths of history can never become the proof of necessary truths of reason." This sentence asserts neither that necessary truths of reason are self-evident, and that history is therefore of no significance for them, nor that truths of history may never under any circumstances become truths of reason. It is true that Lessing points to the "broad and horrid ditch" which separates one's own present from the past, and across which no one can leap, not even by means of Orthodox artificialities. Yet, the thrust of Lessing's dictum is that historical truths which are merely inherited, the significance of which is not newly experienced, cannot become truths of reason. They can become such only if in themselves they become meaningful to a person, thus becoming actually "necessary" to him. In that case, however, they have lost their character as accidental truths.

While Lessing was deeply involved in controversy with the Orthodoxy of his day, and while he posed problems which theology was not able to solve, so that he often appeared to it as an opponent of Christianity, the liberating deed which he performed for the Christian faith and for its affirmations must not be forgotten. To see in the affirmations of faith metaphysical truths revealed in history contradicts not only modern historical thinking, but the nature of faith and of the Christian message as well. When Lessing said that the Christian faith can never be based upon historical proofs, he displayed a better understanding of that faith than did his Orthodox opponents. Faith is possible only on the basis of one's own responsibility. The truth of religion cannot be proved by external means. The only proof there is, is that of the Spirit and of power.

During the two centuries since then the historical thinking which penetrated theology through Semler and Lessing has asserted itself everywhere. At many points, of course, theological study progressed far beyond the results of these two pioneers. Basically, however, we still face the same questions they faced. The problems which were first noted by them cannot be solved once and for all. No *Deus ex machina* can leap across the "horrid ditch" of history. The attempt has frequently been made to underestimate the significance of the questions which Lessing put to theology. During the confessionalistic revival movement of the nineteenth century, men like August Frederick Christian Vilmar (1800-1868) emphasized the authority of the canon and of the confessions without taking account of the results of critical theology. Yet the questions Lessing asked cannot be suppressed in any age.

If one wished to bring the history of dogma, with respect to Protestantism, down to the present day, it would be necessary to write the history of modern biblical scholarship. There is a single line which leads from the Orthodox doctrine of inspiration, past the historical thinking of the Enlightenment, to the problem of the historical Jesus. In this respect the history of dogma has come to be included in the whole range of theological investigation as well as in that of the church's proclamation. The modern problems of the demythologizing of the message of the New Testament, and of hermeneutic, i.e., the right understanding and interpretation of Scripture, are the results of this development. Whether they are welcomed or not, they cannot be undone.

No longer is modern Protestantism concerned merely with the setting forth of certain confessions, as were earlier epochs. It has been drawn into the broad movement of intellectual history. Nevertheless, the end of dogma, or of the history of dogma, has not arrived. It is true, of course, that we face the task of correct interpretation and acceptance of inherited dogma in a measure not known in the past. In this connection it is necessary to warn against the mere repristination of outworn affirmations as well as against a thoughtless rejection of the inheritance of the past. Even though historical thinking is a modern phenomenon, the best thinkers in all periods of the church's history have known that faith is not exhausted in metaphysical propositions. If it is remembered that the ancient church with its dogmas did not want to plumb the mystery of the divine person, but that it meant to confess its faith with reference to certain newly raised problems, it becomes clear that in the history of dogma every attempt at iconoclasm is totally misplaced. If Christianity sees dogmas and confessions in their historical contingency, it may just be possible that it may learn to express its faith in the language of today.

The Barmen Declaration

The history of dogma with respect to Protestantism must not lose itself, however, in theological confrontation with modern thought and in ever new attempts to interpret rightly the inherited affirmations of faith. The church of our day also faces the task of confessing the faith in a way that is new and binding. That this is no less a duty in our day than during past epochs of church history became especially clear to the Protestant church in Germany during the days of the Third Reich. The German church's struggle in that period has considerable significance from the point of view of the history of dogma as well as in other contexts.

It can rightly be maintained that the time to appreciate this struggle fully in its relation both to church history and to the history of dogma has not yet come. We lack the perspective necessary to see the complexities of the recent past in their totality, and thus to be able to place the accents correctly. The struggle of the church with the German Christians (*Deutsche Christen*) and with the representatives of power in the Third Reich has many aspects. For instance, there was the concern to prevent the totalitarian state from encroaching on the domain of the church. To this extent the struggle which ensued is part of the history of the contest between church and state. Then there is the fact that during the years after 1933 the church came increasingly to the realization that it has a responsibility for the world and for men, i.e., that it cannot be content to exist in a ghetto. Hence the struggle of the German church begins a new chapter in the relation between the church and the public domain. The main issue, however, was that the church was forced into a new venture as a result of the demand of the German Christians that the church should perceive in the events of 1933 and in the mission of Adolf Hitler the unambiguous leading of God's hand. It had to rethink the foundations and the criteria of its proclamation and faith in a way which had been made possible by the revival of evangelical theology following World War I, especially as a result of the work of Karl Barth. To the extent that this was the case, the struggle in which the German church became involved belongs to the history of Protestant theology.

This is not meant to be, however, nor could it be, an attempt to make this recent struggle of the church a part of the history of dogma already at this time and thus an attempt to preserve this struggle for posterity. For such a venture the questions involved in the struggle are still much too urgent for both theology and the church. Here we merely want to point out that such a struggle is of significance also for the history of dogma. If making the faith and confession of the church vital in each age is what the history of dogma is all about, if it is never enough simply to hold on to the faith of the fathers, if it is necessary to confess in every new situation once again the totality of the Christian faith, then it is certain that the recent struggle of the German church is also an event in the history of dogma of the Evangelical church as a whole.

In the light of the history of dogma, what is the significance of this struggle? It is to be found in the fact that the church gave an account of itself regarding the sources of its proclamation and its doctrine, that it publicly confessed these foundations of its faith in a new way, and that it thereby drew lines of demarcation not only between itself and the totalitarian state of the Third Reich with its neo-paganism, but also between itself and all attempts to regard certain historical events, or a certain natural, racial disposition of man, as the norm or content of preaching. The Confessing Church's opposition to National Socialism and its insistence upon law and justice were important, to be sure. Yet from the point of view of the history of dogma the real fruit of the church's recent struggle is to be found in its new and unprecedented reflection on God's revelation in Jesus Christ as distinct from all other kinds of revelation.

For this reason the important statements of the Confessing Church, and especially the *Barmen Declaration*, possess a significance which goes far beyond the fending off of certain attempts at state interference with the church. The reasons for the development of the Confessing Church are of course important in themselves. In their attempt to found a national church of which all Protestant state churches were to become members, an attempt supported by many acts of force, the German Christians showed themselves to be manifestly wrong. But from the very beginning the struggle between the Confessing Church and the German Christians involved much more than a controversy concerning certain points of law. For that reason it is a mistake to regard the Confessing Church mainly as an opposing group. Actually it does not bear its name in vain, in that it was primarily concerned with that which is positive, namely, confessing. Its act of confession of course divided the church sharply.

The Synod of Barmen, which met as the first confessional synod of the German Protestant church from May 29 to May 31, 1934, undoubtedly represents the high-water mark of the German church's struggle. It is true that there is no lack of other courageous words, which in certain respects went even further in denying the heresy of the German Christians as well as neo-paganism. In 1936 there was, for instance, the memorandum of the provisional leadership of the Confessing Church, which told Hitler the truth in no uncertain terms. Yet from the point of view of the history of theology and of the history of dogma the Synod of Barmen is undoubtedly more important.

The following are the most important statements of the theological declaration of the Synod of Barmen:

> 1. Jesus Christ, as he is attested for us in Holy Scripture, is the one Word of God which we have to hear and which we have to trust and obey in life and in death.
>
> 2. As Jesus Christ is God's assurance of the forgiveness of all our sins, so in the same way and with the same seriousness he is also God's mighty claim upon our whole life. Through him befalls us a joyful deliverance from the godless fetters of this world for a free, grateful service to his creatures.
>
> 3. The Christian Church is the congregation of the brethren in which Jesus Christ acts presently as the Lord in Word and sacrament through the Holy Spirit. As the Church of pardoned sinners, it has to testify in the midst of a sinful world, with its faith as with its obedience, with its message as with its order, that it is solely his property, and that it lives and wants to live solely from his comfort and from his direction in the expectation of his appearance.
>
> 4. The various offices in the Church do not establish a dominion of some over the others; on the contrary, they are for the exercise of the ministry entrusted to and enjoined upon the whole congregation.
>
> 5. Scripture tells us that, in the as yet unredeemed world in which the Church also exists, the State has by divine appointment the task of providing for justice and peace. (It fulfills this task) by means of the threat and exercise of force, according to the measure of human judgment and human ability. The Church acknowledges the benefit of this divine appointment in gratitude and reverence before him. It calls to mind the Kingdom of God, God's commandment and righteousness, and thereby the responsi-

> bility both of rulers and of the ruled. It trusts and obeys the power of the Word by which God upholds all things.
>
> 6. The Church's commission, upon which its freedom is founded, consists in delivering the message of the free grace of God to all people in Christ's stead, and therefore in the ministry of his own Word and work through sermon and sacrament.[5]

In order to understand these statements, the high point of which is the first thesis, it is necessary to include the condemnation which was added to that thesis:

> We reject the false doctrine, as though the Church could and would have to acknowledge as a source of its proclamation, apart from and besides this one Word of God, still other events and powers, figures and truths, as God's revelation.[6]

Here, as in the condemnations which are added to other statements, it becomes clear that the church has its foundation in Jesus Christ alone, and that it is under no obligation to proclaim anything other than the gospel of Jesus Christ, that, indeed, it recognizes no other sources for its faith but the Word of God.

The objection has been raised that in the last analysis the *Barmen Declaration* is nothing more than a repetition of certain ideas of the theology of Barth. It has been said, furthermore, that the theology of Barth is characterized by an abridgment of the preaching of the law. Even as Barth substitutes for the Lutheran doctrine of the law and the gospel the reversed order of gospel and law, so this declaration, it is said, does not express the Lutheran understanding of the problem of natural revelation, or of the relation between reason and revelation, justice and righteousness. These accusations fail to recognize, however, what was meant to be accomplished at Barmen. In the *Barmen Declaration* the attempt was not to set forth a certain theological epistemology, nor was it to give a definitive explanation of the problem of the relation of natural revelation to God's revelation in Jesus Christ. It is quite true that such a problem cannot actually be solved by means of a brief confession. The question answered at Barmen was whether or not it is permissible to listen to natural revelation—whatever circumstances may surround it—apart from Jesus Christ, which means, without refer-

[5] Translation taken from A. C. Cochrane, *The Church's Confession Under Hitler* (Philadelphia: Westminster, 1962), pp. 239-242. Used by permission.

[6] *Ibid.*, p. 239.

ence to the word of Holy Scripture. Karl Barth himself has said about the first statement of the *Barmen Declaration* "that it does not deny the existence of other events and powers, forms and truths alongside the one Word of God, and that therefore throughout it does not deny the possibility of a natural theology as such."[7] The *Barmen Declaration* does confess, however, that no other events or truths may become the source and foundation of faith and proclamation. To say it differently, the first article of this confession of faith can only be understood in the light of the second.

Of course, the *Barmen Declaration* implies consequences which are of no less importance for the church than they are for theology in general. It indicates that for the Christian there can be no area of life or action to which Christ's claim to Lordship does not apply. The synthesis of Christianity and culture, so often made within modern Protestantism, cannot be regarded as Christian. Theology which loses sight of the center of the church's faith, be that in the interpretation of Scripture, in systematics, in church history, or in the history of dogma, fails in its mission. All efforts toward the renewal of preaching which are not oriented toward that which the church has been given to believe and to preach must necessarily come to nought.

Objection has also been made to the *Barmen Declaration* on the ground that it represents an attempt to be a confession of union between the three Protestant churches in Germany, the Lutheran, the Reformed, and the United. Against this it should again be pointed out that the declaration itself specifically mentions that the German Evangelical Church is a confederation of confessional churches, and that for this reason the *Barmen Declaration,* according to its own self-understanding, ranks lower than the confessional writings of the Reformation. Neither of these charges holds up. The *Barmen Declaration* made no claim to be a confession of church union. It stands neither below nor above the confessional writings of the Reformation. One might say, however, that it constitutes a contemporary embodiment of the Reformation confession in view of new questions which have arisen. As such its claim is unmistakable. The declaration is nothing else but a dogma, in our sense of the term. It is a dogma, of course, which is not simply added to earlier

[7] *CD* 2^1, 178.

dogmas and confessions in the manner of the Catholic *depositum fidei,* and which under certain circumstances may be shelved along with them. It is a dogma, rather, which confesses anew and in a binding way the the whole Christian faith, and whose claim to truth is, therefore, no less valid than that of earlier doctrinal decisions of the church.

Above all the pro's and con's, however, it should at least be acknowledged by all sides that here, for the first time, the Protestant church recognized and again undertook a task from which it had shrunk for centuries, namely, to express its faith in a new and binding way. For this reason the significance of the *Barmen Declaration* for the history of Protestant dogma can hardly be overestimated.

9

The Unity of the Church

The Goal of the History of Dogma

ONLY A FEW DECADES AGO it was possible for Reinhold Seeberg, the author of the most comprehensive history of dogma in the German language, to designate the "Confessional types," i.e., the confessions of the major communions, as the goal of the development of dogma. In that case the history of dogma would end with a doctrinal inventory of the particular churches. The presupposition would be that nothing can be added to that inventory.

The development which has taken place during recent decades in almost all of the churches makes that kind of conception impossible to hold in our day. In many churches a serious quest for the unity of the church has taken the place of self-satisfied seclusion with respect to other churches. Across all communions the attempt is being made to seek among the many churches that which unites, and this is being newly discovered in the confession of Jesus Christ, our common Lord.

During the last century a number of theologians observed that the Protestant church lacks one thing in particular, namely, the experience of what a church is and what it signifies. This insight, which at the time was limited to certain circles within the confessional revival movement, is widely held today. Actually the dogmatic development of all of Christendom during the past few decades is dominated to a remarkable degree by the unity of the church. This is no less true of the Roman Catholic church than it is of Protestant churches. Within the Roman church the doctrine of the church constitutes that complex concerning which the smallest number of official doctrinal decisions have been made. The First Vatican Council was to have given an extensive definition of the doctrine of the church. However, because of the contemporary political situation in Italy, as well as in the rest of Europe, only the doctrine of papal infallibility was accorded dogmatic status, while consideration of other segments of ecclesiology was deferred. Here a great many questions remain to be clarified. The Second Vatican Council considered many of them and gave them dogmatic explication. It is hardly surprising that the position laid down by previous doctrinal decisions was adhered to. However, the importance of the episcopate was emphasized somewhat more strongly than previously, not least through the creation of a conference of bishops from all over the world.

Whatever its status in the Roman church, the problem of the unity of the church does occupy a central place within modern Protestantism. During the last century there were noteworthy mergers of various Protestant churches. The twentieth century witnessed the birth of the ecumenical movement. Whether or not this development will lead to the external unity of the various churches, or whether the unity of the church will find expression only in certain common actions and confessions, rather than in organization, cannot be determined at the present time. There can be no doubt, however, that in our day the unity of the church is the central theme of church history and of the history of dogma, very much as in past epochs this theme was the doctrine of the Trinity, Christology, the doctrine of sin and grace, or the problem of justification.

Though the quest for the unity of the church seems to dominate our present age, there is as yet no clear indication of where it will lead. Nevertheless, this quest raises a multitude of theological questions. Only one of these can be referred to here. It is certain to occasion much diffculty for the churches involved in the ecumenical movement.

If it is a characteristic of the history of dogma that each age is concerned not merely with adding yet another insight to those of the past but with apprehending anew the totality of the Christian faith, this is true also of the present age. It must be admitted, of course, that hitherto Christianity was not sufficiently aware of this fact. This is probably because in our day the doubt about our heritage is entirely different from that of earlier epochs. We are now no longer concerned merely with making older confessions relevant in new situations. The fact is that in the struggle for the unity of the church the problem of the whole doctrinal tradition of the church is once again involved, and on a comprehensive scale. This question becomes apparent in all of its acuteness if we keep in mind the relation of the younger churches of Asia and Africa to western Christendom.

As a result of the intensive confrontation between churches which took place within the context of the ecumenical movement, the significance which nontheological factors had, and still have, in the formation and development of the various churches became evident. Apart from those matters which otherwise contribute to its uniqueness, the Roman Catholic church was formed, in part, by certain geographical and social factors. Perhaps it is not accidental that, generally speaking, Catholicism spread among Latin nations, while Protestantism found its adherents mainly in Germanic lands. The Roman church is at the same time also the church of the European south, while the Protestant church is that of the European north. Doctrinal differences, too, are involved with external factors. When one observes Christianity as it has spread over the face of the globe, it becomes ever more evident that the great communions of the past and present were in some way conditioned by the West, while the younger churches, in spite of the differences which exist among them, have certain characteristics in common. The question of the unification of the divided churches changes its meaning, depending on whether it is asked in the so-called Christian West, or in the context of a dominantly non-Christian environment, as, for instance, in India. Closely connected with these geographical and social factors are certain intellectual and philosophical traditions, which, cutting across denominational lines, shape the churches of a given continent. To a smaller or larger degree all churches of the West have been formed in their thinking, as well as in their doctrinal decisions, by the philosophical heritage of antiquity. Even if a church feels called upon to protest passionately against the philosophical guise of theology, such a church's intellectual heritage and environment will inevitably determine the direction this protest will take.

In setting down these observations we do not mean to advocate a complete relativism, as if the truth were dependent only upon external factors, so that in the last analysis there is no generally binding truth. We never have the truth in anything other than perishable forms; we possess the Word of God only in the witness of human speech. That being the case, the question comes up in our day, with its concern for the unity of the church, whether or not we can and should expect the younger churches to accept the whole heritage of the churches of the West. It is by no means merely a question whether or not, for the sake of truth, the ecclesiastical boundaries of the West must be applied also to Asia and Africa. The problem is a considerably larger one and involves the question, Is the entire philosophical and theological terminology developed in the West in the course of many centuries necessary also for the younger Christianity?

The essential content of the Christian confession undoubtedly belongs to that which cannot be surrendered. The Christian faith is necessarily faith in the triune God. With respect to its essential content the doctrine of sin and grace is no less part of the faith than the Reformation doctrine of justification. Even the rise of historical thinking constitutes a turning point in the history of dogma which certainly cannot be disregarded anywhere. While it is true that the historical thinking of the West has been one-sided in some respects, and may be still in need of refinement, it is also true that a scientific method other than that of historical, critical research is simply inconceivable in theology as well as in other areas.

Still the question remains whether or not the younger churches must be expected to catch up, as it were, with nineteen centuries of western church history and history of dogma. Is it not conceivable that in the theological enterprise in India, for instance, problems may come into focus which are entirely different from those to which we are accustomed in the West, and that for this reason answers may be forthcoming which initially will seem quite as strange to us as do the doctrinal differences of the West to the Christians of Asia? Of course there is always the danger that in certain areas there may arise only a new variant of a theology, like that of the German Christians mentioned in the last chapter. On the other hand, Western Christianity must be careful not simply to force its tradition upon the younger churches.

The tasks confronting the church in this connection are evident in the example of the Church of South India. Here purely Western criteria do not seem to be sufficient to lead to a just appraisal. After lengthy preparations the Church of South India came into being in 1947 through a union of Anglicans, Congregationalists, and Methodists. Here for the first time a church which had preserved the apostolic succession entered into union with nonepiscopal churches. In doing so, ordinations previously undertaken were mutually recognized. During a transitional period of at least thirty years the churches are meant to grow together. Since the union in 1947 ordinations are performed by bishops assisted by pastors. During the transitional period, therefore, there are three kinds of ordination, the episcopal, the nonepiscopal, and the ordination performed under the constitution of the new church. In addition the constitution contains the following important statement: "The Church of South India desires, therefore, conserving all that is of spiritual value in its Indian heritage, to express under Indian conditions and in Indian forms the spirit, the thought and the life of the Church Universal."[1]

Apparently the accustomed standards of the Western church are highly inadequate for appraising the character of the Church of South India. Did the South Indian church sever itself with the sentence just cited from the continuity of the church? Or did it merely free itself from the burden of Western tradition, which under Indian circumstances represents an unnecessary impediment? Even the actual statements of union as such are difficult to appraise from the point of view of the West. It is obviously possible to raise numerous theological objections about the way in which the problem of apostolical succession was solved. In the long run the Church of South India will probably have the apostolic succession in fact and will, most likely, give it a significance similar to that which it enjoys in the Anglican church. Because of a lack of clarity with respect to many important

[1] *The Constitution of the Church of South India* (Madras: The Christian Literature Society, 1952), p. 3.

doctrinal questions, the Lutherans, as well as the Baptists, did not participate in the union. It can certainly not be denied that the constitution of the union contains many problems. Yet, in the eyes of those who united to form the new church in 1947, the division of the church was a much greater problem. It was therefore thought necessary, first of all, to unite, so that in the course of time new ways might be found to meet those problems which have hitherto not been solved satisfactorily. It would seem that the time has not yet come to give a final evaluation of this union. Two things, however, may be said even now. First, during the years of its existence the Church of South India has developed a rich spiritual life. The churches were not absorbed by the new union. Rather, each one contributed its tradition and its peculiar features to the new community. As a result the churches mutually enriched one another. Second, the union of the Church of South India became an example for a number of churches in Asia and in Africa. Quite obviously these "young" Christians are not satisfied with mere administrative mergers. They are concerned, rather, that the separated members will truly grow together into the one body of Christ.

With respect to the history of dogma all of this means that the question of the relevance and of the right interpretation of inherited confessions is raised once again, and under entirely new conditions. We dare not simply accept the scandalous division of Christianity, but neither may we deny the seriousness of the problem of truth for the sake of a questionable compromise. The task with which Christianity is confronted in our day admits of no easier solution than did those tasks which had to be met in ages past.

The Ecumenical Movement

The ecumenical movement grew out of various attempts at the beginning of the twentieth century to draw the churches of the world closer together. The World Alliance for Promoting International Friendship Through the Churches, the Life and Work Movement, as well as the International Missionary Council prepared the way for, and brought into being, the ecumenical movement. During the period between the world wars, the Faith and Order Movement and the Life and Work Movement existed side by side. In 1948 the union of the two was consummated and the World Council of Churches was constituted. Up to the present time three assemblies of the World Council have been held, in 1948 at Amsterdam, in 1954 at Evanston, and in 1961 in New Delhi.

A treatment of the ecumenical movement in the context of the history of dogma might appear to be premature, inasmuch as the ecumenical movement does not regard itself as a church. According to its constitution, the World Council "is a fellowship of churches which accept our Lord Jesus Christ as God and Saviour." This is the wording of the formulation which in 1938, at Utrecht, was taken over from the Faith and Order Movement. Some of the churches which have been brought together in the World Council of Churches are separated from one another by considerable differences. Many of these churches do not practice intercommunion. Some do not even recognize other fellowships as churches, on the ground that these fellowships lack certain essential features such as apostolic succession.

On the other hand, it has become increasingly clear during recent years that the significance of the ecumenical movement is not exhausted in attempts to find a common platform for certain practical questions or to promote mutual understanding among member churches. From its beginnings this movement has generated its own dynamic, which reaches beyond the ideas expressed in its constitution. This dynamic is evident, first, in the fact that, chiefly upon request of the Orthodox churches, another formulation of the first article of the constitution ("Basis") was substituted for the older one cited above. This action was taken at the New Delhi assembly of the World Council, upon the recommendation of the Central Committee at its meeting at St. Andrews in 1960.[2] It is a formula which expresses the common trinitarian faith as follows: "The World Council of Churches is a fellowship of churches which confess the Lord Jesus Christ as God and Saviour according to the Scriptures and therefore seek to fulfill together their common calling to the glory of the one God, Father, Son and Holy Spirit."[3]

[2] See W. A. Visser 't Hooft (ed.), *The New Delhi Report* (New York: Association, 1961), pp. 152-159.

[3] *Ibid.*, p. 426.

This is now the "Basis" of the constitution of the World Council of Churches.

Second, all the work of the ecumenical movement has been directed toward bringing about an increased measure of unity among the churches. In this connection the *Toronto Statement* (1950), which was published under the title *The Church, The Churches, and the World Council of Churches,* has considerable significance. It asserts that the World Council is no "super-church," and that it does not have the task of undertaking negotiations to bring about union between individual member churches. Nor does it have the function of ecclesiastical leadership in reference to member churches. Every member church, says the statement, has the right either to accept or to reject both the statements and the actions of the Council. The authority of the Council is a purely spiritual one; it performs a brotherly service for the member churches. The presuppositions of the World Council are that, according to the New Testament, the church is one, and that for every church the problem of the relation of other churches to the one church should be the subject of discussion. It is not necessary, continues the statement, that every church must regard the other churches as a church in the full sense of the word. The differences between them, however, are to be accepted with mutual respect and, at the same time, in the hope that under the guidance of the Holy Spirit it will be possible to make the unity of the church visible. The statement emphasizes that all Christian churches, including the Roman Catholic church, believe that membership in the one holy church does not entirely coincide with membership in one's own church. They acknowledge that there are members of the one church of Jesus Christ outside of one's own church. The ecumenical movement seeks fellowship with those who are separated by ecclesiastical boundaries, but who are still part of the fellowship of the one body of Christ. The World Council is thus not an end in itself, but merely an instrument for making possible and promoting this confrontation of the churches. Of the members it is expected that they will not merely help one another, but that before the world they will be concerned about a common witness to a common Lord.

The *Toronto Statement* carefully delineates what is basic to the ecumenical movement. It makes clear that, on the one hand, the unity of the church cannot be brought about in a romantic, enthusiastic way through mere unions or compromises, but that, on the other hand, the World Council is not satisfied simply to promote mutual discussion—its stated aim is to help prepare for the visible unity of the church. The fellowship toward which the Council strives is thus a threefold one: *diakonia* (service), *martyria* (witness), and *koinonia* (full fellowship or unity). It is hoped that the churches will come to be united not as a result of negotiations and agreements, but through a spiritual growing together as the separated churches come to recognize their common mission and their unity in Jesus Christ. This represents a new approach that contrasts with earlier attempts at church union.

After the *Toronto Statement* the ecumenical movement actually has developed in the direction indicated by the statement. This was most evident during the third assembly at New Delhi in 1961. Not only was the Russian Orthodox Church received into membership there, but the proposal to integrate the International Missionary Council into the World Council was approved. Thus the missionary dimension of the church was more strongly emphasized than heretofore. Above all, however, the necessity of manifesting the unity of the church was more clearly seen and emphasized than before.

The two first paragraphs of the Report of the Section on Unity read as follows:

> The love of the Father and the Son in the unity of the Holy Spirit is the source and goal of the unity which the triune God wills for all men and creation. We believe that we share in this unity in the Church of Jesus Christ, who is before all things and in whom all things hold together. In Him alone, given by the Father to be Head of the Body, the Church has its true unity. The reality of this unity was manifest at Pentecost in the gift of the Holy Spirit, through whom we know in this present age the first fruits of that perfect union of the Son with his Father, which will be known in its fulness only when all things are consummated by Christ in his glory. The Lord who is bringing all things into full unity at the last is he who constrains us to seek the unity which he wills for his Church on earth here and now.
>
> We believe that the unity which is both God's will and his gift of his Church is being made visible as all in each place who are baptized into Jesus Christ and confess him as Lord and Savior are brought by the Holy Spirit into ONE fully committed fellowship, holding the one apostolic faith, preaching the one Gospel, break-

ing the one bread, joining in common prayer, and having a corporate life reaching out in witness and service to all and who at the same time are united with the whole Christian fellowship in all places and all ages in such wise that ministry and members are accepted by all, and that all can act and speak together as occasion requires for the tasks to which God calls his people. It is for such unity that we believe we must pray and work.[4]

Apropos of this statement the question has been asked, with some skepticism, whether or not the unity of the church is now to be established by force through a revolution from the bottom up, that is, by the local congregations and the national churches.[5] It is felt by some within the confessional world alliances that this would lead to a dissolution of supranational fellowships of doctrine, faith, and confession. It is also pointed out that while the New Delhi assembly announced the goal, it failed to point out concrete ways to reach that goal.

This statement of the New Delhi assembly is misunderstood if it is regarded as an attempt to induce the churches to do the impossible. Paragraph 3 states soberly: "This brief description of our objective leaves many questions unanswered. We are not yet of a common mind on the interpretation and the means of achieving the goal we have described."[6] The statement also denies that the attempt here is to strive for uniformity in rites or in forms of church life. It cannot be gainsaid, however, that here, for the first time in the history of the ecumenical movement, the goal of the movement was clearly stated, namely, to achieve the visible unity of Christendom. The road to its realization may still be a long one. The obstacles to be surmounted may be greater than even critical observers realize. Yet New Delhi has made unmistakably clear that the goal must be the full unity of Christians if the confession of the triune God is really to be taken seriously by all member churches of the World Council. If the ecumenical movement is to accomplish its task this goal must not be lost sight of in the future. In reaching it, romantic daydreams can be quite as dangerous as denominational self-satisfaction and seclusion.

Thus today's generation in the church, no less than former

[4] W. A. Visser 't Hooft (ed.), *New Delhi Speaks* ("Reflection Books"; New York: Association, 1962), pp. 92-93. Used by permission.

[5] E. Kinder, *Lutherische Monatshefte*, 1 (1962), 17.

[6] *Ibid.*, p. 93.

generations, is faced with the task of giving through its witness in word and deed an answer to the question which the Lord once directed to the disciples, "Who do you say that I am?" The answer to this question must be given in a new way. But if it proceeds from faith it will be given in unity with the faith and the confession of the fathers.

Appendixes

Chronological Table

Chapter 1 Canon and Creed

YEAR	EVENTS
Ca. 30	Crucifixion of Jesus.
Ca. 144	Marcion creates his New Testament canon, consisting of the Gospel of Luke (purged of "Jewish" vestiges) and of the first ten letters of Paul. The New Testament canon of the church is simultaneously in process of formation.
Ca. 180	The formation of the New Testament canon is complete in a preliminary way.
End of 2nd century	In both East and West the rule of faith has gained basic significance as a summary of the church's doctrine.
367	In his thirty-ninth Easter Letter, Athanasius, Bishop of Alexandria, mentions a firmly fixed canon of the New Testament containing the twenty-seven books which alone have been regarded as canonical since then. This is the first such reference extant.
382	A Roman synod establishes this same New Testament canon. The synods of Hippo Regius (393) and of Carthage (397, 419) support the Roman decision.

Chapter 2 The Doctrine of the Trinity

YEAR	EVENTS

End of 2nd and beginning of 3rd centuries Irenaeus of Lyons and Tertullian of Carthage are the first to outline an actual doctrine of the Trinity which does not simply set the three persons side by side but expresses clearly the unity of the persons as well as the differences between them; however, the Son is subordinated to the Father, and the Holy Spirit to the Son.

Ca. 200 The two streams of Monarchianism seek to retain the affirmation that God is only one person. For the dynamistic Monarchians, Christ was a man who was filled with the impersonal power of God, and who was adopted as Son of God. (Main representatives: Theodotus the Tanner and Theodotus the Money Changer [both toward the end of the second century]; Paul of Samosata [d. after 272]). For the modalistic Monarchians God was active in various modes, namely, as Father, as Son, and as Holy Spirit. (Main representative: Sabellius, beginning of third century.)

Beginning of 3rd century The two streams of Monarchianism having been excluded from the church, Tertullian's doctrine of the Trinity exercises a decisive influence in the West. In the East, Origen (d. 254) develops his highly speculative doctrine of the Trinity, which already employs the concept of *homoousia* (unity of being), though it emphatically retains the numerical distinctness of the persons and conceives the Godhead to be centered entirely in God the Father; Origen is therefore able to designate the Son as a creature created by the Father. Origen's doctrine of the Trinity was such that it could be developed in various ways, in the direction of Arianism or in the direction of later Orthodoxy.

319 Arius, Presbyter of Alexandria, is excommunicated by the Synod of Alexandria on the grounds that he designates the Son of God as a creature which was not from eternity and whose being therefore does not possess divinity.

325 The Council of Nicaea condemns the doctrine of Arius and in its confession affirms that the Son is one with the Father in his being—he is "very God of very God."

325-361 During the major phase of the Arian controversy the opposition, consisting largely of eastern theologians influenced by Origen, is temporarily successful in substituting creeds of a more or less Arian formulation for the confession of Nicaea. The eastern majority is supported in this attempt by the policy of the emperors. Athanasius and his friends, however, as well as the majority of the Latin West, hold fast to the Nicene confession.

361-381 The last phase of the Arian controversy is marked, first, by the distinction, deriving from the theology of the Cappadocians, between *ousia* (the common substance of the persons of the Trinity) and *hypostasis* (person); a modalistic misunderstanding of the *homoousia* of the Son with the Father is thus avoided. This phase of the controversy is marked, second, by the attention given to the question of the position of the Holy Spirit in the Trinity; it is answered by Athanasius and the Cappadocians in a way which is analogous to the Nicene statements concerning the relation of the Father and the Son.

381 The Council of Constantinople, which brings the Arian controversy to an end, confesses the *homoousia* of the Son and of the Holy Spirit with God the Father.

Beginning of 5th century In his theology Augustine is especially concerned about emphasizing the unity of God. He prefers "relation" to "person," but clings to the distinction of the persons. Augustine's ideas subsequently become normative for the western doctrine of the Trinity, which consequently places more emphasis on the unity of the persons while eastern theology generally develops its doctrine of the Trinity by beginning with the divinity of the Father, although it, too, maintains the *homoousia* of the Son and of the Holy Spirit with the Father. The difference between the Greek and the Latin doctrine of the Trinity is neatly expressed in their divergent formulation of the procession of the Holy Spirit, the Latins asserting that the Spirit proceeds from the Father and the Son, while, according to the Greeks, the Holy Spirit proceeds only from the Father, though he does so through the Son.

Chapter 3 Christology

YEAR	EVENTS

Middle of 2nd century The apologists are the first to outline an actual Christology. Taking over the Logos concept from Greek philosophy, they regard Christ as world reason and cosmic principle, the latter having appeared only imperfectly in ancient philosophy but having revealed itself finally and perfectly in Jesus Christ. Specifically they assert that in order to accomplish the creation of the world God the Father put forth his Word (Logos), which was with him from the beginning.

Beginning of 3rd century Largely as a result of the theological work of Origen, the Logos Christology gains general acceptance. Origen's Christology, however, contains many problems, chief among them being his concept of the human soul of Jesus, which Origen taught was pre-existent. While the other pre-existent souls fell away from God, that of Jesus remained faithful to God and was united with the divine Logos. In the incarnate Christ the soul has a mediating role between the Logos and the body. After the resurrection, however, a progressive absorption of the exalted human body of Jesus begins. This doctrine was susceptible of further development in the direction of both the later Word-flesh Christology and the later Word-man Christology, depending on how one tried to solve the problem of the human soul of Jesus.

Middle of 4th century Apollinaris of Laodicea (d. 390) asserts that the human Jesus had no "spirit," the place of this spirit having been taken by the incarnate Logos. This assertion denies the perfection of the human nature of Jesus. Toward the end of the Arian controversy Apollinaris was condemned by various synods.

Begininng of 5th century Two christological schools face each other: (1) The Antiochenes, who represent a Word-man Christology, and who therefore emphasize the fullness and perfection of the human nature of Jesus Christ but are unable to clarify the unity of divinity and humanity. (2) The Alexandrians, who represent a Word-flesh Christology, emphasizing the "one nature of the incarnate Logos," but who are in danger of slighting the fullness and perfection of the human nature.

431 The Council of Ephesus, which was convened illegally but was later (451) recognized as ecumenical, condemns Nestorius of Constantinople, a prominent representative of the Antiochene party.

451 The Council of Chalcedon, which temporarily ends the christological controversy, confesses in its creed that Jesus Christ is truly God and truly man, possessed of a rational soul and body, and that he is so in (not "of") two natures, inconfusedly, unchangeably, indivisibly, and inseparably, and that both natures are united in one person, while both their completeness and their distinctness remain unimpaired.

End of 5th and beginning of 6th centuries The rise of a variety of Monophysite churches in the Orient, which do not find the unity of the person of Christ sufficiently expressed in the Chalcedonian creed but which are also influenced by national opposition to Byzantium, induces the emperors to undertake various attempts at mediation.

553 The Council of Constantinople (Fifth Ecumenical Council) emphasizes more strongly than the Chalcedonian creed the two natures of Christ and confesses their hypostatic union.

680-681 The Sixth Ecumenical Council, meeting at Constantinople, decides the question, which has arisen in the meantime, whether or not Christ had two wills, corresponding to his two natures. It is asserted that he had two wills and two operations, but that these were undivided, unchanged, unseparated, and unconfused.

Chapter 4 The Doctrine of Sin and Grace

YEAR	EVENTS

Beginning of 3rd century Tertullian is the first to develop the beginnings of a doctrine of original sin according to which even little children are to be regarded as unclean. For a long time the church's opposition to Gnosticism, which regarded all matter, as well as the corporeality of man, as being at enmity against God, hinders the development of a more profound understanding of the Pauline assertions of the power of sin.

Ca. 400 Pelagius and his friend Coelestius, the latter more strongly than the former, emphasize the absolute freedom of the will as over against God. Any insistence upon a doctrine of original sin or of the bondage of the will with respect to divine grace appears to them to constitute a severe impediment to their demands for reform. In Pelagius and Coelestius the moralism of the ancient fathers of the church is elevated to the position of a basic principle. Their concept of God is, in the main, rationalistic; their concept of faith is restricted largely to the observance of the divine law.

Ca. 400 Through his own experiences, which make him aware of the power of sin but, above all, through the intensive study of Scripture, Augustine reaches a much more profound conception of sin and grace. Without denying the psychological freedom of man's will, Augustine recognizes that the human will is free only within the limits of the choices it makes, and that, as a result of original sin, it has no freedom with reference to God and his grace.

411 A synod at Carthage condemns the teaching of Pelagius.

415-418 By sacrificing his friend Coelestius, Pelagius manages to vindicate himself before two Palestinian synods in 415. In 417 both he and Coelestius are even recognized as orthodox by a Roman synod under Zosimus I. Nevertheless, in 418 Pelagianism is condemned by a Carthaginian synod, thus concluding the first stage of the Pelagian controversy. The synod declares that all men are involved in the sin of Adam and need the grace of God not only for the forgiveness of sin, but also to provide them with strength to live a new life.

431 The Fourth Ecumenical Council, meeting at Ephesus, supports the condemnation of the doctrine of Pelagius and of Coelestius.

Ca. 420-529 The semi-Pelagian controversy is waged, first, over the doctrine of predestination as developed by Augustine, and, second, over the question whether sin only weakens man's free will so that he can still cooperate with grace, or whether grace must always precede man's efforts and liberate his will.

529 The Synod of Orange, which ends the semi-Pelagian controversy, basically represents a moderate Augustinianism. It teaches that even man's invocation of divine grace is the work of grace. Predestination to damnation, which Augustine did not teach, is rejected; his idea that grace works irresistibly in those predestined to salvation, is not taken over. Thus there exists a tension between the doctrine of sin and grace as taught by the most outstanding church father of the West and the decisions of the synods. This tension means that the question of sin and grace will persist as a problem in the West.

Chapter 5 Word and Sacrament

YEAR	EVENTS

Ca. 100 The designation of the Lord's Supper as an offering is found first in the East Syrian writing, the *Didache* (14:1). At about the same time, in other sections of the church, Old Testament statements about priests and offerings are applied to ecclesiastical office bearers and to the Lord's Supper. At first this application is only symbolical. In the third century it is a universal conviction that the Supper is the offering of Christians, though the concept of offering is more legalistic in the West than in the East. Alongside the Lord's Supper, baptism is, of course, also of great significance from the very beginning; for baptism, however, there are fewer starting points for a development comparable to that of the doctrine of the Lord's Supper. Besides baptism and the Lord's Supper many other holy acts were known to the ancient church as well as to the early Middle Ages; these were also designated as "sacraments."

Beginning of 5th century The first theologian to elucidate more fully the relation of word and sacrament is Augustine. In him the problem of "word and sacrament" first becomes a topic in itself. Augustine's definition, that the conjunction of word and element constitutes a sacrament, is basic for all later western theology. In his doctrine of the Lord's Supper Augustine does not share the realism of Ambrose (d. 397); his distinction between sign and substance results, rather, in a symbolical interpretation. Thus, both a realistic and a symbolical interpretation are bequeathed to the theology of the Middle Ages.

Ca. 831-ca. 845 The first eucharistic controversy, between Paschasius Radbertus and Ratramnus, clarifies somewhat the questions at issue between the two conceptions of the Supper. Radbertus is inclined more to the realistic conception, Ratramnus more to the symbolical. No decision is reached.

Ca. 1050-1079 During the second eucharistic controversy Berengar is forced to give up his symbolic interpretation and to sign a formula stating that bread and wine really become body and blood as a result of the consecration. This means, first of all, the establishment of the doctrine held already by Ambrose, that through the consecration a change in the elements takes place.

It means, furthermore, that, thanks especially to Humbert, a christocentric view of the Lord's Supper now takes rise.

Middle of 12th century In theology the older and broader concept of the sacraments is displaced by a more precise and narrow one, according to which there are seven sacraments (baptism, confirmation, Lord's Supper, penance, extreme unction, ordination, marriage). This new concept of the sacraments, which is found first in Peter Lombard, rapidly establishes itself everywhere.

1215 At the Fourth Lateran Council the doctrine of transubstantiation is proclaimed as dogma.

13th century The theological systems of the great Scholastics, notably that of Thomas Aquinas, delineate further the theological significance of the sacraments. As a result of the acceptance of Augustinian ideas, the extremely realistic view is softened at a number of points. On the other hand, the sacraments come to be interpreted almost exclusively with reference to man's appropriation of grace: they "contain" grace and infuse it into man. On man's side full saving faith is not necessary; it is sufficient not to "interpose an obstacle."

1439 The Council of Florence confirms the number seven in reference to the sacraments.

16th century Luther's criticism of the sacramental teaching of the medieval church is not directed primarily against the number seven, or against the doctrine of transubstantiation (though he comes to reject both of these), but, rather, against the attempt to make grace a thing and to conceive the sacramental relation to God in legal terms; the latter conception culminates in the idea that the Mass is a sacrifice through which God must repeatedly be propitiated so that he will forgive actual sins. In place of this view Luther emphasizes the words of institution, which he characterizes as a promise that is received only in faith. Since according to the New Testament only baptism and the Lord's Supper have been instituted by Christ, only these are kept as sacraments by the churches of the Reformation.

Chapter 6 Justification

YEAR	EVENTS
(A) 1514	Luther (1483-1546) reaches his Reformation understanding of the righteousness of God and of the justification of man. This insight, which at the same time solves Luther's personal problems as these are related to his moments of anguish, is gained through intensive study of the Scriptures. The critical significance now accorded the Scriptures with reference to both church and tradition means that the inherited doctrinal confessions need to be examined and interpreted from the point of view of Scripture.
1517	The posting of the ninety-five theses concerning indulgences marks the beginning of the confrontation between Luther and Rome.
1525-1529	The eucharistic controversy between Luther and Zwingli (1484-1531) makes apparent basic differences not only in the interpretation of the words of institution, but also in Christology. Luther clings to the literal understanding of "is," emphasizing at the same time—with Alexandrian Christology—the unity of the person of Christ. Zwingli understands the "is" in the sense of "to signify"; with Antiochene Christology he points to the difference between the two natures of Christ. Christ's human nature, he maintains, cannot be omnipresent. In 1529 the Marburg Colloquy draws both sides somewhat closer together, but it does not bring either the common understanding which had been hoped for, or mutual appreciation.
1528	Luther's "confession" in the treatise *Confession Concerning Christ's Supper*.
1529	The *Schwabach Articles*, a confession of the Lutheran theologians of Saxony.
1529	The *Marburg Articles*, which embody the results of the Marburg Colloquy.
1530	The *Torgau Articles*, which are meant to be a preparation of Saxony for the Diet of Augsburg in 1530.
1530	Using these earlier articles Melanchthon writes the *Augsburg Confession* at Augsburg. It contains an outline of the most important doctrines of the Lutheran church. During the same

year he writes the *Apology* in answer to the Catholic *Confutatio*.

1537 Luther writes the *Smalcald Articles.*

1577 After lengthy negotiations and preparations the *Formula of Concord* is accepted; it is intended as a settlement of the controversies which arose after Luther's death.

1580 *The Book of Concord* (the Lutheran confessional treatises) is brought to a conclusion.

(B) 1530 The *Confessio Tetrapolitana,* representing Strasbourg, Constance, Memmingen, and Lindau, is presented to Charles V at the Diet of Augsburg.

1536 Calvin (1509-1564) publishes his *Institutes of the Christian Religion,* a comprehensive, systematic presentation of the Christian faith (the final, thoroughly revised edition appears in 1559).

1536 The *First Helvetic Confession,* written by Bullinger and others.

1549 Calvin enters with Bullinger into the *Consensus Tigurinus,* which brings Geneva and Zurich closer together but accentuates the difference between the Swiss and the Lutherans; most important, it brings about the second eucharistic controversy.

1563 The *Heidelberg Catechism,* the most widely used Reformed confessional treatise, is written by Ursinus.

1566 The *Second Helvetic Confession,* from Bullinger's pen, is accepted by many Reformed churches in various countries.

1618-1619 The Synod of Dort decides various doctrinal controversies which have arisen in the Reformed church.

(C) 1545-1563 The Council of Trent brings not only Rome's final rejection of the entire Reformation, but also an extensive delineation of the Catholic faith. For the scriptural principle of the Reformation the Roman church substitutes the equality of Scripture and tradition. Trent's inadequate definition of apostolic tradition makes it possible for contemporary Roman Catholicism to base its doctrine progressively less upon Scripture and progressively more upon tradition, even without regard for the age of the latter. In this respect the Council of Trent represents a decisive turning point in the history of the development of Catholic doctrine.

Chapter 7 Dogma within Recent Catholicism

YEAR EVENTS

17th and 18th centuries Modern Catholicism defends itself with great tenacity and consistency against the inroads of modern thought, especially against that of the Enlightenment, but also against attempts at renewal and greater depth from within, such as Jansenism, a seventeenth-century Augustinian movement in theology and piety. Resisting such movements, the Roman church continues to build without deviation upon the foundation laid at the Council of Trent.

1854 After the Roman church has not defined a new dogma for several centuries, Pope Pius IX declares the immaculate conception of Mary to be a dogma which is to be believed by all Christians. This is the first time a pope promulgates a dogma without first consulting a council or gaining its support. The new element in this definition is not merely the specific content, which cannot be established from Scripture, but especially the pope's claim to be able to define dogmas on his own authority.

1870 The First Vatican Council defines as dogma the infallibility of the pope, which is contingent upon his addressing himself *ex cathedra* to questions of faith or morals which concern the entire church. Although there is considerable opposition to the promulgation of the dogma, especially in Germany and Austria, the overwhelming majority of bishops and theologians submit. However, a group breaks off from the Roman church to form the Old Catholic Church, which does not recognize the new dogma.

1950 Pope Pius XII defines the latest Roman Catholic dogma, that Mary, after completing her life on earth, was bodily assumed into heaven.

Chapter 8 Dogma within Protestantism

YEAR EVENTS

18th century The general intellectual revolution which takes place in European thought, and which finds expression, among other things, in the rise of the historical-critical method, leads to a serious crisis in Protestantism and demands a profound re-evaluation, which has not yet come to an end. The Protestant church takes up the tasks with which it is confronted, even though at times it is reluctant to do so, and thus faces the inescapable intellectual struggle.

19th century While the influences of the philosophy of Idealism and of Romanticism upon Protestant theology (cf. Schleiermacher) help to vanquish the theology of the Enlightenment, they hinder it from gaining a full insight into the historical nature of existence and into the tasks with which theology is thereby confronted. In the meantime, however, the historical-critical method wins an assured place in theology.

20th century Besides the tasks which are posed for the Protestant church by its confrontation with modern thought, the problem of church and state also arises and demands a new solution.

1933-1945 At stake in the struggle of the German church under National Socialism is not only the repudiation of the heresy of the German Christians (*Deutsche Christen*) and defense against the totalitarian demands of the state, but also a critical self-appraisal of Protestantism and new reflection on the nature of the faith and the sources of theological knowledge and doctrine. The *Barmen Declaration* (1934) confesses that Jesus Christ is the one Word of God, which Christians must hear and obey.

Chapter 9 The Unity of the Church

YEAR	EVENTS
1910	The World Missionary Conference at Edinburgh
1925	and the Life and Work Conference at Stockholm,
1927	and the Faith and Order Conference at Lausanne accomplish, each in its own sphere, a drawing together of the major Protestant churches. These various movements lead to
1948	The founding of the World Council of Churches,
1948	The first assembly of the World Council at Amsterdam.
1954	The second assembly of the World Council at Evanston.
1961	The third assembly of the World Council at New Delhi, where the International Missionary Council is integrated with the World Council.

Glossary

Accidens That which is accidental, added to, mutable.

Adiaphora Things that are permitted, neither commanded nor forbidden.

Alloiosis Literally, "interchange"; Zwingli's idea that the doctrine of the *communicatio idiomatum* does not refer to a real interchange of the properties of the natures of Christ, but that this is merely a figure of speech.

Character Indelebilis An indelible mark which, according to Roman Catholic doctrine, is bestowed through baptism, confirmation, and ordination.

Communicatio Idiomatum Interchange of the properties of the one nature of Christ with those of the other.

Depositum Fidei "Deposit of the faith"; the treasure of the truths of faith which, according to Roman Catholic doctrine, was given by Jesus and the apostles to the teaching office (*magisterium*) of the church, which is charged with transmitting these truths unaltered and, where necessary, with developing them further.

Docetism The doctrine that Christ only appeared to become man.

Dyotheletism The doctrine that Christ has two wills, one divine and one human.

Eschatology Doctrine of the last things.

Ex Opere Operato The Roman Catholic doctrine that the sacraments are efficacious for salvation merely because they are performed, provided the recipient does not "interpose an obstacle."

Homoousia Unity of being, equality of being (or of substance).

Hypostasis Independent being, person.

Logos Word, speech, mediator of Revelation.

Monarchianism The doctrine that God is only one person.

Monophysitism The doctrine that Christ has only one divine-human nature.

Monothelitism The doctrine that Christ has only one divine-human will.

Pneumatomachoi The opponents of the *homoousia* of the Holy Spirit with the Father and the Son.

Soteriology The doctrine of salvation.

SYMBOL Creed (thus used frequently in the history of dogma).

SYNERGISM The doctrine that the free will cooperates with grace in conversion.

OUSIA Being, the state of being, substance; later, an individual being.

For Further Reading

General Histories of Dogma

BETHUNE-BAKER, J. F. *Introduction to the Early History of Christian Doctrine.* 5th ed. Cambridge University Press, 1933.

DANIÉLOU, JEAN. *The Development of Christian Doctrine Before the Council of Nicaea,* Vol. 1. Translated and edited by J. A. Baker. London: Darton, Longman and Todd, 1964.

HARNACK, ADOLF. *History of Dogma.* 7 vols. Translated from the 3rd German ed. by Neil Buchanan. Boston: Little, Brown, 1902 ff.

KOHLER, WALTHER. *Dogmengeschichte als Geschichte des christlichen Selbstbewusstseins.* 2 vols. Zurich: Max Niehans, 1943 and 1951.

LOOFS, FRIEDRICH. *Leitfaden zum Studium der Dogmengeschichte.* 2 vols. 5th rev. ed., edited by Kurt Aland. Halle-Saale: M. Niemeyer, 1951-1953.

MCGIFFERT, A. C. *A History of Christian Thought.* 2 vols. New York: Scribners, 1932.

SEEBERG, REINHOLD. *Text-book of the History of Doctrines.* 2 vols. in 1. Translated by C. E. Hay. Philadelphia, 1905. Reprinted, Grand Rapids: Baker, 1952.

WERNER, MARTIN. *The Formation of Christian Dogma.* Translated by S. G. F. Brandon. London: A. and E. Black, 1957.

Introduction: Dogma and the History of Dogma

ALAND, KURT. "Dogmengeschichte," in *Die Religion in Geschichte und Gegenwart.* 3rd ed. Tübingen: Mohr, 1958.

JOURNET, CHARLES. *What Is Dogma?* Translated by M. Pontifex. New York: Hawthorn Books, 1964.

LOHSE, BERNHARD. "Was verstehen wir unter Dogmengeschichte innerhalb der evangelischen Theologie?" *Kerygma und Dogma,* 8 (1962), 27-45.

LOOFS, FRIEDRICH. "Dogmengeschichte," in *Realencyklopädie für protestantische Theologie und Kirche.* 3rd ed. Leipzig: J. C. Hinrich, 1896 ff.

PELIKAN, JAROSLAV. "Dogma," in Marvin Halverson and Arthur Cohen (eds.), *A Handbook of Christian Theology*. New York: Meridian Books, 1958.

PRENTER, REGIN. "Are We to Abolish Dogmas?" *Lutheran World Review*, 2 (April, 1950).

RONDET, HENRI. *Do Dogmas Change?* Translated by M. Pontifex. New York: Hawthorn Books, 1961.

STECK, KARL GERHARD. *Undogmatisches Christentum?* "Theologische Existenz heute," New Series, No. 48. Munich: Kaiser, 1955.

Chapter 1 Canon and Creed

ALAND, KURT. *The Problem of the New Testament Canon*. "Contemporary Studies in Theology," No. 1. London: Mowbray, 1962.

BINDLEY, T. H. (ed.). *The Oecumenical Documents of the Faith*. 4th ed. London: Methuen, 1950.

BROWN, ROBERT MCAFEE. "Tradition as a Protestant Problem," in *Theology Today*, 17 (1960-1961), 430-454.

CULLMANN, OSCAR. *The Earliest Christian Confessions*. Translated by J. K. S. Reid. London: Lutterworth, 1949.

DILLISTONE, F. W. (ed.). *Scripture and Tradition*. London: Lutterworth, 1955.

FLESSEMAN-VAN LEER, E. *Tradition and Scripture in the Early Church*. Assen: Van Gorcum, 1954.

HANSON, R. P. C. *Tradition in the Early Church*. Philadelphia: Westminster, 1962.

KELLY, J. N. D. *Early Christian Creeds*. 2nd ed. New York: McKay, 1960.

LIETZMANN, HANS. *A History of the Early Church*, Vol. 2. *The Founding of the Church Universal*. 2nd ed. Translated by B. L. Woolf. New York: Scribners, 1950.

MORAN, G. *Scripture and Tradition: A Survey of the Controversy*. New York: Herder, 1963.

Chapter 2 The Doctrine of the Trinity

ANDRESEN, CARL. "Zur Entstehung und Geschichte des trinitarischen Personbegriffes," *Zeitschrift für die neutestamentliche Wissenschaft*, 52 (1961), 1-39.

BURN, A. E. *The Council of Nicaea*. New York: Macmillan, 1925.

GWATKIN, H. M. *Studies of Arianism*. 2nd ed. Cambridge, Eng.: Deighton Bell, 1900.

HEFELE, KARL J. *A History of the Christian Councils*. 5 vols. Translated by William R. Clark. Edinburgh: T. and T. Clark, 1871-1896.

KELLY, J. N. D. *Early Christian Doctrines.* New York: Harper, 1959.

KRETSCHMAR, GEORG. *Studien zur frühchristlichen Trinitätstheologie.* Tübingen: Mohr, 1956.

MCGIFFERT, A. C. *God of the Early Christians.* New York: Scribners, 1924.

PRESTIGE, G. L. *God in Patristic Thought.* 2nd ed. London: S.P.C.K., 1952.

Chapter 3 Christology

BETHUNE-BAKER, J. F. *Nestorius and His Teaching.* Cambridge University Press, 1908.

BIGG, C. *The Christian Platonists of Alexandria.* Oxford: Clarendon, 1913.

DANIÉLOU, JEAN. *Origen.* Translated by W. Mitchell. New York: Sheed and Ward, 1955.

ELERT, WERNER. *Der Ausgang der altkirchlichen Christologie.* Berlin: Lutherisches Verlagshaus, 1957.

GILG, ARNOLD. *Weg und Bedeutung der altkirchlichen Christologie.* 2nd ed. Munich: Kaiser, 1955.

LITTLE, V. A. S. *The Christology of the Apologists.* London: Duckworth, 1934.

LOOFS, FRIEDRICH. *Nestorius and His Place in the History of Christian Doctrine.* Cambridge University Press, 1914.

PATTERSON, L. *Theodore of Mopsuestia and Modern Thought.* London: S.P.C.K., 1926.

RAVEN, C. E. *Apollinarianism.* Cambridge University Press, 1923.

SELLERS, R. V. *The Council of Chalcedon.* London: S.P.C.K., 1953.

———. *Eustathius of Antioch.* Cambridge University Press, 1928.

———. *Two Ancient Christologies.* London: S.P.C.K., 1940.

SULLIVAN, F. A. *The Christology of Theodore of Mopsuestia.* Rome: Apud Aedes Universitatis Gregorianae, 1956.

VINE, A. R. *An Approach to Christology.* London: Independent Press, 1948.

Chapter 4 The Doctrine of Sin and Grace

FERGUSON, J. *Pelagius.* Cambridge, Eng.: W. Heffer, 1956.

GROSS, J. *Geschichte des Erbsündendogmas.* 2 vols. Munich: Ernst Reinhardt, 1960, 1963.

NYGREN, GOTTHARD. *Das Prädestinationsproblem in der Theologie Augustins.* Lund: Gleerup, 1956.

PRESTIGE, G. L. *Fathers and Heretics.* London: S.P.C.K., 1940.

TELFER, WILLIAM. *The Forgiveness of Sins.* Philadelphia: Muhlenberg, 1960.

TURNER, H. E. W. *The Patristic Doctrine of Redemption.* London: Mowbray, 1952.

WARFIELD, BENJAMIN B. *Studies in Tertullian and Augustine.* New York: Oxford University Press, 1930.

WORKMAN, H. B. *Christian Thought to the Reformation.* New York: Scribners, 1911.

Chapter 5 Word and Sacrament

ADAM, KARL. *Die Eucharistielehre des hl. Augustinus.* Paderborn: Schöningh, 1908.

BONNER, GERALD. *St. Augustine of Hippo: Life and Controversies.* Philadelphia: Westminster, 1963.

GRASS, HANS. *Die Abendmahlslehre bei Luther und Calvin.* 2nd ed. Gütersloh: Bertelsmann, 1954.

JETTER, W. *Die Taufe beim jungen Luther.* Tübingen: Mohr, 1954.

LAMPE, G. W. H. *The Seal of the Spirit.* London: Longmans, 1956.

MACDONALD, A. J. M. *Berengar and the Reform of Sacramental Doctrine.* London: Longmans, 1930.

PAISSAC, H. *Theologie du Verbe: Saint Augustine et Saint Thomas.* Paris: Éditions du Cerf, 1951.

RAHNER, KARL. *The Church and the Sacraments.* Translated by W. J. O'Hara. New York: Herder, 1963.

SASSE, HERMANN. *This Is My Body.* Minneapolis: Augsburg, 1959.

STONE, D. *A History of the Doctrine of the Holy Eucharist.* London: Longmans, 1909.

WALLACE, R. S. *Calvin's Doctrine of the Word and Sacrament.* Edinburgh: Oliver and Boyd, 1953.

WILLIS, G. G. *Saint Augustine and the Donatist Controversy.* London: S.P.C.K., 1950.

WISLØFF, C. J. F. *The Gift of Communion: Luther's Controversy with Rome on Eucharistic Sacrifice.* Translated by Joseph M. Shaw. Minneapolis: Augsburg, 1964.

Chapter 6 Justification

ALTHAUS, PAUL. *The Theology of Martin Luther.* Translated by Robert C. Schultz. Philadelphia: Fortress, 1966.

BAEPLER, RICHARD. "Scripture and Tradition in the Council of Trent," *Concordia Theological Monthly*, 31 (1960), 341-362.

BORNKAMM, HEINRICH. *Luther's World of Thought*. Translated by Martin H. Bertram. St. Louis: Concordia, 1958.

DOWEY, EDWARD. *The Knowledge of God in Calvin's Theology*. New York: Columbia University Press, 1952.

ELERT, WERNER. *The Structure of Lutheranism*. Translated by W. A. Hansen. St. Louis: Concordia, 1962.

FARNER, O. *Zwingli the Reformer*. New York: Philosophical Library, 1952.

JANSEN, J. F. *Calvin's Doctrine of the Work of Christ*. London: J. Clark, 1956.

JEDIN, HUBERT. *A History of the Council of Trent*. 2 vols. Translated by D. E. Graf. London: Nelson, 1961.

KÖHLER, WALTHER. *Zwingli und Luther*. 2 vols. Leipzig: Heinsius, 1924; and Gütersloh: Bertelsmann, 1953.

LOHSE, BERNHARD. "Entstehung und Eigenart der Konfessionskirchen des 16. Jahrhunderts," *Studium Generale*, 14 (1961), 692-704.

MCNEILL, JOHN T. *The History and Character of Calvinism*. New York: Oxford University Press, 1954.

NIESEL, WILHELM. *The Theology of Calvin*. Translated by Harold Knight. Philadelphia: Westminster, 1958.

PINOMAA, LENNART. *Faith Victorious*. Translated by Walter J. Kukkonen. Philadelphia: Fortress, 1963.

RUPP, E. GORDON. *The Righteousness of God*. London: Hodder and Stoughton, 1953.

SCHLINK, EDMUND. *The Theology of the Lutheran Confessions*. Translated by Paul F. Koehneke and H. J. A. Bouman. Philadelphia: Muhlenberg, 1961.

VAN BUREN, PAUL. *Christ in Our Place*. Edinburgh: Oliver and Boyd, 1957.

Chapter 7 Dogma within Recent Catholicism

CAROL, J. B. (ed.). *Mariology*. 3 vols. Milwaukee: Bruce, 1955-1961.

COLACCI, MARIO. *The Doctrinal Conflict Between Roman Catholic and Protestant Christianity*. Minneapolis: Denison, 1962.

LOEWENICH, WALTHER VON. *Modern Catholicism*. Translated by Reginald H. Fuller. New York: St. Martin's, 1959.

MIEGGE, GIOVANNI. *The Virgin Mary: The Roman Catholic Marian Doctrine*. Translated by W. Smith. Philadelphia: Westminster, 1955.

SCHROEDER, H. J. (trans.). *Canons and Decrees of the Council of Trent.* St. Louis: Herder, 1941.

SUBILIA, V. *The Problem of Catholicism.* London: SCM, 1964.

TAPPOLET, W. *Das Marienlob der Reformatoren.* Tübingen: Katzmann, 1962.

Chapter 8 Dogma within Protestantism

BARTH, KARL. *Karl Barth zum Kirchenkampf.* "Theologische Existenz heute," New Series, No. 49. Munich: Kaiser, 1956.

CASSIRER, ERNST. *The Philosophy of the Enlightenment.* Boston: Beacon, 1955.

COCHRANE, ARTHUR C. *The Church's Confession Under Hitler.* Philadelphia: Westminster, 1962.

EBELING, GERHARD. "The Significance of the Critical Historical Method for Church and Theology in Protestantism," *Word and Faith.* Translated by James W. Leitch. Philadelphia: Fortress, 1963.

HIRSCH, EMANUEL. *Geschichte der neuern evangelischen Theologie.* 5 vols. Gütersloh: Bertelsmann, 1949-1954.

HORNIG, GOTTFRIED. *Die Anfänge der historisch-kritischen Theologie.* Göttingen: Vandenhoeck und Ruprecht, 1961.

KOCH, GERHARD. *Die christliche Wahrheit der Barmer Theologischen Erklärung.* "Theologische Existenz heute," New Series, No. 22. Munich: Kaiser, 1950.

STEPHAN, HORST. *Geschichte der deutschen evangelischen Theologie seit dem deutschen Idealismus.* New, revised ed. by Martin Schmidt. Berlin: Töpelmann, 1960.

STOEFFLER, F. ERNEST. *The Rise of Evangelical Pietism.* Leiden: Brill, 1965.

WOLF, ERNST. *Barmen: Kirche zwischen Versuchung und Gnade.* Munich: Kaiser, 1957.

Chapter 9 The Unity of the Church

BAUM, GREGORY. *Progress and Perspectives: The Catholic Quest for Christian Unity.* New York: Sheed and Ward, 1962.

BELL, G. K. A. *The Kingship of Christ.* Baltimore: Penguin, 1954.

BRIDSTON, KEITH R., and WALTER D. WAGONER (eds.). *Unity in Mid-Career: An Ecumenical Critique.* New York: Macmillan, 1963.

CAVERT, SAMUEL MCCREA. *On the Road to Christian Unity.* New York: Harper, 1961.

GOODALL, NORMAN. *The Ecumenical Movement, What It Is and What It Does.* New York: Oxford University Press, 1961.

JÄGER, LORENZ. *The Ecumenical Council, the Church and Christendom.* Translated by A. V. Littledale. New York: Kenedy, 1962.

KÜNG, HANS. *The Council, Reform and Reunion.* Translated by Cecily Hastings. New York: Sheed and Ward, 1961.

MARGULL, HANS JOCHEN. *Hope in Action: The Church's Task in the World.* Translated by E. Peters. Philadelphia: Muhlenberg, 1962.

MCNEILL, JOHN T. *Unitive Protestantism.* Revised ed. Richmond, Va.: John Knox, 1964.

MUDGE, LEWIS S. *One Church: Catholic and Reformed.* Philadelphia: Westminster, 1963.

ROUSE, RUTH, and STEPHEN C. NEILL (eds). *A History of the Ecumenical Movement, 1517-1948.* Philadelphia: Westminster, 1954.

RYNNE, XAVIER. *Letters from Vatican City.* New York: Farrar, Strauss, 1963. *The Second Session* (1964). *The Third Session* (1965).

TAVARD, GEORGE H. *Two Centuries of Ecumenism.* Translated by R. W. Hughes. Notre Dame, Ind.: Fides Publishers, 1960.

VISSER 'T HOOFT, W. A. *The Meaning of Ecumenical.* London: SCM, 1953.

VISSER 'T HOOFT, W. A. (ed.). *New Delhi Speaks.* New York: Association, 1962.

Index

A Short History of Christian Doctrine

Index